SADLIER
FAITH AND
WITNESS

LITURGY AND WORSHIP

A Course on Prayer and Sacraments

Annotated Edition

Guide Writer
Isabel F. Blevins

Text Author
Rev. Thomas Richstatter, O.F.M., S.T.D.

William H. Sadlier, Inc.
9 Pine Street
New York, New York 10005-1002
http://www.sadlier.com

Acknowledgments

Scripture selections are taken from the *New American Bible* copyright © 1991, 1986, 1970 by the Confraternity of Christian Doctrine, Washington, D.C. and are used by license of the copyright owner. All rights reserved. No part of the *New American Bible* may be used or reproduced in any form without permission in writing from the copyright owner.

Excerpts from the English translation of the *Catechism of the Catholic Church* for use in the United States of America, copyright © 1994, Unites States Catholic Conference, Inc.— Libreria Editrice Vaticana.

Excerpts from the English translation of *Rite of Baptism for Children* © 1969, International Committee on English in the Liturgy, Inc. (ICEL); excerpts from the English translation of *The Roman Missal* © 1973, ICEL; excerpts from the English translation of *Rite of Confirmation*, Second Edition © 1975, ICEL; excerpts from the English translation of *Ordination of Deacons, Priests, and Bishops* © 1975, ICEL; excerpts from the English translation of *Dedication of a Church and an Altar* ©1978, ICEL; excerpts from the English translation of *Pastoral Care of the Sick: Rites of Anointing and Viaticum* © 1982, ICEL; excerpts from the English translation of *Rite of Christian Initiation of Adults* © 1985, ICEL; excerpts from the English translation of *Book of Blessings* © 1988, ICEL. All rights reserved.

Excerpt from *Conversion: Reflections on Life & Faith.* Copyright © 1993 by James Turro. Published by Tabor Publishing, 200 East Bethany Drive, Allen, TX 75002.

"The Brick" by Michel Quoist, from *Prayers,* copyright © 1985, Sheed & Ward. Reprinted with the permission of Sheed & Ward, 115 E. Armour Blvd., Kansas City, MO 64111.

Excerpt from THE SPIRITUAL LIFE OF CHILDREN. Copyright © 1990 by Robert Coles. Reprinted by permission of Houghton Mifflin Co. All rights reserved.

Reprinted from *Dreams Alive: Prayers by Teenagers,* edited by Carl Koch. Winona, MN: Saint Mary's Press, 1991. Used by permission. All rights reserved. (Written by Elizabeth from Holy Cross High School, Marine City, Michigan.)

Photo Credits

Jim Saylor
Photo Editor

Lori Berkowitz
Associate Photo Editor

Adventure Photo and Film/ Barbara Brown: 86C.
Diane J. Ali: 115 right.
Art Resource: 27 left, 74; Scala: 38 right; Erich Lessing: 80.
Lori Berkowitz: 42 bottom foreground.
Boltin Picture Library: 34, 36, 38A, 110–111, 116 center and left.
Bridge Building Images/ Robert Lentz: 115 left, 116 left.
Karen Callaway: 94A, 99.
Myrleen Cate: 6A, 6C, 50 top, 68 top, 84 top, 94C, 96 left.
Carr Clifton: 62–63.
Catholic News Service: 114 left; Charles Schisla: G21 top; Joe Rimkus Jr.: G24; Nancy Weichec: G25.
Comstock: 49, 106–107.
Crosiers/ Gene Plaisted, OSC: 18, 26, 30C, 32, 33, 35 background, 38C, 42 top left, 46C, 50 left, 52, 54 right, 55, 58 bottom, 62A, 66 right, 72, 76 top right, 78A, 84 bottom, 91 top, 92, 108 right, 110C, 114 center, 119.
FPG: John Terrence Turner: G12–13; D. Dietrich: 38 left; Gerard Loucei: 102C; Miguel Sanchez: 103; Bill Losh: 106 center.
The Franciscans: 31 bottom.
Ken Glaser: 54A, 58 top.
Granger Collection: 42 bottom background, 86A; 89; 110A, 120–121 bottom border.
Anne Hammersky: 16, 30 right, 35 foreground, 43 left & center, 50 right, 75, 88, 96 right.
Image Bank/ Harold Sund: 12; Siquis Sanchez: 54–55; Anthony Boccaccio: 56; Stephen Marks: 102A, 108 left; Michael Melford: 112.
Institute for Our African Ancestors: 114 right.
International Stock/ Tom Stamm: 76 background.
Ken Karp: 30A, 30 left, 40.
Gamma Liaison/ Livio Anticoli: 94–95.
Ron Mamot: 54 left.
Maryknoll: 115 center.

Masterfile/ Courtney Milne: 8–9.
Minden Pictures/ Frans Lanting: 6–7.
National Geographic/ Raymond Gehman: 86–87.
Our Lady of the Most Holy Rosary Catholic Community, Albuquerque, NM: 46A, 51.
Sarma Ozols: 64.
Panoramic Images/ Koji Yamashita: 122–123.
Photo Edit/ Michael Newman: 42 top right, 43 right.
Photo Researchers/ Worldsat: 70–71 background.
Photonica/ Myra Kramer: 79; Yasushi Kurada: 102–103.
Picture Cube/ Larry Lawfer: G18.
Picture Perfect/ K. Schrea: 70C; Warwick Buddle: 78–79.
H. Armstrong Roberts: 63, 78C.
St. Joseph's Abbey/ Br. Emmanuel Morinelli, OCSO: 83.
James Schaffer: 82, 90.
Nancy Sheehan: 17, 31 top.
Chris Sheridan: G16–G17 both, 14A, 62C both, 66 left, 68 right, 76 bottom left, 91 bottom.
Jacquline Srouji: 57.
Stock Boston/ David Ulmer: G21 bottom.
Stock Market/ Joseph Sohn: 46–47.
Superstock: 19, 22A, 24, 106 left.
Sygma/ G. Giansanti: 70A, 70–71 foreground.
Tony Stone Images/ Lawrence Migdale: G9; Gary Holscher: 10 left, 23 bottom left, 31 background; Hugh Sitton: 10 bottom; George Grigoriou: 10 top; Paul Chesley: 10–11; Mary Kate Denny: G19; Penny Tweedie: 14C; M. Townsend: 22 top left, 23 center right; Ralph Wetmore: 22 top right; David Olson: 22 center right, 23 bottom right; John Noble: 22 center right; William J. Herbert: 22 bottom right; Liz Hymans: 22 bottom left, 23 top right; Kevin Morris: 23 top right; Robert Daemmerich: 76 left; Zigy Kaluzny: 118; Emmanuelle Dal Secco: 118A, 120.
Uniphoto: 14–15.
Garth Vaughn: 120–121 top border, 122 left.
Viesti Associates/ Roger Holden: G10; Bavaria: 104.
Westlight/ W. Warren: 48–49.
Bill Wittman: 27 right, 40–41, 59, 65, 68 left, 81.

General Consultant for Texts
Rev. Joseph A. Komonchak, Ph.D.

**Official Theological Consultant
for Texts**
Most Rev. Edward K. Braxton, Ph.D., S.T.D.
Auxiliary Bishop of St. Louis

Publisher
Gerard F. Baumbach, Ed.D.

Editor in Chief
Moya Gullage

Pastoral Consultant
Rev. Msgr. John F. Barry

Scriptural Consultant
Rev. Donald Senior, C.P., Ph.D., S.T.D.

General Editors
Norman F. Josaitis, S.T.D.
Rev. Michael J. Lanning, O.F.M.

Catechetical and Liturgical Consultants
William Sadlier Dinger
Eleanor Ann Brownell, D. Min.
Joseph F. Sweeney
Helen Hemmer, I.H.M.
Mary Frances Hession
Maureen Sullivan, O.P., Ph.D.
Don Boyd

"The Ad Hoc Committee to Oversee the Use of the Catechism,
National Conference of Catholic Bishops,
has found the doctrinal content of this teacher's manual to be in
conformity with the *Catechism of the Catholic Church*."

Nihil Obstat
✠ Most Reverend George O. Wirz
Censor Librorum

Imprimatur
✠ Most Reverend William H. Bullock
Bishop of Madison
February 17, 1998

The *Nihil Obstat* and *Imprimatur* are official
declarations that a book or pamphlet is free of
doctrinal or moral error. No implication is contained
therein that those who have granted the *Nihil Obstat*
and *Imprimatur* agree with the contents, opinions,
or statements expressed.

Printed in the United States of America.

S® is a registered trademark of William H. Sadlier, Inc.

Home Office:
9 Pine Street
New York, NY 10005–1002

ISBN: 0–8215–5665–7
23456789/02010099

A Course on Prayer and Sacraments

This section can be used at any time during the course, e.g., during retreat day, as a "break" week, or in a holiday shortened week. It needs to be scheduled and prepared well in advance.

Sadlier's new FAITH AND WITNESS PROGRAM is a creative response to the needs of adolescents in the Catholic Church. It is rooted in a desire to serve effectively these young people, as well as those adults who teach, guide, and parent them on their faith journey.

It is shaped by an awareness of the multiple challenges and rewards of working with this vulnerable age group, which has been described as having one foot in childhood and the other groping toward adulthood.

At the heart of **Faith and Witness** is "a Person, the Person of Jesus of Nazareth, the only Son from the Father." And its aim is to draw adolescents into "communion with Jesus Christ." (*Catechism of the Catholic Church,* 426)

Just as Jesus himself related to and communicated with people "on their own level," so this program respects and responds to the adolescent's urgent questions: Who am I? Where am I going? What is my purpose in life?

Research done by the Carnegie Council on Adolescent Behavior verifies that many adolescents in our society have not been receiving the kind of guidance and support they need to thrive during this difficult period of metamorphosis. The Council's report warns that youth between ten and fourteen have become "a neglected generation." It notes alarming increases in adolescent suicide, firearm use, smoking, drug and alcohol addiction, pregnancy, and poor grades. Its recommendations stress that schools should create programs better suited to adolescents' developmental needs, and parents should be

INTRODUCING FAITH AND WITNESS

A Five-Course Program for Junior High Students

encouraged to become more involved in their young people's lives.

Sadlier's new **Faith and Witness Program** endeavors to meet these goals through an integration of the specific social, intellectual, religious, and spiritual needs of youth. It addresses "the desire for God [that] is written in the human heart" (*Catechism,* 27) as well as the Church's pastoral mission. Particular attention is paid to the following aspects of that mission: examining the reasons for belief, celebrating the sacraments, being integrated into the faith community, providing and calling forth gospel witness (*Catechism,* 6).

The semester courses that together comprise the program draw young people into relationship with Jesus and the New Testament, Liturgy and Worship, Church History, Morality, and the Creed. Each course invites young people to venture further into the mystery of faith and the challenge of discipleship. Through shared study, reflection, prayer, and action in response to God's word, young people experience themselves as a small faith community within the larger community of the parish and the Church itself.

We asked the writers of the courses to share with you, in a few sentences, their response to the following question:

What hopes do you have for the young people who will use your book?

Creed

"We know what a privilege and a challenge it is to share with young people the dynamic teachings of our Catholic faith. Moreover it is important to share that faith in a clear and meaningful way with the next generation of believers. We do this in two parts: Creed Part I, covering faith and revelation; Creed Part II, covering the Church and the Holy Spirit. Our hope is that young people will come to love Jesus and his Church ever more and take their place in society as committed evangelizers."

**Dr. Norman F. Josaitis, S.T.D., and
Rev. Michael J. Lanning, O.F.M., authors**

Liturgy and Worship

"We all know that it takes a lot more knowledge and skill to do something than to watch something. I hope that this book will provide the students—the next generation of young Catholics—with the help they need to celebrate the sacraments intelligently, joyfully, and fruitfully."

Rev. Thomas Richstatter, O.F.M., S.T.D., author

New Testament

"The purpose of this book is to provide an introduction to the New Testament that will offer young people a mature appreciation of their faith. Knowing all about the good news of Jesus Christ is more than the work of one lifetime. But it is our hope that this book will help young people to become more committed disciples of Jesus and stronger members of his Church."

**Dr. Norman F. Josaitis, S.T.D., and
Rev. Michael J. Lanning, O.F.M., authors**

"This introduction, I hope, will make accessible to young people twenty centuries of Christian reflection on the New Testament."

Dr. Mary Ann Getty, S.T.D., special consultant

Morality

"Too many people think of morality as something negative and limiting. But the truth is that Christian morality is an invitation to become part of the most graced and promising life possible. Morality is all about authentic happiness and rich, lasting loves. My hope with this book is that students will discover that God loves them and wants the best for them, and that people who care for them will always challenge them to be good."

Rev. Paul J. Wadell, Ph.D., C.P., author

Church History

"I love Church history and agree with Cicero who said: 'To know nothing of what happened before you were born is to remain ever a child.' The same is true of Catholics who are unaware of our own religious heritage. The history of the Catholic Church is a marvelous story of saints and sinners, successes and failures, hopes and disappointments. For a person of faith, it is not only a human story but also a divine drama of God's grace at work in our world."

Rev. Thomas J. Shelley, Ph.D., author

CATECHIST'S HANDBOOK

You Are a Catechist

Grace and peace to you! You have been called to be a catechist, a faith-filled minister of the word to adolescents. The aim of your ministry is to bring young people into intimate communion with Jesus Christ, and to draw them more deeply into the faith life of the Church. Think for a moment:

◆ Why do you think you were invited to do this work with young people?
◆ What gifts, talents or experiences do you bring to this ministry?

Ministry to the Needs of Youth

Ministry to young people has two main goals:

• to contribute to the personal and spiritual growth of each young person in your care;

• to invite young people into responsible participation in the life, mission, and work of the faith community. The components of your ministry include:

Evangelization—reaching out to young people who are uninvolved in the life of the Church and inviting them into a relationship with Jesus and the Catholic community.

Catechesis—promoting a young person's growth in the Catholic faith through a teaching process that emphasizes understanding, reflection, and conversation.

Prayer and Worship—guiding young people in developing their relationship with Jesus through personal prayer; drawing them more deeply into the sacramental life of the Church; involving them in a variety of prayer and worship experiences to celebrate their friendship with Jesus in a faith community of their peers.

Community Life—forming young people into the Christian community through programs and relationships that promote openness, trust, respect, cooperation, honesty, responsibility, and willingness to serve; creating a climate where young people can grow and share their struggles, questions, and joys with other young people and feel they are valued members of the Church.

Justice, Peace, and Service—giving direction to young people as they develop a Christian social consciousness and a commitment to a life of justice and peace by providing opportunities for service.

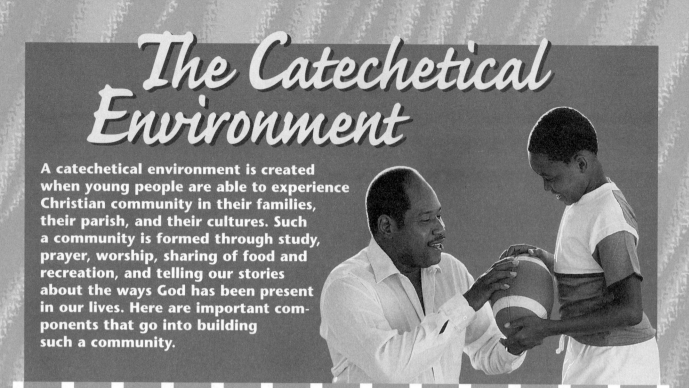

The Catechetical Environment

A catechetical environment is created when young people are able to experience Christian community in their families, their parish, and their cultures. Such a community is formed through study, prayer, worship, sharing of food and recreation, and telling our stories about the ways God has been present in our lives. Here are important components that go into building such a community.

Knowing the Young People

The environment and practices in the home and neighborhood have had, and continue to have, a powerful influence on the faith development of the young people in your group. It is important to be aware of the world the young people inhabit. Here are ways to develop that awareness.

◆ Be sure that your consistency, dependability, and fairness are such to win their confidence.

◆ Review the information you have been given regarding each young person.

◆ Become familiar with where and with whom each young person lives and who has legal custody.

◆ Make sure you are aware of young people who may be neglected or who come from homes that appear to be unhappy.

◆ Be available for private conferences with parents or family members, even if it means rearranging your schedule to meet their employment or family obligations.

◆ Be mindful of and sensitive to the language spoken in the home and the religious affiliation of parent(s) or guardians.

◆ Be alert to the general health and well-being of the young person.

Getting Families Involved

The mission of Catholic education is to support, develop, enhance, and encourage the positive learning that takes place within the home. It is essential, therefore, to involve the family in the catechetical process. Encourage them to participate fully in ongoing religious development of the young person. Regular family conversations about God and religion have a tremendous positive effect on a young person's faith attitudes and practices.

◆ Welcome the families when the program begins. Explain the catechetical program and invite their participation.

◆ Introduce them to the courses. The table of contents for each course provides an excellent overview of what the young people will be expected to learn about our Catholic faith during the program.

◆ Encourage a conversation about ways they can share with their son or daughter the *You Are My Witnesses* page. Duplicate and send home *Highlights for Home* from each chapter of the guide.

◆ Make positive telephone calls to parents. Conversations can be barrier-breakers, and from them catechists can gain great parental support and insight.

◆ Make a "Parents' Day" part of your yearly tradition so that the parents are given the opportunity to share their hopes and dreams for their daughters and sons.

Knowing the Neighborhood

◆ Become aware of the out-of-school activities both of the young people and of those with whom they frequently associate. If possible, attend some of their athletic or musical events.

◆ Be available and willing to listen to the young people without suggesting cures. When necessary, suggest that they seek professional advice as to how to deal with any unhealthy behaviors. Discuss these with the parents as well as any neighborhood influences and/or friends who are adversely affecting the young people's social, emotional, and spiritual development.

◆ Invite professionals to help the young people learn ways to cope with social pressures and problems such as alcohol, drugs, and peer pressure.

Sadlier's **Faith and Witness Program** is designed to nurture in young people a wholesome sense of self and a secure relationship with God in the context of the faith community. By integrating the teaching of Jesus and of the Church with the realities of their lives, they will be better prepared to minister to a world in which secular values often oppose the good news.

Making Discipline Positive

Positive discipline entails creating a climate in which young people feel secure, accepted, and supported. Here are suggestions for establishing and maintaining positive discipline in the group setting.

◆ Establish a sense of order immediately. Clearly and briefly explain to the young people what is expected of them. Rules should be few and easy to remember.

◆ Use affirmation; acknowledge the young people and remember to praise and affirm good behavior.

◆ Provide activities that build healthy self-esteem.

◆ Respect their thoughts and ideas, and expect them to do the same with you and their peers.

◆ Provide activities that challenge them to cooperate with one another.

◆ Deal with those who act inappropriately in a way that will calm them; set aside a space where they can think quietly about their actions and the consequences of them. If correcting is necessary, do it one-to-one, never publicly.

Developing Multicultural Awareness

True Christian community takes place within the context of the cultural heritage and the identity of the young people we teach.

◆ Be aware of and sensitive to ethnic and cultural diversity.

◆ Encourage the young people to express their cultural uniqueness through art, music, dance, food, and dress.

◆ Send communications home in the languages of the families, if possible.

◆ Invite families to share their cultural symbols and food at celebrations.

◆ Be aware of possible conflicts because of ethnic or cultural diversity among young people.

Youth With Special Needs

In recent years, the bishops of the United States have encouraged religious educators to pay particular attention to those young people who have special needs and to integrate these young people, when possible, into regular programs of religious education.

There are many different kinds of special needs. Some young people have *physical* needs that must be taken into consideration. Physical needs may involve any of the five senses, as well as special motor needs. Some have *emotional* needs that require our recognition, attention, and consideration. Still others have *special learning* needs. Learn about the special needs of these young people from the trained professionals who have dealt with them and their families.

Try to ascertain what adjustments or adaptations need to be made for your group. Be aware also of any adaptations necessary to enable the young people to profit from their religion materials. Plan the seating arrangement so that each person feels part of the group. Be sure that the group is aware of and sensitive to the special needs of all.

Recognize how all of us need to receive from as well as give to those who are disabled or challenged in any way. Jean Vanier, founder of the L'Arche communities in which people with disabilities and their caregivers live together, observes that those who are "broken" can reveal to us our own spiritual or psychological "brokenness." By this mutuality, we are strengthened, reconciled, and healed.

Understanding the Adolescent

Adolescence—the period that normally covers the years between eleven and fifteen—is a time of major change, development, and sometimes upheaval in the young person's life. To the young person everything seems to be in flux, in motion—physical development, emotions, ideas, relationships. It is a time of challenge and enormous potential for growth; it can also be a time of frustration and confusion both for the adolescents and for the adults—parents and catechists—who care for them.

Social Development

As young people move into adolescence, their interests begin to extend beyond family and school to wider horizons. As these new interests develop, relationships that had been of primary importance, especially those with family, sometimes seem to recede. Although there is still an essential need for the security and support of family and other adults, it is a time when old ties and the excitement of an enlarging world can conflict. The growing desire of the young people for greater freedom and their continuing need for support and security offer a real challenge to parents and catechists, who must find ways to facilitate this process of progressive emancipation. The sociability of the teenagers should be utilized and their energies channeled into common pursuits. It is the right age for such educational techniques as small-group projects or discussions, debates, panel presentations, retreat days, youth days, and service projects.

Intellectual Development

Young adolescents are increasingly capable of all the intellectual operations. There is specific growth in the ability to deal with abstract ideas and judgments in those young people who have matured beyond the egocentrism of an earlier stage. As they come more and more into contact with the judgments and opinions of others, they will need to be helped and challenged to think more accurately, perceptively, and critically. The broadening intellectual and social world of the young people stimulates a questioning and critical spirit. We can foster a *positive* questioning and critical attitude in the young people by challenging them to explore, probe, and reflect.

Also on a positive level, God's relationship with the young people is often expressed in a more "spiritual" way than before. Prayers become more other-oriented and less egocentric. The Church can be more readily understood as a community of believers, and worship is seen as a natural expression of belief and a way to become a better person.

The catechist should be aware that as real religious insights such as these occur, there can also be a tendency for negative attitudes to develop. This is often especially true for less mature young people, who, when faced with the struggle to move from an egocentric to a more mature religious belief, find it difficult to wrestle with the problems this involves and retreat into indifference or hostility. The challenge to the catechist is great. The first challenge is to recognize some very basic needs of adolescents.

Some Basic Needs

1. *Affirmation and Approval.* Young people must consistently be affirmed by their parents, catechists, and peers. Most have a precarious sense of self-esteem. They suffer anxiety about their physical appearance, their popularity, their skills and talents. They need to be told and shown that they are accepted, appreciated, and approved for who they are right now.

2. *Security and Success.* Because intellectual and other abilities vary so broadly among adolescents, they need multiple opportunities to succeed. An effective catechist discerns and draws out the particular skills of each young person. When a relationship of trust is nurtured between catechist and young person, the young person feels secure enough to do his or her best.

3. *Freedom and Structure.* Like fledgling pilots, adolescents love to fly but they depend heavily on the voice from the control tower. They want freedom to experiment and explore yet they require a reliable home base to return to as needed. Catechists who come to the group well-prepared, who require young people to abide by simple rules, and who consistently offer opportunities for choice and self-expression will do well with this age group. Giving clear directions and guiding young people step-by-step through a new process or ritual reinforces awareness of structure.

4. *Idealism and Self-Definition.* Youth have a great capacity for energetic idealism which can be effectively harnessed in the causes of justice, equality, and peacemaking. When motivated and well directed, they will unselfishly participate in the works of mercy—particularly in one-on-one situations. However, if their idealism and altruism are not channeled by catechists and adult mentors, youth readily take refuge in cynicism and hostility. Their need for self-definition must be met through individual attention from adults and by enlisting their particular abilities in ways that serve others.

5. *Physical Activity and Social Interaction.* Driven by hormonal changes and uncontrollable growth spurts, adolescents literally "cannot sit still" for extended lectures. They need to move from place to place, activity to activity, individual to partnered or group pursuits. Their hunger for interaction with peers can be met in diverse ways (discussions, debates, art or craft projects, sharing food and music, games, dancing, human sculptures).

Thinking Skills for Discipleship

More and more often, a complex and technological society demands critical thinkers. Critical thinkers see beneath surface impressions to the root of an issue or event. They are able to discern causes rather than symptoms, and they are able to project consequences rather than to be satisfied with quick solutions. Above all, critical thinkers are capable of reflection—not only on issues outside themselves, but capable of their own responses and reactions as well. How can we help our young people develop critical thinking skills? And how can we encourage them to use these skills as disciples of Christ?

The ability to think critically can be developed in young adolescents through questions and activities that involve the following:

- solving problems
- making decisions
- imagining outcomes
- setting up criteria
- finding reasons
- reflecting/meditating
- choosing applications to life

"Who do you say I am?" Jesus asked his disciples. It was a question that demanded the disciples to go beneath surface impressions to the heart of the matter. Instead, the disciples responded by repeating what *others* had said— "Some say John the Baptist; others Elijah; still others responded Jeremiah or one of the prophets." Jesus refused to accept the superficial, unreflective answer. He probed further. "But who do you say that I am?"

This is the basic question of our faith. This is the question that we want our young disciples to answer with personal conviction, commitment, and hope.

"You are the Messiah, the Son of the living God" (Matthew 16:13–16).

Prayer and the Young Person

A well-known youth minister was asked what advice he would give to religion catechists. "Be bold about the spiritual," he said. "These kids want and need religious experience. They need help with prayer."

Forms of Prayer

Many young people have experienced prayer as "talking to God" and reciting prayers. They are ready to explore new ways of expressing their relationship with God. In addition to liturgical prayer, the official prayer of the Church, they can enrich their prayer life by using prayer forms like the following:

- **The Breath Prayer**
  Seated with back straight and eyes closed, the person focuses on the flow of breath in and out of the body. As breath is exhaled, one can "breathe" a simple word or phrase like "Jesus" or "Here I am, Lord."

- **Prayer with Scripture**
  Herein lie unlimited riches. Try gospel meditations using imagination, i.e., "place yourself in the scene . . ."; read the psalms in choral fashion; learn personally chosen passages by heart; and practice proclaiming the word of God.

- **The Symbol Prayer**
  Potent symbols from the Bible and the liturgy (water, wind, oil, fire, light, incense) may speak more powerfully to meditating youth than would many words or explanations.

- **The Prayer of Music**
  This native tongue of youth speaks to them of God as they reflect on, participate in, and respond to music (religious, classical, contemporary).

- **The Prayer of Journaling**
  Prayers, Scripture responses, poems, dreams, doubts, questions, dialogues with Jesus and the saints are recorded in words and/or art in the young person's book of life. He or she comes to know God and self more intimately.

- **Traditional Vocal Prayer**
  Traditional prayers—prayers of the Catholic community— are the most used and taken-for-granted form of prayer. When they are prayed slowly and thoughtfully, instead of rattled off, they can be a source of comfort, rootedness, and connectedness for young people. One way to make traditional prayers take on new meaning is to pray them against a background of beautiful music or visual images.

Young people should be invited to help choose and prepare for these and other prayer experiences. Suggestions for these prayer experiences (about 10 minutes) are provided in the *Introduction* and *Conclusion* of each session. However, brief opening and closing prayers (a minute or two) may be used to frame the session itself as an extended prayer. Sources for these include: a line or two from traditional prayers, the Mass, the psalms, inspired songs, prayers of the saints, collections of prayers by teenagers, and the words of Jesus.

Do not assume that young people reject prayer. They are hungry for the spiritual, for relationship with God. Prayer is a way for them to touch the living God who is with them and in them.

Some resources that might be helpful:

Hokowski, Maryann. *Pathways to Praying with Jesus.* Winona, MN: Saint Mary's Press, 1993.

Koch, Carl, FSC. *More Dreams Alive: Prayers by Teenagers.* Winona, MN: Saint Mary's Press, 1995.

Bolton, Martha. *If the Pasta Wiggles, Don't Eat It. . . .* Ann Arbor, MI: Servant Publications, 1995.

Morris, Thomas H. *Prayer Celebrations for the Liturgical Year.* New York, NY: William H. Sadlier, 1998.

Questions That Matter

Questions have to be carefully prepared if they are to be truly effective. Part of preparation for teaching each lesson should be the formulation of questions that stimulate, challenge, and engender deeper thought. Besides simple recall, questions should motivate and stimulate emotion, evaluative thinking, imagination, and creative problem solving. Vary your techniques; allow time for responses (research shows that most teachers wait less than 4 seconds); above all, *listen* to the answers! Here are some sample questioning techniques.

Recall

- List the types of evidence for believing in God. Other "recall" words: name; define; outline; describe.

React

- Imagine a friend tells you that he no longer believes in God. List four questions you would ask your friend about his reasons for not believing.

Compare

- In what ways are the early Church (A.D. 33–300) and today's Church alike?

Contrast

- In what ways are they different?

Preference

- Which would you rather be—a stained glass window or a church bell?
- Which helps you to pray—silence or music?

Personification

- What questions would you like to ask Francis of Assisi (or Mary, or...)?
- What would Jesus think or say about this issue? How might he say it?

Creative Thinking

- What if there had been television in Jesus' time?
- What if you could trade places with Saint Paul (or Catherine of Siena...)?
- Suppose that Jesus had not come. What would the consequences be?

Application

- Give Luther a list of alternatives to leaving the Church.
- Ask several "when" questions about the Church.
- Ask five "why" questions about faith.

Research Skills

- Would it have been possible for Pope John Paul II to meet Hitler?
- Would it have been possible for Catherine of Siena to have dinner with Ignatius Loyola?

Synthesis

- What might be some of the moral consequences of violent or sexual content in some contemporary music?
- The answer is "life." What is the question?

Ways of Learning

In his book *Frames of Mind,* Dr. Howard Gardner identified seven types of intelligence of which educators need to be aware among their students.

Because young people vary so widely in their intellectual abilities, it is especially important that catechists recognize these multiple intelligences.

The following list describes seven intelligence types and suggests appropriate teaching strategies within the context of the FAITH AND WITNESS PROGRAM.

1. Linguistic Intelligence
Exhibits sensitivity to the meaning and order of words

- *Storytelling:* scriptural, traditional, contemporary and imaginary stories to be told, re-told, or written
- *Brainstorming:* unleashing a torrent of ideas on a specific issue or question, i.e., How would we describe Jesus to teen aliens who had never heard of him?
- *Speaking a New Language:* learning a prayer in Aramaic, Spanish, Latin, or American Sign Language
- *Publishing:* collecting and publishing a semester's worth of young people's reflections, prayers, responses

2. Logical-Mathematical Intelligence
Shows ability to discern patterns of reasoning and order; dexterity with numbers

- *Classification:* organizing information (on Church history, Creed, or New Testament) on attribute webs (listing attributes of a person, place or thing as spokes around the subject)
- *Devising Strategies:* for computer or board games on history or Scripture
- *Socratic Questioning:* catechist or leader questions young people's views to sharpen critical thinking skills (e.g., "Do you think human beings will eventually have the power to understand the mysteries of life?")

3. Spatial Intelligence
Demonstrates ability to grasp how things orient to each other in space

- *Making Maps and Architectural Models:* recreating scenes or places from Scripture and Church history
- *Making Timelines and Murals:* visualizing historical, liturgical and creedal developments

4. Bodily-Kinesthetic Intelligence
Using the body skillfully and handling objects with unusual aptitude

- *Drama and Dance:* role-playing moral decision-making; acting out stories from Scripture and history; ritual prayer in which dance or choreographed movement is integrated
- *Human Sculptures and Relays:* small groups form "sculptures" of faith concepts or objects (community, steeple, fishermen's boat) using only their bodies; teams perform physical "feats" and respond to faith questions on relay "batons."
- *Crafts:* using clay, pipe cleaners, papier -maché, looms, wood, beads to make faith-related objects (from Scripture, Church history, prayer traditions)

5. Musical Intelligence

Using sensitivity to sound, melody, instrumentation and musical mood

- *Rhythms, Songs, Chants, Raps:* employing these as aids to internalization and memorization (composing songs on moral issues or chants of favorite prayer lines)

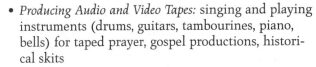

- *Producing Audio and Video Tapes:* singing and playing instruments (drums, guitars, tambourines, piano, bells) for taped prayer, gospel productions, historical skits
- *Collecting Disks:* resource of religious, classical and contemporary music to illustrate, amplify or embody content themes ("Godspell," "Messiah," "Tears In Heaven," plus nature recordings)

6. Interpersonal Intelligence

Showing relationship skills, understanding and empathy

- *Peer Sharing:* interacting with partners or small groups to explore content questions and personal responses; peer tutoring and mentoring by older youth or adults
- *Doing Simulations:* groups participate in "as-if" environments (e.g., "You have just heard Jesus' Sermon on the Mount and are now on the road home. What are you feeling, thinking, planning to do?")
- *Making Murals, Puzzles, Banners:* working cooperatively to produce an art project illustrating a faith theme
- *Peacemaking Strategies:* role-playing ways of reconciliation practiced by Jesus, saints, Gandhi, Martin Luther King, Jr., youth
- *Culture Sharing:* putting together prayer and worship experiences enriched by African-American, Hispanic, Asian, Native American and other cultural expressions within the Church

7. Intrapersonal Intelligence

Showing self-knowledge and self-discipline; awareness of one's inner life

- *Doing One-Minute Reflections:* taking "time out" in the midst of interactive learning for reflection or deep thinking (no talking; occasional background music)
- *Praying, Journaling, Retreats:* responding to youth's hunger for God and need for self-awareness
- *Offering Choices:* enhancing self-discipline and self-expression by offering choices on projects, methods, ways of responding to content
- *Expressing Feelings:* calling forth expressions of wonder, surprise, anger, joy, caring, humor, sadness in response to faith experiences (through stories, poems, videos, photos, music, personal witness, prayer)

The Learning/Teaching Process

Adolescents need to feel some ownership of the learning situation. They do not respond positively to being "talked at" or "talked down to." They need to participate as much as possible in the planning, presentation, and carrying out of the program. Above all, they need to be challenged to take responsibility for their learning.

The courses in SADLIER'S FAITH AND WITNESS PROGRAM are designed with these realities in mind. The process suggested is simple yet comprehensive. Each lesson consists of three steps:

1. Introduction

The lesson begins with an *opening prayer*—preferably led by one or more of the young people. (See page G21.)

- The opening prayer is followed by the *forum* (see page G20) in which the young people present their responses, reflections, or reactions to the assigned reading and activity.

2. Presentation

- The catechist clarifies the material the young people have read. This can be done through a variety of techniques including questions, activities, dialogue, highlighting, guest speakers, and so on.

3. Conclusion

- Young people and/or catechist give a brief summary of the work of the lesson.
- Catechist gives forum assignment for the next lesson.
- Session closes with a brief prayer or song.

This guide will suggest a variety of techniques, activities, questions to facilitate this process. The key with young people is to have a balance of consistency and variety so that every lesson is solid but not predictable.

Preparing a Lesson

If we truly believe that our catechetical work with young people is the most important teaching we can do, it is essential that we go to them prepared. Preparation for religion class is absolutely essential.

Here are a few suggestions for preparing to teach this course. The suggestions are especially intended for those who may be new—either to teaching religion or to teaching adolescents.

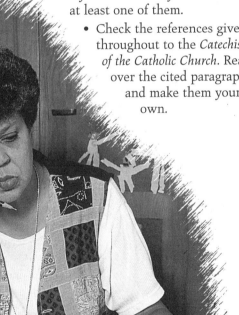

Remote Preparation

- Read the whole text carefully. This will give you an understanding of the scope of the whole course and the sequence of ideas throughout.

- As you read make marginal notes about any ideas you have regarding the material and how to present it.

- Look at the list of resources and try to familiarize yourself with at least one of them.

  - Check the references given throughout to the *Catechism of the Catholic Church*. Read over the cited paragraphs and make them your own.

Immediate Preparation

- Read the chapter for the session.

- As you read highlight what you consider to be the main points of each lesson. The highlighted statements on the reduced pupil pages will help you.

- List these main points for yourself. It will help to clarify and to focus your objectives.

- Write out the questions you feel will help direct the group's understanding of the material. (See the suggestions for questioning on page G15.)

- Plan the activities you wish to use during the lesson. Make sure you know exactly what you wish the group to do. Assemble any materials you will need.

- Plan the *forum* assignment you will give the young people for the following lesson. Make the assignment clear and simple, but be creative.

- Immediately before the lesson begins, talk to those who are responsible for leading the opening prayer to make sure they have what they need.

- Take a minute for quiet reflection. Ask the Holy Spirit to be in your mind, heart, and mouth as you share the faith with your group.

Youth Interaction

Youth interaction is essential to the success of this program. Their participation in and ownership of the learning process provides stimulus, enthusiasm, and energy to the whole program.

The **Faith and Witness Program** is organized on the principle of youth involvement and responsibility. The two most important elements in the program are, therefore, the youth-directed prayer and the youth-led *Forum*.

Forum

The purpose of the *forum* is to involve the young people immediately and interactively in each session. We want them to become not simply passive receivers of information, but active partners and participants in the learning process.

It is essential, therefore, that the young people assume responsibility for the *forum* and for the preparation necessary to take part in it. If this is not done, the religion lesson will become a reading exercise or a lecture. These are not acceptable alternatives.

How Does the Forum Work?

◆ At the end of each lesson ask the young people to prepare for the next *forum* by doing two things:

• Read carefully the next chapter assigned, and underline key ideas.

• Prepare a written or oral response to the question, reflection, or activity assigned.

◆ Following the opening prayer, each lesson begins with the *forum* in which the young people share both the results of their reading and their responses to the *forum* assignment.

The *forum* should take approximately 15 to 20% of the total class time. If the above process is not possible in your situation, see page G26.

Ideas for Forum Assignments

Each *forum* assignment should act as an interesting and creative "doorway" for the young people into the work of the lesson. Their responses and reactions at the outset of the lesson should provide an initial dialogue that helps them enter enthusiastically into the ideas and content of the lesson. Some ideas:

◆ Always the first part of the assignment is to read the pages of the lesson. Encourage the young people to underline in pencil sentences that they feel are key ideas on these pages.

◆ Some of the suggestions on *Questions That Matter* are excellent ideas for *forum* assignments—especially those under *Recall, React, Personification, Creative Thinking, Application, and Synthesis.* (See page G15.)

◆ *Journaling* could occasionally be the *forum* assignment. Be careful not to require a response that would be too personal or too revealing for a young person to share with the group.

◆ *Simple Research* to discover more information about an idea is helpful if the young people have access to computer on-line services.

Journaling

The young people keep a journal throughout the course. Journal suggestions appear in each chapter. There is a *Sadlier Journal* for *Creed, Morality, Liturgy and Worship,* and *New Testament.*

Purpose:
It provides an outlet for private, ungraded, uncensored expressions of the young people's thoughts, reflections, imaginations, feelings.

Outcomes:
• young people become more in touch with themselves, their feelings, their personal questions;

• young people become better writers;

• young people have something to look back on that will give them insights into their own change and growth.

Youth-Led Prayer

Purpose:
- provides immediate responsibility for and involvement by the young people in the spiritual dimensions of their learning;
- gives them the opportunity to express their own spiritual concerns and to lead others in prayer.

Outcomes:
- young people are enabled to be less self-conscious about their faith;
- they are given the freedom to express their relationship with God and their concerns in personal and creative ways;
- the experience can draw them deeper into their personal life of prayer with God.

Needs:
- especially in the beginning: the catechist's help, support, and suggestions;
- scriptural and other resources (see *Teaching Resources* chart for each chapter);
- partners! Sometimes it is easier with a friend.

How to:
- at the end of each session meet with the young people who will be leading prayer during the next session;
- if they request help, make resources available;
- encourage them—prayer does not have to be perfect; it only has to be sincere.

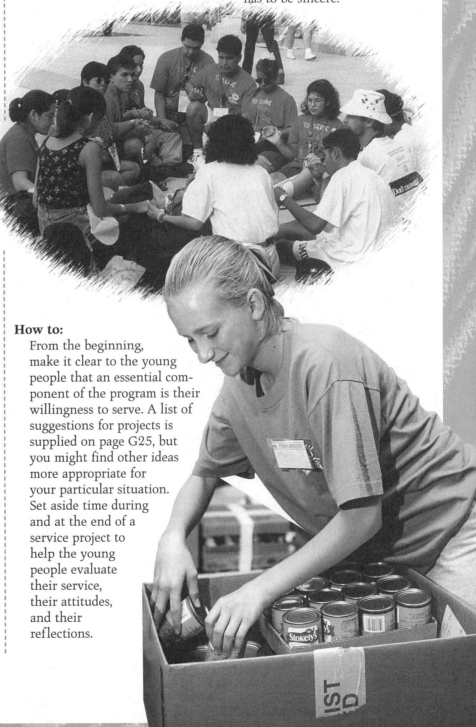

Faith in Action

*I*nvolvement in active service for others is an integral part of the FAITH AND WITNESS PROGRAM.

Purpose:
Young people have so much to give—energy, generosity, enthusiasm, idealism, compassion. It is essential that we help them find practical and immediate ways to share these gifts.

Outcomes:
They will find that they receive far more than they give—a humbling and joyful discovery. They will begin to develop and to live the values of God's kingdom in very real, practical, and sometimes demanding ways.

Needs:
Ideas and suggestions from the parish and communities concerning needs and opportunities the young people can address.

How to:
From the beginning, make it clear to the young people that an essential component of the program is their willingness to serve. A list of suggestions for projects is supplied on page G25, but you might find other ideas more appropriate for your particular situation. Set aside time during and at the end of a service project to help the young people evaluate their service, their attitudes, and their reflections.

FAITH AND WITNESS Program

Morality A Course on Catholic Living

We were made for happiness, a happiness that God alone can provide. Modeling our lives on Christ, we know that the only way to achieve happiness is by rejecting sin and freely choosing to do what is right. Through God's law and God's grace, we are called upon to form our consciences and make moral decisions as followers of Christ and members of the Church. The Church itself is the authentic teacher of the ways of Christ and the manner in which we are to live a moral life in the world.

Within this deeper framework of moral decision making, we explore the Ten Commandments in greater detail. Likewise, we concentrate on gospel formation (the Beatitudes) and what it means to live a life of virtue. This course will enable young people to navigate through challenging times with a clear and positive moral attitude that is essential for Catholics in the new millennium.

Liturgy and Worship A Course on Prayer and Sacraments

It is in the Church's liturgy, especially the seven sacraments, that Catholics celebrate all that God has done for us in Christ Jesus through the working of the Holy Spirit. Our salvation was made possible through the paschal mystery of Christ's passion, death, resurrection, and ascension. This mystery is made present to us in the sacred actions of the Church's liturgy.

As members of the Church, we are called upon to enter into this mystery of faith and truly be people of both word and sacrament. This is where our lives of faith are proclaimed, formed, and nourished. If young people are to be strong and faithful followers of Christ, they must make the liturgical life of the Church their own.

New Testament A Course on Jesus Christ and His Disciples

Young Catholics need to rub shoulders with the culture of Jesus and his times. Likewise, they need to know that in Scripture things are not always what they appear to be. Scripture presents so much more, and young people should never be afraid of the truth as presented in Scripture. This text will introduce them to questions people have asked over the ages: Were the Magi historical figures? Did Jesus really raise people

from the dead, or were they just asleep? Did Jesus really die, and did his body really come out of the tomb? By tackling such questions, this course will help young people to appreciate the contemporary Catholic understanding of Scripture and give them tools to avoid fundamentalistic leanings that distort real Catholic doctrine and Scripture itself.

Creed A Course on Catholic Belief in Two Parts

It is through divine revelation that we come to know God through the knowledge God has of himself. The gift of faith enables us to respond to this divine revelation.

Because our first parents rejected God's plan of original holiness and justice, the whole human race is born in the state of original sin. God promised us a savior and that promise was fulfilled through his only Son, who became flesh and took on our human nature. Jesus, the

Son of God and the son of Mary, is true God and true Man. He offered himself as the perfect sacrifice for us and for our salvation.

We are the Church, the people of God. Jesus promised that he would be with the Church until the end of time. He sent the Holy Spirit to guide the Church in all things. The course concludes with Mary and the saints and our belief in the communion of saints and life everlasting.

Church History A Course on the People of God

How important it is for young Catholics to be in touch with their roots, roots that took hold about two thousand years ago!

Beginning with the apostolic age and the age of persecution, young people will be introduced to the accomplishments of men and women of faith throughout the centuries. The successes and difficulties that the Church

has faced, both within and without, will be studied, but always with a view to help young Catholics of today face the challenges of their own time. As Catholics, we stand on the shoulders of giants. In helping others to know the story of this great Church community, we are preparing leaders for the new millennium.

Liturgy & Worship
Scope and Sequence

Chapter 1

MORE THAN MEETS THE EYE: the use of symbols to express one's deepest beliefs; the awareness of the divine, the sacred in human cultures; the meaning and characteristics of ritual

Chapter 2

THE PRAYER OF THE CHURCH: Catholic symbols and rituals; liturgy—the public prayer of the Church; characteristics of liturgy; the paschal mystery

Chapter 3

GOD'S MASTERPIECES: God's plan of salvation; Jesus, the Word made flesh; definition of sacrament

Chapter 4

THE SACRAMENT OF SACRAMENTS: Eucharist: source and summit of the Christian life; the Mass: sacrifice and meal; liturgical time; the eucharistic prayer

Chapter 5

CELEBRATING EUCHARIST: the Liturgy of the Word, the Liturgy of the Eucharist; the berakah form of the eucharistic prayer; the meaning of the Eucharist for our lives

Chapter 6

THE SACRAMENTS OF INITIATION: the process of becoming a Catholic; the need for conversion; initiation: Baptism, Confirmation, Eucharist; celebrating these sacraments

Chapter 7

OUR HOUSE OF PRAYER: need for sacred space; the parish—visible sign of faith; design that serves four liturgical functions; a place of worship

Chapter 8

SEASONS OF PRAISE: the liturgical year, an unfolding of the whole mystery of Christ; Sunday, the day of resurrection; the Lenten retreat; the solemn liturgies of the Triduum

Chapter 9

A YEAR OF GLORY: seasons of change, preparation and new beginnings; Easter, a season of fifty days; reflecting on the gospels; Pentecost, the Holy Spirit in the Church; the gift of mission; Advent and Christmas: the Kingdom of God among us

Chapter 10

THE SACRAMENT OF RECONCILIATION: Jesus and forgiveness; a reconciling Church; Reconciliation today; celebrating the sacrament: communal and individual rites; sign of the sacrament

Chapter 11

THE ANOINTING OF THE SICK: Jesus and healing; healing in the early Church; essential sign: anointing with oil; a public prayer directed toward healing; celebrating the sacrament

Chapter 12

THE SACRAMENT OF HOLY ORDERS: call to Holy Orders; the three ranks; a share in Christ's priesthood through ministry, divine worship, authority; an indelible mark; ordination of bishops, priests, deacons; essential signs of the sacrament

Chapter 13

THE SACRAMENT OF MATRIMONY: the meaning of marriage; preparation for marriage; life-giving sign of grace; ministers and sign of the sacrament; the marriage commitment; celebrating the sacrament

Chapter 14

MARY AND THE SAINTS: the communion of saints; the meaning of holiness; celebrating the saints; Mary, the mother of God and first disciple

COURSE OVERVIEW

Why a Course on Liturgy and Worship?

By the time young people are in junior high they might have the feeling that they have "had" sacraments and liturgy ever since second grade. It is important to involve them in looking at the liturgical life of the Church in a new and more mature and profound way. In the liturgy, which is the public prayer of the Church, we share in the "work of God." What is the work of God? It is the work of our redemption; it is what Christ did for us. In the liturgy the work of Christ—his passion, death, resurrection, and ascension—continues today in the Church—in us.

The liturgical prayer of the Church makes present in our lives today redeeming actions of Christ in his paschal mystery. When Jesus passed from death to life, all creation was made new—including ourselves. His new life is now our new life. Why a course on liturgy and worship? Because it is the central vocation of every Christian to discover, to celebrate, and to live the meaning of Christ's passion, death, and resurrection in today's world.

Objectives

◆ To deepen the young people's understanding of the Church's liturgy as prayerful celebration of all that God has done for us in Christ through the working of the Holy Spirit.

◆ To develop a richer awareness that our salvation is made present to us in the sacred actions of the liturgy.

◆ To encourage them to enter more fully into this mystery of faith and to become truly people of both word and sacrament.

Faith in Action

Active, attentive, responsible service of others should be the hallmark of the Christian moral life. Involve your group in individual or communal service projects to be carried out throughout this course. The young people should reflect on their commitment in their journals and give a report at the end of the course. (Note: All projects will need your support and coordinating efforts.) Some suggestions follow.

◆ Invite a friend who is not a Catholic to come with you to a sacramental celebration in your parish. Explain the significance of the sacrament and what it means to you. Help your friend follow the liturgy and to feel part of the celebration. Take time afterwards to discuss the liturgy you have shared.

◆ If possible, arrange to accompany a eucharistic minister in your parish when he or she brings the Eucharist to the sick in their homes. Join in any prayers that are offered and take a minute afterwards to talk to the sick person. Find out what it means to be a eucharistic minister.

◆ During this course, ask Jesus to help you become a healing presence in someone's life. "Adopt" a sick, handicapped, or elderly person. Each day pray that your friend may be healed spiritually and physically. Once a week visit or call or send a card to that person.

Cross Curriculum Projects

◆ Young people with an interest in music could research the vast treasury of Church music: chant, polyphony, congregational, oratorio, and modern, for example. They might prepare a program for the group with explanations and musical selections.

◆ Young people with an interest in the visual arts might research the area of modern liturgical art and architecture. They should prepare a report explaining the developments in the field in the last twenty years.

◆ Young scientists might compare and contrast Einstein's thoughts on time with the concept of liturgical time–God's time.

HOW TO USE THIS GUIDE

Preparation

Well in advance:

◆ Read the entire text before meeting for the first time.

◆ Carefully prepare each session, using both text and guide.

Planning

◆ Go over *Teaching Resources.*

◆ Gather materials.

◆ Plan each *Forum* assignment.

◆ Estimate time you will allot for *Introduction, Presentation,* and *Conclusion* of the session. A place is provided to write your estimate beside each head on the guide.

◆ Prayer is an integral part of the catechetical process. It should be a priority in each session.

◆ At this age young people like to feel ownership and some control of the work of the session. If at all possible, encourage them to bring the text home so that they can become familiar with the theme, identify main ideas, and prepare for the *Forum.* (See page G20.)

◆ In order to become active partners and participants in the learning process, it is essential that the young people have time to prepare and that they be encouraged to assume responsibility for their learning. The *Forum* and the opening prayer especially require their preparation and interaction. All of this presumes that the young people can take their books home.

◆ Preview any videos or films to be used; listen to suggested music.

◆ Learn as much as possible about the young people with whom you will be meeting.

◆ Interaction and dialogue are key to the development of a deep and personal understanding of the ideas presented. We urge you to use the *Forum* activity to this end.

Other Options

If your situation does not allow for the books to be taken home, be creative. Find ways to help the group be ready to participate actively and fully in the work of the chapter. Here are some ideas:

◆ Have a small group prepare the chapter presentation and do the *Forum.* Select a different group each week.

◆ Provide reading and *Forum* preparation time at the beginning of each session. *This would work best with sessions of 90 minutes or longer.*

◆ Prepare and begin each session with a summary presentation of the key ideas of the chapter. *Invite and encourage discussion before moving on.*

Features

Adult Focus

helps you to focus on and be comfortable with the theme of the chapter.

Enrichment Activities

provide additional activities to enhance the sessions.

Teaching Resources

give an overview of the session including opening prayer suggestions and optional supplemental resources.

Journaling

Suggestions are provided for each session. A separate *Faith and Witness* Journal is available for each course. There is one journal for *Creed Part I* and *Creed Part II.*

Assessment

An optional assessment in standardized test format is provided as a blackline master. There is one at the end of each chapter in the guide. A blackline-master test book will be provided for use with the program.

Highlights for Home

This blackline master is provided as a communication to encourage family involvement.

The **Faith and Witness Program** provides a genuine opportunity for young people—with your guidance—to come to a powerful understanding of the faith through study, dialogue, and prayer. You, the catechist, have the challenging role of preparing them and calling them to be people of faith and witness.

The semester courses that together comprise Sadlier's **Faith and Witness Program** may be used for young people at the junior-high and high-school levels. You have the opportunity to develop the curriculum to suit your own needs.

Some considerations in choosing your semester course combination are:

- ◆ diocesan guidelines for specific grade levels
- ◆ maturity of students
- ◆ pre-Confirmation catechesis guidelines.

MORE THAN MEETS THE EYE

Adult Focus

As you gather together with the young people at the beginning of this course on Liturgy and Worship, help your group experience Christ's presence and the Holy Spirit's guidance. If the young people are to be strong and faithful followers of Christ, they must make the liturgical life of the Church their own. It is in the Church's liturgy, especially the seven sacraments, that we celebrate all that God has done for us in Jesus Christ through the working of the Holy Spirit. Our salvation was made possible through the paschal mystery of Christ's passion, death, resurrection, and ascension. This mystery is made present to us in the sacred actions of the Church's liturgy. As members of the Church, we are called upon to enter into this mystery of faith and truly be people of both word and sacrament. This is where our lives of faith are proclaimed, formed, and nourished.

In this chapter the young people explore the Church's teaching that an understanding of symbol and ritual is essential to a mature understanding of our worship as Catholics. And if we are aware and willing to participate, each ritual draws us more deeply into the life of faith that it expresses.

Catechism Focus

The theme of Chapter 1 corresponds to paragraphs 1145–1148 of the *Catechism of the Catholic Church*.

Enrichment Activities

More Than Meets the Eye

Have the young people make a cloth or paper banner with four sections. Provide fabric swatches or construction paper for the young people to use to make symbols. Suggest that they place a symbol of their favorite gift of God in nature in the first section of the banner. In the second section they may place a symbol of their favorite interest or hobby. In the third section they may place a symbol of peace and in the fourth section a symbol of happiness.

Computer Connection

Have the young people use an electronic-mail feature of an on-line information service, such as *Prodigy*™, to exchange letters explaining their understanding of Matthew 18:20: "Where two or three are gathered together in my name, there am I in the midst of them." Also have them invite the young people with whom they are communicating to be part of a prayer "web."

Locate and verify other groups of Catholic young people that are willing to exchange letters. Have the young people in your group compose their letters off-line using an appropriate writing software program, such as *Student Writing Center*™. Then have them upload their letter files to the on-line information service in order to send the letters. Have the young people print and present to the class the letters and any responses they may receive.

Teaching Resources

Overview

To explore the ways that we humans use symbols to communicate our belief in the sacred; to discover three of the most important characteristics of ritual.

Opening Prayer Ideas

Look at the photo on pages 6 and 7. Reflect on 1 Corinthians 13:12.

or

Look at the photo on pages 6 and 7. Ask God to help you strengthen your roots of faith.

Materials

- Bibles, journals, and highlighters
- large tub of water
- small pieces of sponge (one for each person)

Liturgy and Worship Journal:
For Chapter 1, use pages 4–7.

REPRODUCIBLE MASTERS
- *Thinking Symbolically,* page 6C
- *Chapter 1 Assessment,* page 13A (optional)
- *Highlights for Home,* page 13B

Supplemental Resources

VIDEOS
The Wonders of God's Creation
Vision Video Inc.
2030 Wentz Church Road
P.O. Box 540
Worcester, PA 19490–0540

William
Franciscan Communications/
St. Anthony Messenger
1615 Republic Street
Cincinnati, OH 45210

Thinking Symbolically

Draw or write a description of a symbol for four concerns that many young people have. Choose from those listed here.

Concerns: peer pressure, gaining more independence, friendship, favorite activities or hobbies, environmental concerns, peace in the world, God's love for you, your faith in God.

More Than
Meets the Eye

At present we see indistinctly,
as in a mirror,
but then face to face.
1 Corinthians 13:12

Objectives: To explore the ways that we humans use symbols to communicate our belief in the sacred; to discover three of the most important characteristics of ritual.

Introduction ___ min.

Note: Encourage the young people to assume leadership roles in preparing and leading the opening prayer for each session. There is a prayer activity described in the *Introduction* section of each session. The time allotted for this prayer should be about ten minutes. Also, if your opening-prayer time is brief, ideas are listed on the *Teaching Resources* chart at the beginning of each chapter. Let the volunteer prayer-leader teams read these ideas and add or adapt them for your group's needs and circumstances.

Opening Prayer: Before the session begins, have the prayer leaders gather a large tub of water and sponges (as many as needed to provide each student with a small square piece).

Give to each young person a sponge piece. Then have the prayer leader read the following script.

> We have gathered in Jesus' name. Place the sponge piece you are holding in the water. Let this action symbolize your willingness to absorb a deep knowledge about the prayers and sacraments of the Church.

Invite the young people to look at the photo on pages 6 and 7. Read together 1 Corinthians 13:12.

Forum: Explain that in this chapter you will be looking at ways humans engage in symbolic thinking. Have a prepared volunteer lead the discussion of the symbolism of the lily pads and examining the roots and veins of the lily pads rather than just looking at them as they float on the water surface.

Presentation ___ min.

◆ Take a few minutes to explain the *Forum*—its purpose and the students' participation in and responsibility for it. Here are some points to cover.

• *Forum* is a Latin word for the place where the ideas and work of the community were explored and discussed. It was the center of public life in a Roman city. So important was this concept that in English the word *forum* refers to an intense exchange of ideas, thoughts, and opinions.

• Each day's work will begin with this kind of exchange and dialogue. The *Forum Assignment* is given in the *Conclusion* section of each chapter. It includes two steps to be prepared before the next meeting.

1. The next lesson is read thoroughly. Key ideas are underlined in pencil.

2. The *forum* activity or question is prepared for discussion. Stress the importance of both preparation for and participation in the *forum*.

◆ Have a volunteer read the poem at the top of page 8. Ask the young people, "What do you think about when you see or hold a rock?" "Do you think about strength or durability?" Then ask how all the things mentioned in the poem are much more than they seem.

A rock, a flower, a fire, a stream,
A touch, a smile, a good-bye, a dream—
Oh, how these are so much more than they seem!
In what ways can things such as these be
"much more than they seem"?

The Real World

You are about to enter into a whole new way of looking at life and faith. Now that you are more mature, it is time to go deeper in understanding exactly what Christ meant when he said, "Where two or three are gathered together in my name, there am I in the midst of them" (Matthew 18:20).

Jesus is with us, especially when we gather to celebrate the liturgy. But how does this happen? To begin our challenging exploration, we must get back to basics and start with our human experience of signs and symbols.

Have you ever heard the expression, "There's more here than meets the eye"? It means that often things can suggest images, emotions, or meanings beyond what we can see with our eyes. When this happens, the things become symbols. A *symbol* is something that stands for or suggests something

else. *Symbol* comes from a Greek word that means "to throw together." When something we observe with our senses is "thrown together" with the unseen—a memory, a feeling, or an idea—it can become a symbol.

How does this happen? To answer this question let's take a look at fire. The discovery of fire was an earthshaking moment in human history. And down through the centuries the image of fire has become a symbol of great power. Human beings see in fire so much more than simple scientific combustion. Fire has many symbolic meanings: light, energy, safety, warmth, even godlikeness.

Over time and cultures certain things or acts have come to have deeper meanings that are recognized by the people of that culture. There is a kind of "sign language" that uncovers a

8

Sacred Space

We can see from the signs that have been left us that ancient peoples used symbols to express their deep beliefs and concerns about the great mysteries of life, concerns that we share today: Who are we? Who made us? Why are we here? Who directs our lives? Does anyone care for us?

This awareness of the divine, the holy, the sacred appears in every human culture. It is expressed differently in different cultures; but in all of them, symbols are part of the way we humans communicate our belief in the sacred. And just as we do today, the ancient peoples set aside symbolic *places* in which to celebrate the sacred mysteries of life.

In every age and culture, the holy place—a shrine, forest grove, temple, church—has been symbolically set apart as a sacred area.

The ancient Greeks saw their highest mountain, Mount Olympus, as the dwelling place of the gods, where they lived shrouded from men's eyes by the mists. The Athenians chose the highest hill in their city, the Acropolis, as their sacred place.

The remains of Machu Picchu, the sacred city of the Inca, lie at the top of the Andes mountains, close to the heavens and suggesting symbolically the efforts humans must make to approach the sacred.

Have you ever been to a place sacred to a culture other than your own? If so, share your experience.

deeper world of meanings, ideas, and emotions. That sign language is made up of symbols. A multicolored piece of cloth, as we have seen, arouses feelings of patriotism. A dove suggests the human desire for peace.

Among all the creatures of earth, we humans are the only ones who have the power and the imagination to think symbolically, to interpret and make sense of our lives, and to express in symbols our deepest beliefs and concerns. What does all that have to do with our Catholic faith and with this course on liturgy and worship?

You're about to find out. This book will invite you to celebrate your faith in a way you have never done before. It will challenge you to look at things you thought were familiar in a whole new way.

9

◆ Ask a different volunteer to read each paragraph of "The Real World." Have the students highlight or underline the definition of symbol.

◆ Have the young people read "Sacred Space" quietly. Allow them a few minutes to respond to the ☀ **thought provoker** on page 9. Then invite volunteers to share their experiences.

Note: Throughout the text you will see a sunburst icon. The directives and questions here are meant to be thought provoking. They will help the young people to internalize the key concepts presented. Throughout the guide these directives and questions will be referred to as ☀ **thought provokers**.

Presentation (cont'd)

◆ Have a volunteer read *Catholic ID*. You may want to show photographs of St. Peter's Basilica. They may be found in encyclopedias or at the following web sites:

• *Feature Story: St. Peter's Basilica, Rome* at http://www.christmas 95.com/ xmas/features/story010.htm

• *Photographs of the Vatican City, Italy* at http://www.crols.com/gbrown/ travels/vatican.htm

◆ Allow a few quiet moments for the young people to read "Symbols in Action." Discuss the symbols included in the description of the President's funeral after listing the following on the board:

• a soldier leading a riderless horse (*a fallen leader*)

• no music, only muffled drums (*silence and grief caused by murder*)

• folding of flag (*service of person to his or her country*)

• playing of "Taps" (*eternal sleep*)

• lighting of eternal flame (*the person's good deeds that live on*)

Note: *FYI (For Your Information)* is a feature that will appear frequently throughout the guide. Its purpose is to provide you with some additional information about one of the topics mentioned on the pages. If you wish share the information with your group.

What about us? What do our sacred places symbolize? Our sacred places and spaces express our deepest beliefs as Catholics. Our most profound belief is that Jesus Christ, the Son of God, became one of us. He suffered, died, and rose again so that we might have new life. All our sacred places, objects, and actions help us to enter more deeply into this mystery of our salvation through Jesus Christ.

Symbols in Action

It is 1963. An assassinated president is being laid to rest. President Kennedy's flag-draped coffin is brought from the cathedral and placed on a horse-drawn gun carriage for the procession to Arlington National Cemetery. Behind the gun carriage a soldier leads a riderless horse. There is no music for this procession, only the sound of muffled drums and the creaking of the carriage wheels.

At the cemetery members of the military fold the flag, with solemn precision, into an intricate and prescribed triangle and present it to the widow. Three

buglers play in echoing sequence the plaintive *Taps*, the sound that ends a soldier's day. Mrs. Kennedy then lights an "eternal flame," a light that will never go out, on the president's grave.

This event, indelibly imprinted on the memories of those who witnessed it, is rich in symbols. How many can you discover?

When symbols are connected like this in meaningful action, we have what is called a ritual. *Rituals*, then, are symbolic actions that often express our deepest beliefs or concerns. Some rituals, of course, are very simple, such as placing candles on a birthday cake, or giving a teammate a high five after a victory.

Other rituals, such as the funeral described above, the opening ceremonies of the Olympic Games, or a graduation ceremony, have deeper and more complicated symbolism.

10

For us Catholics, all our churches are sacred spaces. Each is the "house of God" because Christ is present there in the Eucharist. Your own parish church is a sacred space. Some places, however, hold deeper significance for us because of their location or because of something that happened there. St. Peter's Basilica in Vatican City is one such sacred space. From the earliest centuries of the Church, Christians believed that this was the place where Saint Peter was martyred and buried. Excavations beneath St. Peter's have uncovered a *necropolis*, a "city of the dead." Inscriptions and bones found there seem to confirm that this is indeed the burial place of Saint Peter.

What Makes a Ritual?

Anthropologists tell us that rituals, or symbolic actions, are at the heart of human experience. From earliest times human beings have developed rituals to celebrate, remember, and express in a public way their deepest concerns, their most profound beliefs. Rituals often mark transitions from one stage of life to another. They help us make sense of life's mysteries.

What are some characteristics of ritual? Here are three of the most important ones.

• Ritual is *interpersonal*. It is something one does not alone but with others who share the same beliefs or concerns. When symbolic action is expressed by people as a community, its deepest meanings are revealed and experienced.

• Ritual is *repetitive*. Humans repeat rituals because these actions express what is most constant, most meaningful in their lives. We celebrate ritually what is unchanging to us in a changing world. If an action is true and meaningful to us, it must be repeated, celebrated, over and over again.

• Ritual is *acted out*. It uses symbolic movements and gestures to express deeper meaning.

For example, do you know why the ritual of greeting someone by shaking hands arose? What to us is now an automatic action of greeting was once a very serious and very symbolic action. In the early Middle Ages, it was a sign to strangers or possible foes that one was not holding a weapon and therefore was not a threat to the other. Once men shook hands, both were committed by honor to obey its meaning and not to attack one another during their meeting. The symbol persisted into later ages, when a man's handshake was equivalent to his word. "Let's shake on it" came into the language of business and diplomacy as a symbol of one's word of honor.

 Can you describe some other symbols that are universally recognized?

11

◆ Have the young people form small groups to discuss specific rituals they may have celebrated. Ask the groups to note any ritual that was marked by the three important characteristics described in "What Makes a Ritual?" on page 11: interpersonal, repetitive, and acted out.

◆ Have the young people highlight the key ideas highlighted on the reduced pupil pages.

◆ Direct attention to the ⸾⸾⸾ **thought provoker** on page 11. Have volunteers share their descriptions of universally recognized symbols.

If time allows, have the young people write their thoughts about symbol and ritual in their *Liturgy and Worship Journal*, pages 8–11.

FYI Saint John Damascene (about A.D. 675–749) was a monk and priest who was also a gifted writer and speaker. In 726, when the Byzantine ruler, Leo the Isaurian, condemned the use of religious images by Christians, John wrote the following defense:

What a book is for those who can read, such is an image for those who cannot. What a word is for hearing, such is an image for sight. The holy images are a memorial of God's work.

Presentation (cont'd)

◆ Have the young people highlight the key ideas highlighted on reduced pupil page 12.

◆ Ask the young people to work in pairs to complete the "Symbol and Meaning Chart" on page 12.

◆ Have two volunteers read *Scripture & My Life* and *Catholic Teachings*. Discuss with the students objects that help them recall God's presence. (*stained-glass windows, medals, statues, God's gifts in nature*)

Then ask the students to name the ways we express and have a deeper awareness of our spirituality through language. (*our prayer, the Bible, the teachings of the Church, reading about the saints, our responses at Mass, hymns or songs*)

◆ Direct attention to the  **thought provoker** on page 12. Have the young people form small groups to describe a celebration ritual.

Then have them remain in their groups to discuss the two points in *Things to Share*.

Conclusion ___ min.

Assessment: If you wish to give a standardized format test for this chapter, administer *Chapter 1 Assessment* on page 13A. Allow a brief period (about five to ten minutes) for the young people to complete the test.

An understanding of symbol and ritual is essential to a mature understanding of our worship as Catholics. All the sacraments of the Church involve ritual. And if we are aware and willing to participate, each ritual draws us more deeply into the life of faith it expresses.

In this chapter we have explored symbols: objects, places, and actions that have meanings beyond what we can perceive with our physical senses alone. All people of a given culture recognize and identify with these meanings. Of course a person has to have had some cultural experiences and a certain maturity to be aware of symbolic meanings. You are certainly ready to begin to think symbolically.

See if you can recognize the meanings of these symbols. If you are not sure, use your imagination. See how close you can come to the universal understanding of each one.

Ritual Celebrations

Like symbols, rituals, such as a salute or a handshake, can be very simple. They can also be much more complex, much richer, especially those dealing with people's cultural memories and deepest beliefs.

We have spent a great deal of time on symbol and ritual in this opening chapter. Why? Because symbolic thinking is one of the most essential and profound things humans can do. Symbolic thinking is certainly the most essential and profound thing we do as Catholics. And when we grow in appreciating and understanding the symbols and rituals of our faith, they will speak to us as nothing else in the world does.

Describe a ritual that is part of your Thanksgiving, Christmas, or Fourth of July celebration.

Symbol	Meaning
A bishop carries a shepherd's staff. It is called a *crosier*. Why a shepherd's staff?	
A traditional symbol of justice is a statue of a woman. She wears a blindfold and holds balanced scales in her hands. What do these symbols say about justice?	

12

Answers for Chapter 1 Assessment

1. c   **2.** b   **3.** c   **4.** a   **5.** b

6. a   **7.** a   **8.** c   **9.** d   **10.** See page 13.

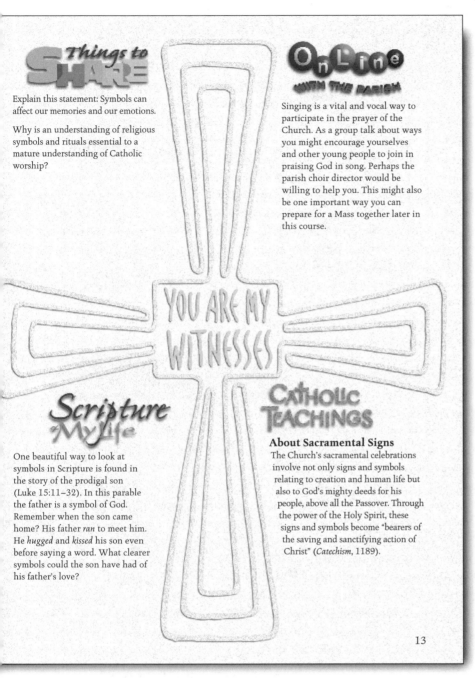

Things to SHARE

Explain this statement: Symbols can affect our memories and our emotions.

Why is an understanding of religious symbols and rituals essential to a mature understanding of Catholic worship?

OnLine WITH THE PARISH

Singing is a vital and vocal way to participate in the prayer of the Church. As a group talk about ways you might encourage yourselves and other young people to join in praising God in song. Perhaps the parish choir director would be willing to help you. This might also be one important way you can prepare for a Mass together later in this course.

Scripture of My Life

One beautiful way to look at symbols in Scripture is found in the story of the prodigal son (Luke 15:11–32). In this parable the father is a symbol of God. Remember when the son came home? His father *ran* to meet him. He *hugged* and *kissed* his son even before saying a word. What clearer symbols could the son have had of his father's love?

Catholic Teachings

About Sacramental Signs

The Church's sacramental celebrations involve not only signs and symbols relating to creation and human life but also to God's mighty deeds for his people, above all the Passover. Through the power of the Holy Spirit, these signs and symbols become "bearers of the saving and sanctifying action of Christ" (*Catechism*, 1189).

13

Conclusion (cont'd)

◆ *On Line with the Parish*, which appears in each chapter, will suggest ways the young people can connect with, participate in, and serve their parish. Take time to talk about these suggestions with the students and find ways to facilitate their parish endeavors.

Note: The *Forum Assignment* is written in the voice of the catechist addressing the group.

FORUM Assignment

✔ Read pages 14–21. Underline in pencil the statements that express six key ideas.

✔ Complete the handout *Thinking Symbolically*. Write a brief prayer about your concerns.

Closing Prayer: Invite the young people to look again at the photograph of the pond on pages 6 and 7. Encourage them to reflect silently on what they have discovered and explored "beneath the surface" during this session.

Evaluation: Have the young people discovered that symbols can affect our memories and emotions? Do they recognize that an understanding of religious symbols and rituals is essential to a mature understanding of Catholic worship?

FOR CHAPTER 2

- copies of handout *To Proclaim God's Love*, page 14C
- *Chapter 2 Assessment*, page 21A
- *Highlights for Home*, page 21B
- words and music for a joyful psalm

Assessment

 1 *Symbol* comes from a Greek word that means

a. "a sacred place."

b. "a repeated action."

c. "to throw together."

d. "an important discovery."

 2 _____ involve ritual.

a. Only the sacraments of initiation

b. All the sacraments of the Church

c. Only Baptism and Confirmation

d. Only Marriage and Holy Orders

 3 We say that ritual is _____ because it is expressed by people as a community.

a. repetitive

b. acted out

c. interpersonal

d. none of the above

 4 We say that ritual is _____ because rituals express what is most constant, most meaningful in our lives.

a. repetitive

b. acted out

c. interpersonal

d. frequent

 5 We say that ritual is _____ because we use symbolic movement to express deeper meaning.

a. repetitive

b. acted out

c. interpersonal

d. frequent

 6 Which is an example of symbolic thinking?

a. seeing fire as warmth and safety

b. seeing fire as scientific combustion

c. both a and b

d. neither a or b

 7 Which is the true statement?

a. Catholics consider all our churches to be "houses of God."

b. Catholics consider only St. Peter's Basilica to be sacred.

c. The Church teaches that symbols are non-essential to human life.

d. Sacred places have nothing to do with belief.

 8 Rituals are _____ that often express our deepest beliefs or concerns.

a. symbolic objects

b. sacred places

c. symbolic actions

d. symbolic words

 9 Which of the following would be considered a complex ritual?

a. a handshake

b. a victory sign

c. wishing someone "Happy Anniversary"

d. a wedding

 10 Explain briefly the symbolism found in the story of the prodigal son. Write your response on the reverse side of this page.

13A HANDOUT

CHAPTER 1: More Than Meets The Eye

Highlights for Home

Focus on Faith

During this course, *Liturgy and Worship*, the young people will examine closely the uniqueness of Catholic worship: its roots, its transforming power, and its deep spirituality. It is in the Church's liturgy, especially the seven sacraments, that we Catholics celebrate all that God has done for us in Jesus Christ through the working of the Holy Spirit. Our salvation was made possible through the paschal mystery of Christ's passion, death, resurrection, and ascension. As members of the Church, we are called upon to enter into this mystery of faith and truly be people of word and sacrament. This is where our lives of faith are proclaimed, formed, and nourished. If our sons and daughters are to be strong and faithful followers of Christ, they must make the liturgical life of the Church their own. In this chapter the young people will begin to see that if they are to be men and women of prayer and mature people who know how to celebrate God's presence in their lives, they must be at home with the rituals, signs, and symbols that are part of our Catholic identity.

Conversation Starters

. . . . a few ideas to talk about together . . . .

◆ What places do I consider sacred?

◆ What symbols or rituals help me make sense of life's mysteries?

◆ What religious symbol causes pleasant memories or emotions?

Feature Focus

Scripture & My Life on page 13 describes the symbolic actions of the loving father in the story of the prodigal son (Luke 15:11–32). Instead of waiting to be approached, the father *ran* to meet his son, who was returning after a long period of time. He *hugged* and *kissed* his son before the young man said a word. Reflect on the ways the relationship between the father and son symbolizes the relationship between God, our loving Father, and each of us.

Reflection

What images come to mind as you reflect on Psalm 91:1–4?

You who dwell in the shelter of the Most High,
who abide in the shadow of the Almighty,
Say to the Lord, "My refuge and fortress,
my God in whom I trust."
God will rescue you from the fowler's snare,
from the destroying plague,
Will shelter you with pinions,
spread wings that you may take refuge;
God's faithfulness is a protecting shield.

THE PRAYER OF THE CHURCH

Adult Focus

It is essential that our young people develop a deep understanding and appreciation for the public prayer of the Church, which is called *liturgy*. In this chapter they will learn that the liturgy is public because each liturgical celebration includes, concerns, and affects the whole Church. It is the official prayer of the Church.

Liturgical prayer is different from private prayer in an important way. Liturgical prayer is the prayer of Christ himself and as such has unique value far beyond what we ourselves can do. Liturgical prayer is always a prayer to the Blessed Trinity offered to God the *Father* in, through, and with his *Son, Jesus Christ*, in the unity of the *Holy Spirit*. In liturgical prayer we use the words and actions given to us by the Church. These words and actions have been treasured and handed down to us across the centuries in the rites and rituals of the liturgy.

Above all, our liturgy celebrates our relationship with the Father in and through the paschal mystery of Jesus Christ. Liturgy is a communal, public experience and, at the same time, a personal experience because of that relationship. That is why we say that good liturgy is never private, but good liturgy is always personal.

Catechism Focus:

The themes of this chapter correspond to paragraphs 1146–1152 of the *Catechism*.

Enrichment Activities

Video View

You may want to show the video *Journey to the Mountain Top,* the story of World Youth Day 1993. Viewing this dialogue of the Church with the young people from around the world and watching Pope John Paul II celebrating Mass with the youth may help the young people to understand the concerns of Christ that we pray for in liturgical prayer. Watching various youth groups in their ministry to the needy will demonstrate the statement in *Catholic Teachings:* "Liturgy sends us out to serve others, and that experience sends us back to celebrate liturgy."

The video is made available by Liguori Publications. The address is:

Redemptorist Pastoral Communications
Liguori, MO 63057
(314) 464-2500

Teaching Resources

Overview

To explore the characteristics of liturgy, in which we proclaim and celebrate the paschal mystery of Christ.

Opening Prayer Ideas

Look at the photo on pages 14 and 15. Lift up your minds and hearts to God by praying together Psalm 63:5.

or

Pray together the prayer said upon waking on page 124.

Materials

Liturgy and Worship Journal:
For Chapter 2, use pages 8–11.

- Bibles, journals, and high-lighters
- words and music for a joyful psalm

REPRODUCIBLE MASTERS
- *To Proclaim God's Love,* page 14C
- *Chapter 2 Assessment,* page 21A (optional)
- *Highlights for Home,* page 21B

Supplemental Resources

VIDEO

Gregorian Chant: The Monks and Their Music

Ignatius Press
P.O. Box 1339
Ft. Collins, CO 80522

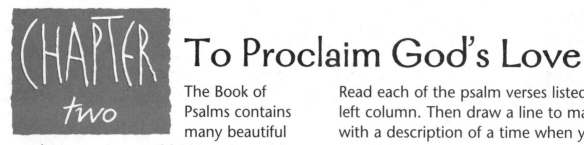

CHAPTER two

To Proclaim God's Love

The Book of Psalms contains many beautiful words our ancestors of faith used to address God. Jesus prayed the psalms, and today when we celebrate and live out the paschal mystery, we pray these verses.

Read each of the psalm verses listed in the left column. Then draw a line to match it with a description of a time when you would find it helpful to pray these words.

1. Psalm 148:1–14   a. after the sacrament of Reconciliation

2. Psalm 34:2–4   b. when you are upset and want God's guidance

3. Psalm 130:1–8   c. when you want to praise God for his gifts of creation

4. Psalm 59:17–18   d. a national holiday

5. Psalm 96:7–13   e. when you want to ask God's forgiveness

6. Psalm 121:1–8   f. when you want to invite others to pray

7. Psalm 103:1–18   g. when you want God's help to overcome temptation

8. Psalm 143:4–11   h. when you want to ask God to help you be strong and courageous

Write your favorite psalm verse. Think of the ways the words help you to lift your mind and heart to God.

_____

_____

_____

_____

_____

_____

_____

_____

_____

_____

_____

_____

The Prayer
of the Church

Lord, teach us to pray.
Luke 11:1

Objective: To explore the characteristics of liturgy in which we proclaim and celebrate the paschal mystery of Christ.

Introduction ___ min.

Opening Prayer: Explain to the young people that when we pray, we lift up our hearts and minds to God. Invite them to stand and extend their arms as if each of them was one of the tree branches shown in the photograph on pages 14 and 15. Ask all to pray the following response from Psalm 63:5 to each of the situations listed.

Response: I will lift up my hands, calling on your name.

Situations: When I am happy and my life is running smoothly. . . .
When I am upset and everything seems topsy-turvy. . . .
When I cannot seem to overcome a stumbling block. . . .

Invite any one who wishes to share the prayer he or she has written for the *Forum Assignment*.

Forum: Ask the young people to form small groups to share the symbols of concerns that they have drawn or described on the handout *Thinking Symbolically*. Allow about five minutes for discussion. Then have a prepared volunteer invite the young people to look at the photo on pages 14 and 15 as he or she reads aloud Ephesians 3:14–21.

Presentation ___ min.

◆ Brainstorm with the young people about ways we as Catholics express our hopes and beliefs. List the responses on the board.

◆ Direct attention to the photographs on these pages. Explain the following symbolism:

• The fragrant smoke that rises when incense is burned is a symbol of the people's prayers rising to God.

• By the lighting of the paschal candle, the priest expresses our hope in Christ our Light, who has risen from the dead.

During solemn celebrations of the Mass, the altar, the gifts of bread and wine, the celebrant and the participants, and the paschal candle are incensed as a sign of reverence.

◆ Discuss with the students some of their ordinary daily rituals. Ask, "Does performing these rituals make you feel secure?" "bored?"

◆ Then ask:

• What do our Catholic rituals help us to do? (*celebrate Christ's saving action in our lives*)

• What should we never forget about the signs and symbols of our faith? (*They put us in touch with the divine. Through them we share in God's own divine life.*)

◆ Have the students highlight the statements that are highlighted on the reduced pages of this chapter.

In every culture human beings express their beliefs and hopes in symbolic ways. Think of the ways that we as Catholics express our hopes and beliefs.

Catholic Symbols and Rituals

Words alone can never fully express the deep meanings of our Catholic faith. Because we are human beings, because we have bodies and live in the world of created things, we often use symbols to express our thoughts and feelings, our understandings and insights. When we Catholics pray together, we celebrate in and through *symbolic* activity. Catholic worship is filled with symbols: eating and drinking, being plunged into water and anointed with oil, standing and sitting, processing from place to place, raising our hands, speaking out and singing together. As Catholics we must never forget that these signs and symbols of our faith put us in touch with the divine. Through them we share in God's own divine life.

The church, the sacred place where we meet for worship, is full of symbols: light, fire, water, word, incense. Often the very architecture of a church is symbolic. Many of our churches are

16

cross-shaped in design, a symbol of our redemption. Others are circular, symbolic of the public nature of our worship.

The prayer of the Church is not only *symbolic* activity; it is also *ritual* activity. We do things over and over in prescribed, formal, and set ways. Rituals are characteristic of Catholic worship. At Mass, for example, Catholics know "what happens next," what to expect. When the priest greets us with, "The Lord be with you," we respond, without any thought or hesitation, "And also with you." When the priest invites us, "Let us pray," we stand up. Our rituals help us to do together what we came to do: celebrate Christ's saving actions in our lives.

Catholics perform many ritual actions during our liturgical celebrations. Perhaps you have never thought about the meaning of these rituals. But understanding what is being said and done through ritual helps us to participate in the prayer of the Church.

In order to pray well and to come to know what that prayer means in daily life, it is important for us to acquire the skills and understanding that are necessary to celebrate the prayer of the Church with enthusiasm and joy.

In this course we will discover how Catholics have traditionally prayed and worshiped God. We will explore the liturgy and the sacraments, the Church year, and Catholic devotions. We will learn about the rituals and ceremonies that Catholics have used through the centuries to celebrate God's presence in our lives. In this way we, too, can come to know how much we are loved by God and come to appreciate even more what it means to belong to his Church.

The Prayer of the Church

Liturgy is the public prayer of the Church in which we proclaim and celebrate the mystery of Christ. Originally the word *liturgy* meant "a public work"—literally, a work for the people, for everyone.

Because the public prayer of the Church is for everyone, it came to be called *liturgy*, which now means "the participation of the people in the work of God." What is the work of God? It is the work of our redemption; it is what Christ did for us. Liturgy is a work by and for the people, but above all it is God's work. In liturgy the mission of Christ—the work of his passion, death, resurrection, and ascension—continues today.

Liturgical prayer, as God's work and the work of the people, the Church, is a very particular kind of prayer. What are some of its characteristics?

Public   First, as we have already seen, liturgical prayer is *public* prayer. Yet it is public in a very special way. Not all prayers said in public are liturgical. For example, a group of people may gather in church to say the rosary. This is certainly a public act, but liturgical prayer is public in a deeper sense.

Liturgical prayer is public because each liturgical celebration, such as the Mass or the sacraments, includes, concerns, and affects the whole Church community. And because liturgical prayer is always for the entire Church, it is public even when only a small number of people are present.

Prayer of Christ   Liturgical prayer is the prayer of Christ himself. Because it is the prayer of Christ, liturgical prayer has unique and special value above and beyond anything else we, as Church, could possibly do.

17

◆ Ask volunteers to explain why it is important for us to look more closely at the liturgy and the sacraments, the Church year, and Catholic devotions. What value do they have for us? How can they help us?

Have the young people describe in their journals their current attitudes about celebrating the prayer of the Church. Encourage them to be honest. Emphasize that they should respect one another's privacy as they write in their journals.

◆ Ask, "What would you say to a friend who told you, 'I don't think liturgical prayer is for me. I'll stay at home and pray privately'?" Allow about two minutes for discussion.

◆ Ask the young people, "Would you consider the opening prayer to be liturgical prayer?" Then write the following statement beginnings on the board and have the students complete them:

• The prayer service was public prayer because . . .

• We included personal prayer when . . .

• It was not liturgical prayer because . . .

◆ Ask volunteers to explain the characteristics of liturgical prayer that are described in the chapter.

If time allows, have the young people write their thoughts about liturgical prayer in their *Liturgy and Worship Journal*, pages 8 through 11.

Presentation (cont'd)

◆ Have volunteers read the  thought provoker on page 18. Ask a volunteer to list the young people's responses on the board.

◆ Ask a volunteer to summarize *Catholic Teachings About Liturgy* on page 21. On the board draw a large circle, and divide it into four equal segments. As you point to each segment, use the following script to demonstrate that "liturgy and loving service form one unbroken circle."

- Segment 1: You have a concern about peace in the world.
- Segment 2: During the general intercessions at Sunday's Mass, the assembly prays for peace.
- Segment 3: At the dismissal the celebrant prays "Go in peace to love and serve the Lord."
- Segment 4: During the week you help to defuse rather than escalate an argument among your friends.

Then point to the second segment, and explain that during next Sunday's liturgy you will give thanks for the peace Christ brings and that sometimes you can be an instrument of his peace.

Ask the young people to think of other examples of liturgy that send us out to serve others and of experiences that send us back to celebrate liturgy.

A deacon accepting the offerings of bread and wine at the preparation of the gifts

Worship of the Trinity   Every liturgical celebration is offered in, with, and through *Jesus Christ*, in the unity of the *Holy Spirit*, to the honor and glory of the *Father*. Liturgical prayer is always worship of the Trinity.

Addressed to God   Liturgical prayer is always addressed to God. Even when we honor Mary and the other saints in the liturgy, we praise and thank God for them.

In the Words of the Church   In our private prayer we are encouraged to pray freely and spontaneously, both alone and sometimes with others. In liturgical prayer, however, we pray in the words and with the actions given to us by the Church.

Communal and Personal

In the liturgy we pray with Christ, the head of the Church, and with his whole body, the Church on earth and in heaven. Now that's public!

18

Do you think it is possible to be both *public* and *personal* at the same time? Have you ever been with a group of people celebrating a victory, a memorial, or another special moment in life? You are all experiencing something together, but at the same time you are feeling it personally, individually.

That is what liturgy is like. It is a communal experience and a personal experience at the same time. Good liturgy is never private, but good liturgy is always personal.

Liturgical prayer is the prayer of Christ. What do you think might be some of the concerns of Christ that are expressed in the liturgy?

There is an ancient saying in the Church: "The way we pray shows what we believe." The liturgy is the official way we pray as Catholics. In what way does the prayer of the Church show what we believe?

What makes us who we are as Catholics is our relationship to the Father in and through Jesus Christ. We believe in Jesus Christ—in who he is and in what God has accomplished in him. What makes us Catholic is our belief in the paschal mystery of Jesus. By the *paschal mystery* we mean all that God has done to redeem us in Christ Jesus, especially in his suffering, death, resurrection, and ascension. We proclaim this paschal mystery at every Eucharist when we say, for example:

Christ has died, Christ is risen, Christ will come again.

The word *paschal* refers to Passover, the feast of freedom for the people of Israel. During this great feast, the Jewish people celebrate their deliverance, their passing over, from slavery to freedom. During Holy Week and Easter, we Christians celebrate the "passing over" of Jesus from death to new life. As the liturgy tells us, Jesus Christ is now and always "our Passover and our lasting peace."

Mystery means more than just something that cannot be fully understood. It also means *a truth that continually calls us to deeper understanding*, a truth so wonderful that we are continually drawn to investigate the depths of its meaning.

Catholics believe that the birth, life, suffering, death, resurrection, and ascension of Jesus Christ is the very center of all that exists. When Jesus passed from death to life, all of creation was made new—including ourselves. His new life is now our new life. It is the central vocation of every Christian to discover and live the meaning of the paschal mystery, Christ's passion, death, and resurrection, in today's world. How do we do this?

The first step is to begin to develop a personal relationship with God, for it is our *person* that we bring to the public prayer of the Church. We do not come to the celebration of Christ's paschal mystery as strangers in God's presence or even as mere acquaintances. We come as Jesus' own friends and disciples, just as his first followers did.

Usually friendship does not just happen. We have to work at a relationship. We have to spend time with the other person. We have to develop common interests. We have to want what is good for the other, and we need to be willing to sacrifice for the other.

We become friends with God in much the same way, spending time with him, developing common interests, learning about God, sharing our concerns, our dreams, our hopes. That is what praying really is.

And even though we may not realize it, God is waiting for us to come to him. God, after all, tops the list of those who love us. He sees, knows, and loves us as we really are. God shows his love for us through Jesus Christ and through the Church. And it is in praying with the Church "through Jesus Christ, our Lord" that we come to recognize and respond to him in a personal way.

What is your relationship with God like? Do you come to celebrate liturgy as a stranger, as an acquaintance, or as a friend?

The Crucifixion, Georges Rouault, 1939

19

◆ Write the words *paschal* and *mystery* on the board. Have volunteers explain the meaning of both. Then ask what we mean by the term *paschal mystery*. *(all that God has done to redeem us in Christ Jesus, especially in his suffering, death, resurrection, and ascension)*

Emphasize that when we proclaim the paschal mystery at Mass, we remember what Jesus has done for us, we thank him for his great love, and we proclaim our belief that he will return in glory.

◆ Have the young people form small groups to prepare dramatic readings of the following Scripture accounts:
• Jesus' crucifixion (John 19:16–30)
• Jesus' resurrection (John 20:1–10)
• Jesus' ascension (Luke 24:36–53).

Allow the groups a few minutes preparation time. Then ask them to present their readings to the entire group.

Have volunteers name ways in which we live the paschal mystery. List the responses on the board. Then invite the young people to respond in their journals to the questions in the ⁓⁓⁓ **thought provoker** on page 19.

FYI Share the following reflection of James Turro, an author of contemporary spiritual books:

Man is God's most precious thought. This is one of the truths the sacraments disclose to us. Just as in the human community signs are used by men to manifest their thoughts and intentions toward one another, so God uses these signs to put beyond doubt his affection for us. No need to wonder or fear what God thinks of us; he declares himself through the sacraments.

Presentation (cont'd)

◆ Distribute the handout *To Proclaim God's Love*. Have the young people work in pairs to complete the matching activity. Allow about five minutes for the work.

Then have the young people check their papers as you share with them the following matches. (Answers: 1. *c*, 2. *f*, 3. *e*, 4. *h*, 5. *d*, 6. *g*, 7. *a*, 8. *b*)

◆ Have volunteers explain the ways in which the liturgy is still celebrated as it was by the early Christians. Have the group chart the similarities and differences.

Conclusion ___ min.

◆ Discuss with the young people what will never change about our liturgical celebrations. Emphasize the first paragraph. Then invite volunteers to describe various unique cultural expressions in liturgical celebrations.

Assessment: If you are administering *Chapter 2 Assessment*, allow about ten minutes for the young people to complete the test.

A Little History

How did liturgy come to be the way it is today? Our liturgical family has a history, a rich and interesting one formed by many languages, cultures, and historical events.

What are the roots of our liturgical life? Where do these symbols and rituals come from? We begin with Jesus himself. As we shall see, it is really Jesus who gives us the sacraments and entrusts them to the Church.

When the Son of God became one of us, he did so in a particular culture: Jesus was a Jew who lived in first-century Palestine. His first followers were also Jews. After the resurrection and ascension of Jesus, they continued to pray in the Temple in Jerusalem on the Sabbath. But now they did something new as well.

We read that "every day they devoted themselves to meeting together in the temple area and to breaking bread in their homes" (Acts 2:46). In the Temple they listened to readings from the Old Testament and responded with psalms and prayers. In their homes they shared the Eucharist, as Jesus had instructed them. Even at this early date, we can trace the origin of the two parts of the Mass as we know them today: the Liturgy of the Word and the Liturgy of the Eucharist.

The liturgy is a major part of the tradition of the Church. The word *tradition* means "what is handed down." Because the liturgy is handed down to us from the earliest days of the Church, we look to the teaching authority of the Church to guide our liturgical celebration.

But the liturgy is also flexible and open to various cultures. Can you discover unique cultural expressions in African liturgical worship? Latin American? Asian? Magazines from missionary societies may help you with your search.

20

As the good news of Jesus spread from Palestine to the ends of the Roman Empire, the message was translated into new languages and planted in new cultures. Greek was the common language spoken at that time, so the gospels and the letters of Saint Paul were written in Greek. Later, when Latin became the official language of the Roman Empire, the Bible and the liturgy were translated into Latin.

In what ways do we still celebrate the liturgy as the early Christians did? How are we different?

We no longer go to the Temple for prayer; instead we go to our parish churches. But we still read the same readings and pray the same psalms as the first Christians did. We no longer read the Scriptures in Latin, as the Romans did; now we read them in our own languages. We celebrate the same breaking of the bread, the same Eucharist. The most important parts of the liturgy have not changed. They have been given to us just as they were given to the first followers of Jesus.

Yet our culture today does influence some aspects of liturgy because our culture expresses our experience of life. The question of change—of what should or should not be changed based on changing culture—is always a very important and serious question for the Church. It is the Church that teaches and guides us in what can be changed and what can never be changed. For example, for two thousand years we have celebrated the Eucharist as the memorial of Christ's death and resurrection. Through sacramental signs we share in this mystery of faith. Bread and wine are transformed into the Body and Blood of Christ. This will never change. The words of institution will never change. How wonderful it is that the Church guides us to this truth and will do so for all time.

"The way we pray shows what we believe." Give one example from the liturgy that shows what we believe as Catholics.

Answers for Chapter 2 Assessment

1. d   **2.** b   **3.** d   **4.** a   **5.** c

6. c   **7.** b   **8.** a   **9.** b   **10.** See page 20.

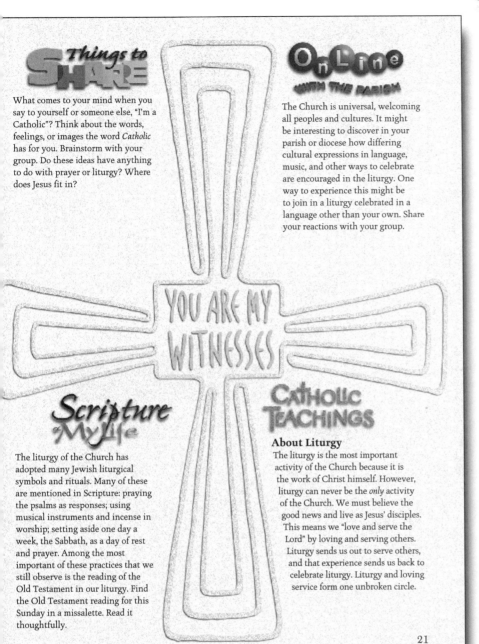

Things to SHARE

What comes to your mind when you say to yourself or someone else, "I'm a Catholic"? Think about the words, feelings, or images the word *Catholic* has for you. Brainstorm with your group. Do these ideas have anything to do with prayer or liturgy? Where does Jesus fit in?

OnLine WITH THE PARISH

The Church is universal, welcoming all peoples and cultures. It might be interesting to discover in your parish or diocese how differing cultural expressions in language, music, and other ways to celebrate are encouraged in the liturgy. One way to experience this might be to join in a liturgy celebrated in a language other than your own. Share your reactions with your group.

Scripture of My Life

The liturgy of the Church has adopted many Jewish liturgical symbols and rituals. Many of these are mentioned in Scripture: praying the psalms as responses; using musical instruments and incense in worship; setting aside one day a week, the Sabbath, as a day of rest and prayer. Among the most important of these practices that we still observe is the reading of the Old Testament in our liturgy. Find the Old Testament reading for this Sunday in a missalette. Read it thoughtfully.

CATHOLIC TEACHINGS

About Liturgy

The liturgy is the most important activity of the Church because it is the work of Christ himself. However, liturgy can never be the *only* activity of the Church. We must believe the good news and live as Jesus' disciples. This means we "love and serve the Lord" by loving and serving others. Liturgy sends us out to serve others, and that experience sends us back to celebrate liturgy. Liturgy and loving service form one unbroken circle.

21

Conclusion (cont'd)

Have a volunteer read *Scripture & My Life*. Read the Scripture passage from the Old Testament for the previous or upcoming Sunday.

FORUM Assignment

✔ Read pages 22–29. Underline in pencil the statements that express six key ideas.

✔ Discuss *Things to Share* questions with one more of the adult members of your family. Be prepared to share their and your responses.

Closing Prayer: Have the young people write their favorite psalm verse on the handout. Then proclaim together or sing a joyful psalm. After each verse, you may want to suggest that the young people use the Latin words of praise *Gloria in excelsis Deo* (**Glow**-ree-a in ex-**chel**-sees **day**-oh), meaning "Glory to God in the highest."

Evaluation: Have the young people explored the differences between private prayer and liturgical prayer? Have they discovered the meaning of the paschal mystery in our lives?

FOR CHAPTER 3

- lectionary
- copies of handout *Poetic Expression*, page 22C
- *Chapter 3 Assessment*, page 29A
- *Highlights for Home*, page 29B

Assessment

 1 Which of the following is not characteristic of liturgical prayer?
a. prayer of Christ himself
b. prayer to the Blessed Trinity
c. always addressed to God
d. includes our own words

2 _____ are characteristic of Catholic worship.
a. Personal words
b. Rituals
c. Foreign languages
d. Prayers to the saints

 3 Today Catholics define *liturgy* as
a. a work for the people.
b. personal and public prayer.
c. reading.
d. the participation of the people in the work of God.

4 The word *tradition* means
a. what is handed down.
b. being flexible.
c. cultural expression.
d. not changeable.

5 Circle the true statement.
a. Good liturgy can be private.
b. Liturgy may sometimes be the only activity of the Church.
c. Liturgy sends us out to serve others.
d. Liturgy is never personal.

 6 Current culture
a. never influences liturgy.
b. has completely changed the liturgy.
c. does influence some aspects of liturgy.
d. none of the above

 7 *Paschal* refers to
a. the birth of Jesus.
b. the feast of Passover.
c. Jesus' ascension.
d. a psalm response.

8 The two parts of the Mass originated
a. at the time of the early Christians.
b. after the fall of the Roman Empire.
c. during the Middle Ages.
d. in recent times.

9 The most important parts of the liturgy
a. have always been changed.
b. will never change.
c. may change in the future.
d. can be changed at any time.

 10 Name two ways we celebrate the liturgy as the early Christians did. Write your responses on the reverse side of this page.

Highlights for Home

Focus on Faith

In this chapter the young people have learned that when we Catholics pray together, we do so through symbol and ritual. It is essential that your son or daughter develop a deep understanding of and appreciation for the liturgy, the public prayer of the Church. You can help him or her to do this through your example.

In liturgical prayer we use the words and actions given to us by the Church. These words and actions have been treasured and handed down to us across the centuries in the rituals of the liturgy.

Help your son or daughter understand that the Church's liturgy celebrates our relationship with God the Father in and through the paschal mystery of Jesus Christ.

Conversation Starters

. . . . a few ideas to talk about together . . . .

◆ What words and symbolic gestures help me to lift up my mind and heart to God?

◆ What symbols or rituals help me make sense of life's mysteries?

◆ How do I discover and live the meaning of Christ's paschal mystery in today's world?

◆ Do I come to celebrate liturgy as a stranger, as an acquaintance, or as a friend?

Feature Focus

Catholic Teachings on page 21 explains that liturgy sends us out to serve others and that those experiences of love and service in turn send us back to celebrate liturgy. We hear the good news at Mass and we show our belief by living as Jesus' disciples.

Reflection

Think about and pray these words (Psalm 36:6–10) that have been repeated since the time of David.

Lord, your love reaches to heaven;
your fidelity, to the clouds.
Your justice is like the highest mountains;
your judgments, like the mighty deep;
all living creatures you sustain, Lord.
How precious is your love, O God!
We take refuge in the shadow of your
wings.
We feast on the rich food of your house;
from your delightful stream you give us
drink.
For with you is the fountain of life,
and in your light we see light.

GOD'S MASTERPIECES

Adult Focus

On December 17 the Church begins praying the "O antiphons" as we wait for the celebration of Jesus' coming into the world to save us from sin and death. On this day we pray:

O Wisdom, O holy Word of God,
you govern all creation with
your strong yet tender care.
Come and show your people the way to
salvation.

Jesus came to show us what God is like by what he did, what he said, and what he was. The invisible life of God, first made visible in Jesus Christ, is now made visible in the Church. Jesus has given the Church seven sacraments, visible and effective signs, through which we share in God's grace. Through the sacraments our faith is nourished and made strong.

When we celebrate the liturgy and the sacraments, we celebrate God's plan and our Christian story, which is part of that plan. That is why we can say that Catholics are truly people of word and sacrament.

Catechism Focus

The themes of this chapter correspond to paragraphs 1077–1109, 1114–1118, and 1122–1130 of the *Catechism*.

Enrichment Activities

Sacraments Are . . .

Explain to the young people that the sacraments have been referred to as "doors to the sacred" because through the sacraments we enter into communion with our God. Have the young people choose a word or a picture that says best what sacraments mean to them. On construction paper have them draw a personal symbol or logo that best illustrates the word or visualization they have chosen. Then have them mount the illustrations on black construction paper. Make stained-glass doors by hanging the young people's work on the doors of your room.

Computer Connection

Have the young people use a multimedia software program, such as *Hyperstudio*®, to make a multimedia Sunday Readings Journal. Using the *Hyperstudio*® program, they can set up the Journals as a stack of cards by making "buttons" that allow them to manipulate the stack and progress from card to card. Have them add a button for each date. Inform them that any word or icon can be used as a button.

Journal entries may take the form of questions to God, prayers, and reflections about Sunday readings. The young people may also wish to include scanned-in pictures, digitized photographs, imported sounds, and clip art. Encourage them to use different borders, backdrops, and features such as fading to black or white from card to card.

Teaching Resources

Overview

To understand that Jesus has given the Church seven sacraments through which we share in his saving work.

Opening Prayer Ideas

Look at the photos on pages 22 and 23. Meditate on the Scripture passages listed on guide page 22–23.

or

Look at the stained-glass collage on page 26. Reflect on the ways we encounter Christ in the sacraments.

Materials

- Bibles, journals, and highlighters
- lectionary

Liturgy and Worship Journal:
For Chapter 3, use pages 12–15.

REPRODUCIBLE MASTERS
- *Poetic Expression,* page 22C
- *Chapter 3 Assessment,* page 29A
- *Highlights for Home,* page 29B

Supplemental Resources

PAMPHLETS
- *Youth Update:* "Why We Have Sacraments"
Catholic Update
- "Sacraments: It All Starts with Jesus"
- "The Seven Sacraments— Symbols of God's Care"
- "What Are Sacraments?"

Saint Anthony Messenger
1615 Republic Street
Cincinnati, OH 45210

CHAPTER three

Poetic Expression

Use poetic form to express your thoughts about the sacraments or your thanks to Jesus for them. You may wish to follow one of the patterns given below:

Haiku

Example

You gave us signs of
your great love for us, Jesus.
For these, I thank you.

Cinquain

Example

Sacraments,
Jesus' signs,
Showing the way,
Filling, energizing, making holy,
Celebrations!

Pattern

Line 1 has five syllables.
Line 2 has seven syllables.
Line 3 has five syllables.

Pattern

In Line 1, one word names the subject.
In Line 2, two words describe the subject. In Line 3, three words describe an action about the subject. In Line 4, express your feelings using four words. In Line 5, one word renames the subject.

Your poetic verse

_____
_____
_____
_____
_____
_____
_____
_____
_____
_____
_____

THROUGH HIM
WITH
HIM
IN
HIM

God's Masterpieces

How great are your works, LORD!
Psalm 92:6

Objective: To understand that Jesus has given the Church seven sacraments through which we share in his saving work.

Introduction ___ min.

Opening Prayer: Invite the young people to look at the panoramic view on pages 22 and 23. Proclaim together Psalm 92:6. Use the following script to guide the young people's meditation. Have them imagine they are with the disciples in Jerusalem after Jesus' ascension. They are sharing their memories of many things Jesus has told them about himself.

• One in your midst remembers Jesus telling the Samaritan woman, "Whoever drinks the water I shall give will never thirst; the water I shall give will become in him a spring of water welling up to eternal life" (John 4:14).

• Another person remembers Jesus telling his disciples, "I am the bread of life; whoever comes to me will never hunger, and whoever believes in me will never thirst" (John 6:35).

• John reminds everyone of Jesus' words after the Passover meal: "I am the true vine, and my Father is the vine grower. He takes away every branch in me that does not bear fruit, and everyone that does he prunes so that it bears more fruit" (John 15:1–2).

• Mary, the mother of Jesus, asks the group to recall her son's words: "I am the good shepherd. A good shepherd lays down his life for the sheep" (John 10:11).

• You remind everyone about Jesus telling people that he. . . . (Have the young people take turns sharing their memories.)

As a response to Jesus' words, look again at the photos on pages 22 and 23. Pray Psalm 23 together with confidence and trust in God's great love.

Chapter Warm-up: Have a volunteer write on the board the symbols Jesus used in the Scripture passages read during the meditation. Discuss the significance of these symbols.

Forum: Refer to *Things to Share* on page 29. Have the young people form two groups. Tell the members of each group that they are on a panel discussion show. They are to discuss the words, feelings, and images that they and those they have questioned associate with being a Catholic.

Have each group choose a moderator who will share the group's ideas about prayer and liturgy.

Presentation ___ min.

◆ Ask the young people to look at the reproduction of *Jesus as the Comforter*. Invite them to share their thoughts about what Jesus might be saying.

◆ Have a volunteer read the questions in the introductory paragraph on page 24. Ask the young people to explain what a sacrament is.

◆ Allow a few minutes of quiet time for the young people to reflect on the following question: "We've already learned about the sacraments; why are we going to study about them again?"

After the quiet time, have the young people discuss their responses with a partner.

Jesus as the Comforter, August Jerndorff, 1846–1906

Is a sacrament something we pray? something we do? something we receive or something we watch? or something else? What do you think a sacrament is?

God's Master Plan

What is a sacrament? To answer this question, we go back to the very beginning. At the very beginning, when God created the world and everything in it, he had a plan. He did not just create one thing after another without knowing from the very beginning what it would be when it was all finished. The Father had a plan in mind.

Throughout the Old Testament we read about God's plan. Little by little the plan is revealed in

the history of his chosen people and through his prophets and messengers. And when the right moment came, this plan was revealed in all its wonderful mystery in the birth, life, passion, death, and resurrection of Jesus Christ. The plan God had in mind was Jesus Christ! In Jesus, God would reveal himself to us most fully. In Jesus, we see God made visible, at once truly human and truly divine.

24

Jesus, the Word Made Flesh

In the first chapters of the Book of Genesis, we glimpse the harmony God plans for the world. Men and women are at peace *with each other*: They are partners and helpers to each other. The human creatures are at peace *with the earth*. They are also at peace *with God*: Adam walks and talks with him in the garden. This is God's plan: He wants all creation to be reconciled and at peace.

Then sin shatters the dream. Peace between human beings dissolves; peace with the earth becomes toil and struggle. And peace with God? When God calls to Adam, Adam hides. He no longer walks and talks freely with God. This is the first sin—the *original* sin. And all of us share in its effects: weakness of will, tendency to sin, suffering, and death.

But God did not give up on the plan. When the time was ripe, God sent his only Son to bring it to fulfillment. This is Jesus, the Word made flesh. Jesus spent his life showing us how to be at peace with one another, with creation, and with his Father and ours. He spent his life teaching love and forgiveness, healing sickness and division. His resurrection and ascension was his victory over death and sin. Jesus is our redeemer. Through him we are saved from sin. His sacrifice on the cross and his victory over sin and death made the Father's plan of peace and harmony possible for us and for our world. The paschal mystery is the promise that God's plan will be fulfilled.

The Son of God, the second Person of the Blessed Trinity, became one of us in Jesus. In Jesus the invisible God becomes visible! In Jesus we see and come to know the invisible God, whom no eye has ever seen.

Think for a moment. How are you at peace with others, with creation, and with God? How can you deepen and strengthen this peace?

The Sacraments

The plan of God did not end with the death of Jesus. After his resurrection, the risen Christ appeared to his apostles and said, "Receive the holy Spirit" (John 20:22). In handing over the Spirit, Jesus handed over to his descendants—his followers, the Church—his own life.

This life of Jesus, this Spirit, dwells now in the Church, in us. The invisible life of God, first made visible in Jesus Christ, is now made visible in the Church. And Jesus has given the Church seven special signs to draw us into union with him and the Father through the power of the Spirit. Through the sacraments we encounter Christ. Through the sacraments we share in the saving work of Jesus Christ our redeemer.

Sacraments are unique signs. They do more than point the way; they *are* the way. For example, the water of Baptism is not only a sign of life. Through the water of Baptism, we truly receive *life*. In the Eucharist the bread and wine are not only signs of the Body and Blood of Christ. They *become* the Body and Blood of Christ.

A sacrament actually brings about—that is, makes real and present—what it signifies. When we celebrate the sacraments, we do not simply celebrate salvation, forgiveness, and union with God. We are in fact saved, forgiven, and made one with Jesus Christ.

25

◆ Discuss the ways original sin shattered the harmony of God's plan for the world and how all of us share in its effects.

Then ask, "What made the Father's plan of peace and harmony possible for us and for the world?" (*Jesus' sacrifice on the cross and his victory over sin and death*)

◆ Allow the young people a brief period to reflect on the **thought provoker** on page 25.

If the young people are using the *Liturgy and Worship Journal,* you may wish them to respond to the questions for this chapter found on pages 12 through 15.

◆ Have the young people highlight the statements highlighted on reduced pupil pages 24 and 25.

Presentation (cont'd)

◆ Direct the young people's attention to the collage of stained-glass windows on page 26. Have volunteers identify the sacrament symbolized in each window. (*Starting with Baptism, shown in upper left, and moving in clockwise direction: Confirmation, Reconciliation, Anointing of the Sick, Holy Orders, Matrimony, and Eucharist*) Ask, "Why do you think the window for Eucharist is in the center?"

Have the young people turn to page 29. Read together *Catholic Teachings.* Discuss briefly the sacraments the young people have received.

◆ Discuss the four essential qualities that are always present in the celebration of each sacrament.

Also discuss the **thought provoker** on page 26. Write the following statements on the board. Have a volunteer underline the verbs in each statement.

• We *celebrate* salvation, forgiveness, and union with God.

• We *share* in God's grace.

• We *praise* and *worship* God.

• We *remember* and enter into the paschal mystery.

Have a volunteer summarize *Catholic ID* on page 26.

A *sacrament* is a visible and effective sign, given to us by Christ, through which we share in God's grace. No wonder that the Church calls the sacraments "God's masterpieces" (*Catechism*, 1091).

Celebrating the Sacraments

The Church celebrates the seven sacraments. In the celebration of each sacrament, four essential qualities are always present.

Ritual Action   A sacrament is God's life in us—grace—expressed in ritual action. Each sacrament has its own symbols and gestures, its own ritual way of expressing the gift of grace being shared. For example, in the sacrament of the Anointing of the Sick, the sick person is anointed with oil in the sign of the cross. The oil and the cross are signs of the healing given by Christ.

Worship of God   In every sacrament we praise and worship the Holy Trinity in liturgical prayer.

Paschal Mystery   In every sacrament we remember and enter into the paschal mystery and are made part of it in a deeper way.

The Power of the Holy Spirit   The sacraments make the paschal mystery present and effective by the power of the Holy Spirit—by what God does.

Are sacraments something we only receive? Explain.

God's Plan in Writing

Each of the seven sacraments celebrates some aspect of the plan of God that has come to fulfillment in Christ and in the Church. Sacred Scripture is the written record of this divine plan as it unfolds in history. Sacred Scripture is the inspired word of God. When it is proclaimed, God is speaking to us. So when we Catholics celebrate the liturgy, we hear the word of God.

The proclamation of Sacred Scripture plays a prominent role in every liturgical celebration. In every liturgy we read aloud some part of the story of God's plan. Through the Scriptures we are reminded continually of what God has done for us and what God still plans to do—with our cooperation.

CATHOLIC ID   Because the sacraments are so important, the Church reminds us that the sacramental rites cannot be changed by anyone. Even the supreme authority in the Church can only change the liturgy after faithful reflection and "with religious respect for the mystery of the liturgy" (*Catechism*, 1125).

26

When we celebrate the liturgy and the sacraments, we celebrate God's plan and our Christian story, which is part of that plan. We need the word of God in the Scriptures to help us to hear our story with faith and understanding and to urge us on to complete the work of Christ in the world. That is why we can say that Catholics are truly people of word and sacrament.

Let us look more closely at the ways the Scriptures are used in our liturgical celebrations.

• The readings and the psalms are from Scripture.
• The prayers and liturgical songs are drawn from Scripture.
• The symbols and rituals in the liturgy take their meaning from Scripture.

In recent times the Church expanded the amount and the variety of the Scripture readings to be proclaimed. These readings are found in an official liturgical book called the *lectionary*.

The *lectionary* contains the Scripture readings assigned to the various days of the Church year. It provides us with a great variety of Scripture readings all through the year. Because it contains the word of God, we treat the lectionary with great respect.

In Every Liturgy

The liturgy of the Church has been influenced by many cultures and many languages. We use important words rooted in Hebrew, Greek, and Latin to explain the meaning behind the rituals and symbols of our liturgy. Some of these important words common to every sacrament are *anamnesis, presence, doxology, epiclesis,* and *berakah.* At first these terms may seem strange. But after we are introduced to them and we see how they function in each of the sacraments, they will begin to seem like old friends.

27

◆ If possible, show the parish's *lectionary* to the young people.

Emphasize the importance of listening to the Scripture readings during our liturgical celebrations. Give some suggestions for learning how to listen to the Scriptures.

• Listen for key words.
• Listen for key questions.
• Listen for the ending sentence.
• Ask, "What is God asking me to hear?"

Ask the young people to write in their journals what they remember about the readings of last week's liturgy. Have them use this as a way to privately evaluate their listening skills during liturgical celebrations.

◆ Turn to *Scripture & My Life* on page 29. Have the young people form small groups to read the Scripture passages and make their choices. When a representative from each group is receiving its choice for each sacrament, have him or her give the group's reason for the choice.

Just in case...
some pronunciation helps

> *anamnesis* . . . . . an-am-**nee**-sis
> *epiclesis* . . . . eh-peh-**klee**-sis
> *berakah* . . . . beh-**rah**-kah

Presentation (cont'd)

◆ Have the young people highlight the statements highlighted on reduced pupil pages 26 through 28.

◆ Write the words *anamnesis* and *presence* on the board. Point to the word *anamnesis*. Explain that this special kind of remembering helps us to keep in mind that Jesus loved us so much that he suffered, died, and rose again to save us.

Then point to the word *presence*. Ask a volunteer to explain the ways the risen Christ is present and active with us in each and every liturgy.

◆ Write the words *doxology*, *epiclesis*, and *berakah* on the board. Have a different volunteer explain the meaning of these words.

◆ Have the young people read the ☼ **thought provoker** and indicate the parts of the prayer by proclaiming each.

Assessment: If you are administering *Chapter 3 Assessment*, page 29A, allow about ten minutes for the young people to complete the test.

Conclusion ___ min.

◆ Encourage the young people to share *Highlights for Home*, page 29B, with their families.

Remembering   As we have already seen, recalling and celebrating the paschal mystery is at the heart of liturgical prayer. The term for this "remembering" is *anamnesis*. This word from the Greek means "memory," as in, "Do this in memory [*anamnesis*] of me." *Anamnesis* is the liturgical act of remembering. This special kind of remembering not only calls to mind a saving act of God that happened in the past but also makes that event present to us now.

When we celebrate the sacraments, we are not merely recalling events that happened long ago and far away. We are celebrating events that are present to us now. What began in the past, in the death and resurrection of Jesus, is continued into the present. *Now* Jesus Christ is risen. *Now* the Holy Spirit comes upon us. And *now* we are sent forth by Christ to love and serve.

Presence   The risen Christ is present and active with us in every sacrament and in every liturgy.
- He is present in the Mass under the signs of bread and wine and in the person of the priest.
- He is present in his power in the sacraments.
- He is present in his word when the Scripture is read.
- He is present in the assembly. Jesus himself said, "Where two or three are gathered together in my name, there am I in the midst of them" (Matthew 18:20).

Glory   Whenever we recall and make present God's plan for us, we experience feelings of thanksgiving and praise, and we give God glory. Each sacrament and liturgical action is a *doxology*, a prayer that gives God glory.

Calling Upon the Holy Spirit   In each sacrament we call upon the Spirit to make us holy and to build up the body of Christ. The technical term for this petition is *epiclesis*. For example, at the Eucharist we ask God:

Let your Spirit come upon these
    gifts to make them holy,
so that they may become for us
the body ✝ and blood of our Lord,
    Jesus Christ.

As we explore each of the seven sacraments, look for this prayer of petition, the epiclesis, and see what the prayer asks for. The epiclesis is often the key to understanding the meaning of a sacrament.

Blessing   One of the prayer forms familiar to Jesus and to the early Church was the berakah. The *berakah* is not a specific prayer; rather, it is a prayer *form*. The berakah usually involves three elements: We call on the name of God (invocation). We gratefully remember (anamnesis) all that God has done for us. We make our petition (epiclesis). Here is an example:

Blessed are you, Lord, God of all
    creation.
Through your goodness we have
    this bread to offer,
which earth has given and human
    hands have made.
It will become for us the bread
    of life.

This last sentence is really a prayer of petition meaning, "God, make it become for us the bread of life."

 In the prayer above indicate the invocation, anamnesis, and epiclesis.

Answers for Chapter 3 Assessment

1. c   2. b   3. d   4. d   5. c
6. b   7. a   8. c   9. a   10. Refer to page 26.

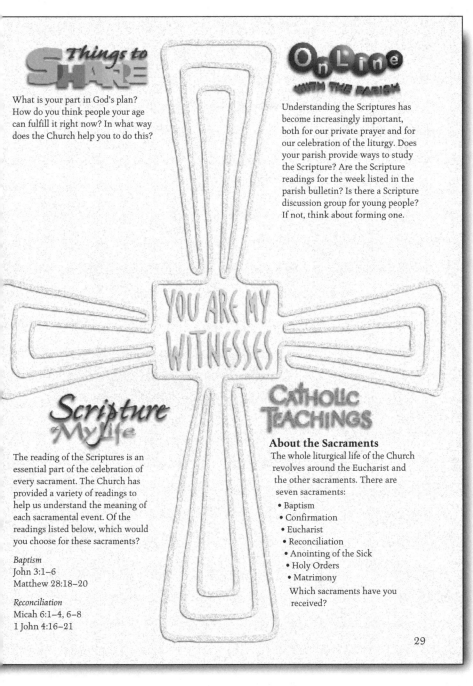

Things to SHARE

What is your part in God's plan? How do you think people your age can fulfill it right now? In what way does the Church help you to do this?

OnLine WITH THE PARISH

Understanding the Scriptures has become increasingly important, both for our private prayer and for our celebration of the liturgy. Does your parish provide ways to study the Scripture? Are the Scripture readings for the week listed in the parish bulletin? Is there a Scripture discussion group for young people? If not, think about forming one.

Scripture in My Life

The reading of the Scriptures is an essential part of the celebration of every sacrament. The Church has provided a variety of readings to help us understand the meaning of each sacramental event. Of the readings listed below, which would you choose for these sacraments?

Baptism
John 3:1–6
Matthew 28:18–20

Reconciliation
Micah 6:1–4, 6–8
1 John 4:16–21

Catholic Teachings

About the Sacraments
The whole liturgical life of the Church revolves around the Eucharist and the other sacraments. There are seven sacraments:

• Baptism
• Confirmation
• Eucharist
• Reconciliation
• Anointing of the Sick
• Holy Orders
• Matrimony
Which sacraments have you received?

29

Conclusion (cont'd)

Distribute the handout *Poetic Expression*. Have a volunteer read the directions. Explain that the young people may use a poetic form with which they are most comfortable.

FORUM Assignment

✔ Read pages 30–37. Underline in pencil the statements that express six key ideas.

✔ Complete the handout *Poetic Expression*.

Closing Prayer: Pray the following words written in the form of a berakah:

> Jesus, Good Shepherd,
> you always show me
>   the right path
> when I take time to ask
>   for your help.
> Help me this week, especially
>   when. . . .

Evaluation: Have the young people discovered that through the sacraments we encounter Jesus Christ? Have they explored the prominent role the proclamation of Scripture plays in every liturgical celebration?

FOR CHAPTER 4

• *Jesus Broke Bread with Them*, page 30C
• *Chapter 4 Assessment*, page 37A
• *Highlights for Home*, page 37B
• construction paper and markers
• missalettes or hymnals

Assessment

1 _____ is the liturgical act of remembering.
   a. Epiclesis
   b. Presence
   c. Anamnesis
   d. Berakah

2 The word _____ comes almost directly from Latin and means "to be before one."
   a. epiclesis
   b. presence
   c. anamnesis
   d. berakah

3 _____ is a prayer that gives God glory.
   a. Berakah
   b. Anamnesis
   c. Epiclesis
   d. Doxology

4 _____ is the technical term for calling upon the Holy Spirit to make us holy.
   a. Berakah
   b. Doxology
   c. Anamnesis
   d. Epiclesis

5 The proclamation of Sacred Scripture _____ every liturgical celebration.
   a. is not part of
   b. is not important in
   c. plays a prominent role in
   d. is the most important part of

6 In _____, God reveals himself to us most fully.
   a. the Book of Genesis
   b. Jesus
   c. Baptism
   d. the gifts of nature

7 Sacramental rites
   a. cannot be changed by anyone.
   b. can be changed at any time.
   c. are changed every ten years.
   d. can be changed by those participating in them.

8 The whole liturgical life of the Church revolves around _____ and the other sacraments.
   a. Baptism
   b. Reconciliation
   c. the Eucharist
   d. Confirmation

9 A sacrament is a _____ and _____ sign, given to us by Christ.
   a. visible, effective
   b. invisible, effective
   c. visible, ineffective
   d. invisible, ineffective

10 Explain briefly why the Church calls the sacraments "God's masterpieces."

   _____
   _____
   _____
   _____
   _____

Highlights for Home

Focus on Faith

Jesus came to show us what God is like by what he did, what he said, and what he was. The invisible life of God, first made visible in Jesus Christ, is now made visible in the Church. Jesus has given the Church seven sacraments, visible and effective signs, through which we share in God's grace. Through the sacraments our faith is nourished and made strong.

In previous years, the young people have studied the sacraments. Help your son or daughter to avoid the "Been there; done that" syndrome. Help them to deepen their understanding and heighten their participation as people of word and sacrament. When we celebrate the liturgy and the sacraments, we celebrate God's plan and our Christian story, which is part of that plan.

Conversation Starters

. . . . a few ideas to talk about together . . . .

◆ How is Jesus a sign of God's love?

◆ In what ways are the sacraments "doors to the sacred" for me?

◆ How can I, as a member of the Church, be a visible and effective sign of God's love?

Feature Focus

In reading *Scripture & My Life* on page 29, the young people learn that the reading of the Scriptures is an essential part of the celebration of every sacrament. The Church provides a variety of readings to help us understand the meaning of each sacramental event.

Reflection

In this chapter your sons and daughters learned about the berakah, a prayer of blessing. In some parishes it is a custom that homes be blessed during the Easter season by a parish minister or a member of the household. Reflect on and pray the following blessing:

Lord,
we rejoice in the victory of your Son over death:
by rising from the tomb to new life
he gives us new hope and promise.
Bless all the members of this household
and surround them with your protection,
that they may find comfort and peace
in Jesus Christ, the paschal lamb,
who lives and reigns with you and the
*   Holy Spirit*
one God, for ever and ever.

THE SACRAMENT OF SACRAMENTS

Adult Focus

In the Eucharist Jesus gave his Church a memorial of his saving passion, death, and resurrection. Now and for all time, we, the followers of Jesus, can gather in the presence of the risen Savior at the Eucharist and enter into his paschal mystery. We can be united with the sacrifice of Jesus Christ and give praise to the Father through him.

The Eucharist is a sacrifice. Sacrifice is a ritual action that brings about our joyful union with God. Through the sacrifice of Jesus on the cross our sins were forgiven and we were reunited with God. Every celebration of the Eucharist makes present the sacrifice of Jesus. The Eucharist is also a sacred meal. The *meal* is the external sign of the sacrifice. In the eucharistic celebration what we *see* is a meal; what the meal *makes present* is the sacrifice.

In this chapter we want the young people to come to a deeper and richer understanding of this great sacrament of love in which our redemption is carried on, we are filled with grace, and a pledge of future glory is given to us (*Catechism*, 1402, 1405).

Catechism Focus

The themes of this chapter correspond to paragraphs 1324–1332 of the *Catechism*.

Enrichment Activities

Video View

Note: It is essential that all videos be previewed before showing them to the group. This is part of teacher preparation. Choose the particular part of the video you wish to share with the students. Develop the questions or ideas you wish to use as follow-up.

The film *Jesus of Nazareth* (Zeffirelli) is one that can be used over and over again, each time showing and discussing a different segment. You might wish to add it to your library.

From *Jesus of Nazareth* show the segment on the Last Supper. Invite reactions, comments, and responses to your questions. Then, as time allows, show the segment again as part of a *Closing Prayer*. Allow time for silence and reflection. (See *Supplemental Resources*.)

Guided Meditation

Invite the group to pray using a guided meditation on the Eucharist. An excellent source is *Guided Meditations for Youth on Sacramental Life*, Arsenault and Cedor, St. Mary's Press, 702 Terrace Heights, Winona, MN 55987–1320, 1–800–533–8095. The meditations are on audio cassette. There is also a leader's guide available.

Teaching Resources

Overview

To discover in a deeper way that the Eucharist is the source and summit of the Christian life.

Opening Prayer Ideas

Reflect on 1 Corinthians 10:16.   or   Pray or sing one verse of a eucharistic hymn.

Materials

- Bibles, journals, and high-lighters
- construction paper and markers
- missalettes or hymnals

REPRODUCIBLE MASTERS
- *Jesus Broke Bread with Them,* page 30C
- *Chapter 4 Assessment,* page 37A (optional)
- *Highlights for Home,* page 37B

Liturgy and Worship Journal:
For Chapter 4, use pages 15–19.

Supplemental Resources

VIDEOS
Jesus of Nazareth
Vision Video, Inc.
2030 Wentz Church Road
P.O. Box 540
Worcester, PA 19490–0540

Sacraments—Loving Actions of the Church: "Eucharist"
Ikonographics
P.O. Box 600
Croton-on-Hudson, NY 10520

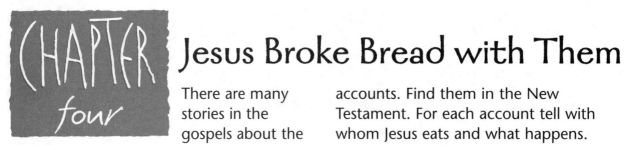

CHAPTER four

Jesus Broke Bread with Them

There are many stories in the gospels about the times when Jesus shared a meal with others. From those listed below, choose two accounts. Find them in the New Testament. For each account tell with whom Jesus eats and what happens. Select a line from the account that you wish to remember and write it.

Matthew	**Mark**	**Luke**	**John**
9:9–13	6:34–44	7:36–50	13:1–15
14:13–21	14:3–9	14:1–6	21:9–17

Gospel Account: _____

_____

Description: _____

_____

_____

_____

Quote: _____

_____

_____

_____

_____

Gospel Account: _____

_____

Description: _____

_____

_____

_____

Quote: _____

_____

_____

_____

_____

Objective: To discover in a deeper way that the Eucharist is the source and summit of the Christian life.

Introduction ___ min.

Opening Prayer: Give each person a piece of construction paper. Make sure markers are available. Ask the young people to draw or outline on the paper a symbol that stands for the truest thing they know about themselves right now. For example, a person might feel the truest thing is that he or she is honest or creative or confused or energetic or lonely. Allow about five minutes for the group to illustrate the truest things. Then gather together near the prayer table on which is placed wheat or bread and grapes or grape juice.

The Leader prays: Lord, be present with us. We bring you ourselves.

(*In turn, each person quietly places his or her symbol on the table, saying, "Here I am, Lord."*)

(*When all have done this, the bread and grape juice or wheat and grapes are passed slowly and quietly around the circle. Have music playing softly. The last person returns the symbols to the table.*)

Leader: Lord Jesus, you give yourself to us as life-giving food. In the Eucharist you say to us, "Here I am."

All: "I am the living bread that came down from heaven; whoever eats this bread will live forever" (John 6:51).
(*All return quietly to their places.*)

Forum: Allow a few minutes of quiet time for the young people to add their finishing touches to the poems they wrote on the handout *Poetic Expressions.* Encourage a supportive atmosphere by asking the young people to listen attentively to each poet who shares his or her poem with the group.

Presentation ___ min.

◆ Have a volunteer read the opener on page 32. Discuss the importance of the Eucharist. Then share examples of the power of this sacrament in the lives of people:

• Missionaries in Africa tell of people who walk twenty miles or more just to take part in the Eucharist.

• When the communists banned religious services in countries of Eastern Europe, people risked their lives to meet together secretly to celebrate Mass.

Ask, "What is your attitude toward the Eucharist?" Ask the young people to write a response to this question in their journals.

◆ Have the young people highlight the key ideas highlighted on reduced pages 32 and 33.

◆ Write the word *memorial* on the board. Ask for brief descriptions or definitions of this word. Help the young people to see that the Eucharist is not just a memory of Christ's passion, death, and resurrection as events that happened long ago; it is a living memorial. Each time we celebrate the Eucharist, we enter into and become part of the one sacrifice of Jesus Christ. This is a great mystery and we grow in understanding the mystery of the Eucharist only by coming to it as often as we can.

Why is it that we call one sacrament by so many names—Eucharist, the Lord's Supper, the breaking of Bread, the Holy Sacrifice, the sacred mysteries, Holy Communion, and Holy Mass? Why do you think this sacrament is so important?

The Body and Blood of Christ

The Eucharist is the center of our lives. The early Christians knew this. That is why, even under threat of persecution and death, they would risk their lives to come together and celebrate this sacrament. Contemporary Catholics know the same truth. All over the world, whenever and wherever the Mass is celebrated, Catholics will travel for miles or take any risk to be present. Despite any suffering the Church may endure, men and women will always come together as a eucharistic assembly of faith.

What draws people to this sacrament? After all, it has not really changed that much in two thousand years. We still offer the simple gifts of bread and wine. We still gather around the priest who presides at each Mass. Let's take a moment to look more

32

deeply at this "sacrament of sacraments" that the Church says is the source and summit of our life.

The first thing that Catholics must understand is that the sacrament of the *Eucharist* is really and truly the Body and Blood of Christ. The bread and wine are not just symbols to remind us of Christ. In the Eucharist they have become Christ—body and blood, soul and divinity. Jesus himself told us this. Even before the Last Supper, he said, "I am the living bread that came down from heaven; whoever eats this bread will live forever; and the bread that I will give is my flesh for the life of the world" (John 6:51).

On the night before he died for us, Jesus instituted this sacrament of his Body and Blood. At the Passover feast commemorating God's saving action of bringing the Jewish people from death to life, Jesus took the gifts of unleavened bread and wine and said, "This is my body which will be given up for you. This is the cup of my blood, the blood of the new and everlasting covenant. Do this in memory of me." What had Jesus done? He had given to his Church a living memorial of his saving passion, death, and resurrection. Now, for all time, his disciples could gather together in the presence of their risen Savior and enter into his paschal mystery. They could make themselves part of the one sacrifice of Jesus Christ and give praise to God the Father through him.

How wonderful! How simple and yet full of mystery. The Savior of the world would now be with his Church for all time in a most marvelous way. In this sacred meal the Church would be nourished as the body of Christ by Christ himself. In the liturgy the Church would give thanks—the meaning of Eucharist—for all that God had done through his Son. By the power of the Holy Spirit, the Church would unite itself to Christ by sharing in his Body and Blood.

When we assemble at the Eucharist, we are Christ's body, the Church, and we make this reality visible. We are never more the Church than when we are celebrating the Eucharist around the table of the Lord. In this sacrament of love, our redemption is carried on, we are filled with grace, and a pledge of future glory is given to us (*Catechism*, 1402, 1405).

Our Time, God's Time

Remembering (anamnesis) is at the heart of each of the sacraments. This is especially true of the Eucharist. Every time we celebrate the Eucharist, we hear the words "Do this in memory of me." We remember what Jesus did on Holy Thursday at the Last Supper. We remember what he did for us on Calvary on the first Good Friday. We remember how he rose from the dead on Easter Sunday. Indeed we remember the

entire life of Jesus, all that he said and did for us as our redeemer.

When we remember these events at the Eucharist, we do not merely think about events that happened long ago in Jerusalem. The liturgy makes them *present* to us here and now.

How? Imagine that you are looking at a house you have never seen before. If you are standing in front of the house, for example, you see only the front; you can only imagine what the back is like. If you are directly above the house, you have a completely different view, but you still do not see *all* of it. Time is something like that for us. We see only what is before us: the present. We can only read about the past; we can only imagine the future.

For God, however, our past, present, and future are all one. For God all time is *now*. This is a hint of what "God's time of salvation" means. In the liturgy the events we might think of as "past" are actually present. In the liturgy we do not just recall the events of Holy Thursday, Good Friday, and Easter Sunday. These events are made present.

33

◆ Draw a very large circle on the board. Ask, "Where is the past in the circle?" "Where is the present?" "Where is the future?" Explain that a circle is a whole with no beginning and no end. It is all one. It is all now. This is true of our past, present, and future with God. It is all one; it is all now.

Divide the circle into three equal sections. In each part write one of the following days: Holy Thursday, Good Friday, Easter Sunday. Invite volunteers to tell the events that happened to Jesus and the disciples on each of these days. List the information in the appropriate section of the circle. Direct attention to the language that has been used in describing the events. Point out that all the verbs are in the past tense!

On the entire circle, write "God's time is *now*." Underline the word *now*. Remind the students that in the liturgy, especially the celebration of the Eucharist, we enter into God's time. Ask, "How can the Last Supper be now? Does Christ die and rise again for us every time we celebrate the Mass?" Encourage a discussion of these ideas.

Presentation (cont'd)

Write the word *mystery* on the board. Ask for a definition. (*a truth that we cannot fully understand*) Ask the young people to reflect for a moment about the Eucharist. Then encourage them to write in their journals one question they would like to ask Jesus about the Eucharist.

◆ If possible, have a mobile in the room. Ask the young people to describe what a mobile is. If some have made mobiles in the past, ask them to explain the necessity of *balance* among all the parts. Point out that a true understanding of Eucharist demands that we keep in balance the three mysteries of Holy Thursday, Good Friday, and Easter Sunday.

◆ In large letters print the word *sacrifice* on the board. If available, use colored chalk. First ask, "What do you think of when you hear this word?" Have one or two student "scribes" list these word associations on the board, but *not* under the word *sacrifice* itself.

Now invite someone to describe animal sacrifice in the Old Testament (see page 34). Ask, "What did the sprinkling of blood symbolize?" (*God's life being shared with the people*) "What is the major emphasis of the ritual?" (*the people's joyful union with God*) Write this response on the board under *sacrifice*.

This does not mean that these events are repeated. No. Only the celebrations are repeated. But "in each celebration there is an outpouring of the Holy Spirit that makes the unique mystery present" (*Catechism*, 1104). When we celebrate the liturgy, the mysteries of our faith are made present. We enter into the event. We encounter the presence of Christ, and we are filled with God's grace. When we celebrate the liturgy, we stand in God's time and God's presence.

We must keep in balance the three mysteries—Holy Thursday, Good Friday, and Easter Sunday—and not let any one outweigh the others. A true Catholic understanding of the Eucharist is achieved only when we balance all three. If we think of the Mass as a meal but do not see the relation of the meal to Christ's sacrifice on Good Friday, we do not have a balanced understanding. If we reverence Christ present in the Eucharist but fail to reverence Christ present in the Church (in one another and in the poor), we do not have a balanced understanding of the Eucharist.

We begin with Good Friday in order to understand what we mean when we say the Mass is a *sacrifice*. When we think of sacrifices in the Old Testament,

Crucifixion, Sadao Watanabe, 1970

34

we might picture the sacrifice of an animal. The blood of the animal was a symbol of life. On the Day of Atonement, the high priest sprinkled this blood on the community. This ritual action was a sign that it was God's own life which gave life to the people. In the life the people now shared with God, their sins were forgiven; they were at one (*at-one*-ment) with God and with one another.

The emphasis in this ritual is not on the killing of the animal but on the celebration of *the people's joyful union with God*. The central meaning of sacrifice, then, is union with God. For the Hebrews, for Jesus, for the early Church, and for us today, *sacrifice* is a ritual action that brings about and celebrates our joyful union with God.

As the early followers of Jesus began to reflect on his death and resurrection, they began to understand the Good Friday event as a sacrifice. Jesus began to be seen as the Lamb of God, the paschal victim—slain, yes, but victorious in the end. Jesus broke the chains of death. Through his sacrifice our sins were forgiven and we were reunited with God. Only Jesus, the spotless victim, could have done this.

We believe that the celebration of the Eucharist makes present to us the sacrifice Jesus offered once and for all on the cross. At the Eucharist we remember Good Friday not merely as an event from the past. The sacrifice of Jesus is a *mystery*; it is more than words can say. It is a mystery we remember and make present each time we celebrate the Eucharist.

 Have you ever made a sacrifice that gave life, even in a small way?

The Eucharistic Prayer

At each Eucharist we hear these or similar words:

While they were at supper,
he took bread, said the blessing, broke the bread,
and gave it to his disciples, saying:
Take this, all of you, and eat it:
this is my body which will be given up for you.

What a wonderful phrase to reflect on: "my body which will be given up for you." In joining with

Christ to celebrate this Holy Thursday meal, we celebrate and make present the sacrifice of Good Friday. Sacrifices are celebrated in many different ways. One form of sacrifice known to Jesus and the early Church was the sacred meal: Eating and drinking together symbolized and brought about joyful union with God.

Today, at the Holy Sacrifice of the Mass, the meal is the external sign of the sacrifice. We do not ask whether the Mass is a sacrifice *or* a meal; it is *both*. The sharing of food and drink, the meal itself, is the sacrament. It is the external sign of the sacrifice. What we *see* is a meal; what the meal *makes present* is the sacrifice.

Before meals most Catholics "say grace." They say a prayer thanking God for the food they are about to eat and asking God to bless them as they share their meal. At the Eucharist, the greatest of all meals, we say, through the priest, the eucharistic prayer, the greatest of all meal prayers.

The basic shape of this meal prayer is that of the prayer of blessing (berakah) known to Jesus and the apostles. In this prayer:
• We call upon the name of God (invocation).
• We gratefully remember all that God has done for us (anamnesis).
• We make our petition (epiclesis).

The eucharistic prayer begins with a dialogue between the priest and the

people, "The Lord be with you. . . . Lift up your hearts. . . ." Then we call on God, our loving Father, and give thanks for all the wonderful things he has done for us. We thank God most especially for Jesus. We remember what Jesus did for us at the Last Supper; we remember his passion, death, and resurrection. And we make our petition. We ask God to send the Holy Spirit to change the bread and wine into the Body and Blood of Christ. We ask that we who eat the Bread and drink the Cup may become one body in that same Spirit.

When we listen closely to the words of the eucharistic prayer and understand the meaning of this greatest "grace before meals," we understand the relationship between Holy Thursday and the meaning of the Eucharist.

In order to understand the Eucharist well, we must hold these images of Good Friday and Holy Thursday in their proper balance. And to these two we add a third: the image of Easter Sunday.

 Find a song about the Eucharist in a hymnal or a missalette. What does it say about a meal? a sacrifice?

We Are One Body

Jesus told us, "I am with you always, until the end of the age" (Matthew 28:20). The Eucharist is the celebration of this abiding presence of Jesus in our midst. The risen Jesus makes us one with him in the Church. Through Baptism, Confirmation, and Eucharist, we have become the body of Christ.

CATHOLIC ID The words that Catholics use reflect what they believe about the Eucharist. Out of deep respect for Christ's real presence in the Eucharist, we call the consecrated Bread the *Host*, and the consecrated Wine the *Precious Blood*.

◆ Point out the thought provoker on page 34. Allow a brief time for reflection.

◆ Have a volunteer read *Catholic ID* on page 35. Discuss receiving Holy Communion under both species, the Host and the Precious Blood.

◆ Have the students tell what key ideas they have underlined on pages 34 and 35. Ask them to give reasons for their choices. Then have the group highlight the main ideas that are highlighted on the reduced pages.

◆ Do a quick review of the following terms by writing each word on the board and asking a volunteer to define it: berakah (*a prayer of blessing*), anamnesis (*the liturgical act of remembering*), epiclesis (*the prayer of petition*), invocation (*calling on God's name*), doxology (*praise to God*), and sacrifice (*a ritual action that brings about and celebrates joyful union with God*).

Repeat the definition of *sacrifice*. Then ask the young people whether they have ever thought of a meal as a sacrifice. Ask why the Eucharist is a sacrifice. (*The sacred meal of the Eucharist is a sacrifice because it symbolizes and brings about our joyful union with God.*)

◆ Have the young people answer the questions in the thought provoker on page 35.

Presentation (cont'd)

◆ Have a volunteer read *Catholic Teachings* on page 37. Ask the young people to highlight the definition of *transubstantiation*.

◆ Ask, "What was the important revelation Paul received when Jesus said, 'I am Jesus, whom you are persecuting'" (Acts 9:5)?

The young people should be able to see that Jesus is so united to us that what we do to one another we do to him.

◆ Discuss the ☼ **thought provoker** on page 36. Encourage thoughtful responses, not rote replies.

Have a volunteer read *Things to Share*. Ask the young people to write their responses in their journals.

Conclusion ___ min.

◆ Have volunteers read *Scripture & My Life* and *On Line with the Parish*. Discuss the questions.

Assessment: If you are planning to administer *Chapter 4 Assessment*, page 37A, allow about ten minutes for the young people to complete the test.

Supper at Emmaus, Ivo Dulčić, 1916

This is the heart of Easter Sunday: Christ is totally identified with us, his followers, his Church. Our work now is to be the presence of Christ in the world.

This is what Paul the Apostle, once called Saul, learned on the road to Damascus. In the Acts of the Apostles we see Saul on his way to persecute the followers of Jesus. Suddenly, "he fell to the ground and heard a voice saying to him, 'Saul, Saul, why are you persecuting me?' He said, 'Who are you, sir?' The reply came, 'I am Jesus, whom you are persecuting'" (Acts 9:4–5).

This experience taught Paul that Christ cannot be separated from his members. The risen Lord is so united to us, his followers, that what we do to one another we do to Christ. This fact is central to our understanding of the real presence of Christ at the Eucharist. Paul met Christ who was so identified with us that to persecute Christians was to persecute Christ himself.

Around A.D. 50, Paul wrote to the Corinthians regarding some concerns he had about the way they were celebrating the Eucharist. At issue was their understanding of the presence of Christ in the Eucharist. Paul had heard of the divisions between the rich and the poor that separated the community.

36

The poor are going hungry while the rich eat and drink all they want. Paul scolds the Corinthians for celebrating the Eucharist without recognizing the body of Christ— his Church. He tells them that this is the "body of Christ" they must see at the Eucharist if they are to celebrate worthily. He reminds them that all who eat and drink without recognizing *this* body eat and drink judgment on themselves. Sharing the Eucharist is a promise that we will treat all people as Christ would treat them—indeed, as we would treat Christ himself. This is also what it means to "do this in memory of me."

So the next time you hear the words "Body of Christ" at Communion remember and believe that:
• Christ is really and truly present in the Eucharist.
• We the Church are the body of Christ.

If we believe these things about the Eucharist, then the words of Saint Augustine can both make sense to us and challenge us: "We become what we eat"—that is, in the Eucharist we can be transformed into Christ.

☼ *Why do you think it is so important to prepare to receive Christ in the Eucharist and to receive him worthily?*

Answers for Chapter 4 Assessment

1. b   **2.** b   **3.** c   **4.** b   **5.** c
6. a   **7.** b   **8.** d   **9.** b   **10.** See pages 32–33.

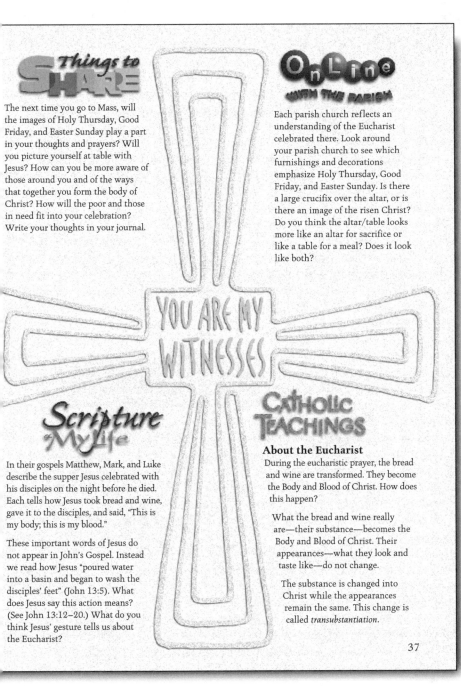

Things to SHARE

The next time you go to Mass, will the images of Holy Thursday, Good Friday, and Easter Sunday play a part in your thoughts and prayers? Will you picture yourself at table with Jesus? How can you be more aware of those around you and of the ways that together you form the body of Christ? How will the poor and those in need fit into your celebration? Write your thoughts in your journal.

OnLine WITH THE PARISH

Each parish church reflects an understanding of the Eucharist celebrated there. Look around your parish church to see which furnishings and decorations emphasize Holy Thursday, Good Friday, and Easter Sunday. Is there a large crucifix over the altar, or is there an image of the risen Christ? Do you think the altar/table looks more like an altar for sacrifice or like a table for a meal? Does it look like both?

Scripture My Life

In their gospels Matthew, Mark, and Luke describe the supper Jesus celebrated with his disciples on the night before he died. Each tells how Jesus took bread and wine, gave it to the disciples, and said, "This is my body; this is my blood."

These important words of Jesus do not appear in John's Gospel. Instead we read how Jesus "poured water into a basin and began to wash the disciples' feet" (John 13:5). What does Jesus say this action means? (See John 13:12–20.) What do you think Jesus' gesture tells us about the Eucharist?

Catholic Teachings

About the Eucharist

During the eucharistic prayer, the bread and wine are transformed. They become the Body and Blood of Christ. How does this happen?

What the bread and wine really are—their substance—becomes the Body and Blood of Christ. Their appearances—what they look and taste like—do not change.

The substance is changed into Christ while the appearances remain the same. This change is called *transubstantiation*.

37

Conclusion (cont'd)

FORUM Assignment

✔ Read pages 38–45. Underline in pencil the statements that express six main ideas.

✔ Complete the handout *Jesus Broke Bread with Them*. If possible choose passages from two different gospels.

Closing Prayer: Hand out strips of paper. Ask each person to think of one way he or she wants to share Christ with others. Have the young people write their thoughts on the strips of paper, using this formula: "Jesus, help me to bring you to others by _____." Collect the strips of paper in a basket. Then gather in a prayer circle. Invite the young people to pass the basket around the circle. As each person receives the basket, have him or her draw a paper and read the prayer. After each prayer the whole group should respond: "Body of Christ. Amen."

Evaluation: Have the young people come to a deeper understanding of the Eucharist as the source and summit of their lives as Catholics? Do they recognize the Eucharist as both meal and sacrifice?

FOR CHAPTER 5

• copies of handout *For Granted*, page 32C
• copies of *Chapter 5 Assessment*, page 45A
• copies of *Highlights for Home*, page 45B

Assessment

 1 Christ is in the Eucharist
a. through anamnesis.
b. body and blood, soul and divinity.
c. in the Church.
d. in the priest.

 2 God's time is
a. a memorial.
b. always now.
c. "straight line" time.
d. past time.

3 In each liturgy the mysteries of the faith are
a. repeated.
b. simply symbols.
c. made present to us.
d. recalled.

 4 In the Old Testament the animal's blood
a. was poured on the earth.
b. was a symbol of life.
c. was a sign of atonement.
d. both b and c

 5 The emphasis of ritual sacrifice is on
a. killing of animals.
b. instilling fear.
c. the people's union with God.
d. the reminder of death.

 6 In the Mass the meal is
a. the external sign of the sacrifice.
b. the most important part.
c. the least important part.
d. both a and c

 7 The greatest of all meal prayers is the
a. berakah.
b. eucharistic prayer.
c. words of consecration.
d. Our Father.

 8 The eucharistic prayer includes three elements:
a. berakah, epiclesis, great Amen.
b. invocation, anamnesis, sanctus.
c. berakah, anamnesis, epiclesis.
d. invocation, anamnesis, epiclesis.

9 The change of bread and wine into the Body and Blood of Christ is called
a. consecration.
b. transubstantiation.
c. invocation.
d. atonement.

 10 Explain this statement: The Eucharist is the center of our lives. Write your response on the reverse side of this page.

Highlights for Home

Focus on Faith

Often teenagers tend to feel that they have "had" lessons on the Eucharist since second grade. They can be unaware that the mystery of the Eucharist is so profound and so transforming that even a lifetime of prayer and study would never be sufficient. The Church teaches that "the Eucharist is 'the source and summit of the Christian life'" (*Catechism*, 1324). The Eucharist is Christ himself, the giver of life, the nourishment of our souls.

In this chapter on the Eucharist, the young people are asked to deepen their understanding of what it means to enter into the paschal mystery of Christ—his saving passion, death, and resurrection—made present in each celebration of the sacrament through which our redemption is carried on, we are filled with grace, and a pledge of future glory is given (*Catechism*, 1402, 1405).

Conversation Starters

. . . . a few ideas to talk about together. . . .

◆ What do I find most difficult to understand about the Eucharist?

◆ What efforts do I make to deepen my understanding?

◆ When was the last time I fully participated in the Eucharist, tuning out distractions?

Feature Focus

Scripture & My Life on page 37 points out that John's Gospel does not relate the words Jesus said over the bread and wine. Instead John recounts the action of Jesus in washing the feet of his disciples. This was a task usually reserved for servants. This action of Jesus tells us something very important about the Eucharist. What do you think it is?

Reflection

Saint Paul reminds the Corinthians that simply to receive the Eucharist without recognizing the body of Christ—the Church—is to miss the whole point of the sacrament. We are fed by the Body and Blood of Christ so that we, in turn, may be "bread" for others. Saint Augustine reminds us that "we become what we eat." In the Eucharist we become Christ.

This week:
How can I be Christ for others?
How can I be bread for the poor?

CELEBRATING EUCHARIST

Adult Focus

*This is the Lamb of God . . . .
Happy are those who are called to his supper.*

The celebration of the Eucharist is the focus of this chapter. We who are called to share the Bread of Life understand that we are called to celebrate both a meal and a sacrifice. We celebrate this sacrificial meal within a fourfold structure that can be found in any celebratory meal: 1) We gather (the Introductory Rites); 2) We tell our stories (the Liturgy of the Word); 3) We share our meal (the Liturgy of the Eucharist); 4) We return home (the commissioning).

As the young people follow this outline, they are gradually led to a deeper and more complete understanding of each part of the Mass. They are encouraged to examine in detail the celebration they have experienced countless times, in order that the meaning of these familiar rites might emerge in a new and more profound way.

A complete understanding of the celebration of the Eucharist requires a broad view—a view of the past (the Last Supper), the present (Christ's living presence today), and the future (a foretaste of the banquet of heaven). As this broad view comes into focus for the young people, they can be encouraged to put this new understanding into practice through a more informed participation in the holy sacrifice of the Mass.

Catechism Focus

The theme of this chapter corresponds to paragraphs 1346–1355, 1384–1387, and 1396–1405 of the *Catechism*.

Enrichment Activities

Computer Connection
Have the young people use a writing program to compose letters thanking Jesus for the wonderful gift of himself in Holy Communion.

If your class is using the *Student Writing Center*™*, begin by selecting the letter icon and then "With Letterhead" from the Letter Layout window. Instruct the young people to choose an appropriate letterhead from the "Choose a Letterhead" window. Make sure they clear the letterhead of any existing text by highlighting the text and then pressing the delete key. Encourage the young people to add pictures to enhance their letters either before or after they finish writing. To access the picture library, they should click on the picture icon or select "Choose Picture," listed under "Graphics" in the main menu.

Have the young people print their letters. Have each person roll up his or her letter and tie a decorative ribbon around it. Collect the scrolled letters into a box, and present them at a group prayer service or liturgy.

Sacred Vessels
Invite a priest to show and explain the use of the sacred vessels used during the celebration of the Eucharist.

Teaching Resources

Overview

To discover that the celebration of the Eucharist has a fourfold structure: gathering, storytelling, meal sharing, and commissioning.

Opening Prayer Ideas

Spend quiet time in prayer to Jesus. Express your thoughts about celebrating the Eucharist.

or

Pray or sing together the Our Father. Invite the young people to exchange a sign of peace with those who are near them.

Materials

- Bibles, journals, and highlighters
- notepaper and envelopes or tape or stapler for sealing letters
- basket
- missalettes

REPRODUCIBLE MASTERS
- *For Granted*, page 38C
- *Chapter 5 Assessment*, page 45A
- *Highlights for Home*, page 45B

 Liturgy and Worship Journal:
For Chapter 5, use pages 20–23.

Supplemental Resources

VIDEOS
Living Eucharist
A Eucharist Parable
Saint Anthony Messenger
http://www.american catholic.org

A Teen's Guide to Living the Mass
Liguori Publications
1 Liguori Drive
Liguori, MO 63057

CHAPTER five

For Granted

Imagine that thirty-five years have passed and that you have been stationed on Space Base 10 for a few years. Your chaplain has not been able to visit to celebrate Mass for almost a year. On the lines below, finish the conversation with the chaplain to express your feelings about this matter.

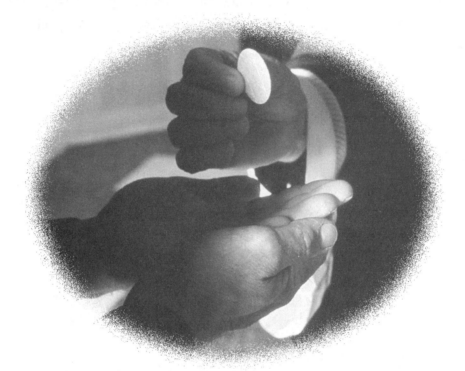

You: I think I took for granted the privilege of participating in Mass and receiving Jesus' Body and Blood every Sunday while I was based on earth!

Chaplain: _____
_____
_____

Chaplain: _____
_____
_____

You: When I return home, _____
_____
_____
_____

You: I really miss _____
_____
_____

Chaplain: _____
_____
_____

Celebrating Eucharist

He was made known to them
in the breaking of the bread.
Luke 24:35

Objective: To discover that the celebration of the Eucharist has a fourfold structure: gathering, storytelling, meal sharing, and commissioning.

Introduction ___ min.

Opening Prayer: Ask the young people to write a note to Jesus to express their thoughts about attending and participating in Mass each week. Encourage them to be honest, and assure them that no one will read their notes.

When you see that most people have finished writing, ask them to read over and then fold the notes. You may want to provide envelopes, tape, or staples for sealing the notes. Then ask the young people to print their initials on the outside of the notes. Have a volunteer take around a basket to collect the notes. Then place the basket on the group's prayer table.

Invite the young people to look at the photos on pages 38 and 39. Have them imagine that Jesus is walking with them on the road through the field. He is speaking to them personally, responding to their notes. Allow a few minutes of quiet time.

Direct the young people's attention to the painting of the supper at Emmaus on page 39. Have a volunteer read the account in Luke 24:28–35. Ask the young people to pray quietly, answering Jesus' request to celebrate the Eucharist.

Forum: Have the young people form small groups to share their responses they have written on the handout *Jesus Broke Bread with Them*. After the brief discussion time, invite a representative from each group to summarize the members' responses.

Presentation ___ min.

◆ Have the young people form small groups to discuss the following questions:

• Do you notice a pattern to the parts of the parties or celebrations you have been going to in the past year?

• What is the pattern you would describe to friends who have moved to another community?

• Do you enjoy the parties if you go with a poor social attitude or in a bad mood?

◆ Then read the following scenario: You have invited all of your best friends to a party at your home. A few of the guests do not speak or participate in the party activities.

Ask, "How do these people affect the spirit of the entire group?"

While the young people are discussing, write on the board the four parts of any meal of celebration listed by number on page 40. Have the groups compare and contrast their patterns with this list.

◆ Invite the young people to turn to *Scripture & My Life* on page 45. Have a volunteer read the paragraph and then have everyone read the story of Emmaus quietly. Ask volunteers to respond to the questions.

What would you say if a friend who had never been to Mass asked you, "What do you Catholics do when you go to church on Sunday?"

Owning the Eucharist

Most of us have been celebrating the Eucharist almost all our lives, so we may think we know it well. But the Eucharist is a great mystery, so there is always more to understand, more to appreciate, more to celebrate. The Eucharist is a community action, a liturgical action. It requires the participation of each and every one of us, the entire body of Christ.

"Doing" is different from just "watching." Doing requires information and skills. Playing the trumpet in the band requires more information and skills than watching the parade go by. At the Eucharist we are the "players"; we *all* celebrate the Eucharist together. We each have an active part, whether that be reading, listening, bringing up the gifts, singing, or responding together with our "Amen!" In the last chapter we studied what the Eucharist means. Now we want to learn how to celebrate that meaning.

The external shape of the Mass is a meal. It will help us understand how to celebrate the Eucharist if we first think of what we do when we celebrate a special meal in our homes. For example, how might you celebrate Thanksgiving dinner at your grandmother's house?

Each person's Thanksgiving might be a little different, but we would probably find these same four parts in any meal of celebration: (1) We gather. (2) We tell our stories. (3) We share our meal by putting food on the table, saying the blessing, and eating and drinking. (4) We return home.

The Eucharistic meal has a similar four-fold structure:
• gathering
• storytelling
• meal sharing: preparation of the gifts, the eucharistic prayer, the communion rite
• commissioning.

40

Each of these elements has its own special purpose. The better we understand each of these four parts of the Eucharist, the better will we be able to celebrate the Eucharist with meaning.

Gathering

We come together in one place for the eucharistic assembly. We gather together as the Church to make the body of Christ visible.

The priest invites us to make the sign of the cross. He greets us, saying "The Lord be with you." We respond, "And also with you." This greeting is used

several times during the Mass. It is intended both as a wish, meaning "*May* the Lord be with you" and as a profound statement of faith, meaning "As you assemble for worship, the Lord *is* with you." The Introductory Rites are intended *to gather us together into a worshiping assembly.* We are asked to pause and recall our common need for salvation (the penitential rite). On Sundays and feasts, we sing or recite the hymn "Glory to God in the highest." At the close of the Introductory Rites that gather us together, the priest asks us to join our hearts and minds in prayer. After a few moments of silence, the priest "collects" our intentions into one prayer. We make it our own by responding "Amen."

Storytelling

When we gather for a meal, we usually begin with conversation: telling our stories. At the Eucharist, after the Introductory Rites, we sit down and enter into the ritual of conversation with Sacred Scripture, the inspired word of God. We do this in the Liturgy of the Word.

Through the reading of the Scriptures, we listen to the Father's story once again. On Sundays we have three opportunities, because there are three readings. The first reading is ordinarily taken from the Old Testament and is related in theme to the gospel of the day. This Old Testament reading recalls, in some way, God the Father's original covenant with us.

41

◆ Distribute parish missalettes. If possible, have the young people find the prayers in the Introductory Rites. Explain that the celebrant has the option of using one of two greetings and one of the three penitential rites. Also explain that there is a different set of two opening prayers that the priest may choose to use for each Sunday.

◆ Explain to the young people that the rite of blessing and sprinkling of holy water may be used in place of the penitential rite. The prayer of blessing reminds us that water brings new life to the earth and that in Baptism water is the sign of being cleansed from sin.

◆ Invite volunteers to list on the board the different parts of the Liturgy of the Word in the correct sequence. Remind the group that Scripture is the inspired word of God. As God's word, Scripture has a unique power in our lives. We can truly say that Scripture is God's word in power, which brings about what it proclaims.

FYI The prayer of blessing used during the Easter season reminds us that the Israelites were led through the waters of the Red Sea to freedom, and that we are led through the waters of Baptism to life in Christ and freedom from sin. In this prayer we ask to share the joy of all who were baptized at Easter. After the people are sprinkled with the holy water, the priest faces the people and says:

> May almighty God cleanse us of our sins,
> and through the eucharist we celebrate
> make us worthy to sit at his table
> in his heavenly kingdom.

Presentation (cont'd)

◆ Discuss with the young people the statements they underlined in this chapter. Then have them highlight the key ideas highlighted on the reduced pupil pages.

◆ Ask a volunteer to summarize "General Intercessions" on page 42. Direct attention to the ☼ **thought provoker**. Have the young people form four groups. Designate for each group one of the four categories listed. Have the group write a general intercession for this category. Explain that the groups will pray for these intentions during the *Closing Prayer*.

◆ Ask volunteers to explain the words and actions of the preparation of the gifts. You may want to discuss the following points with the young people:

• In the past, when society was agricultural, the gifts given at the Eucharist often included garden and farm produce. Some of this food helped to support the parish priest; some of it was given to the poor.

Preparation of the Gifts   *The Dialogue*

Following the first reading we sing or recite a psalm, a song from the Book of Psalms. The second reading is usually from one of the letters of Paul or from another apostolic writing. The first two readings conclude with "The word of the Lord." To this we all respond with our liturgical "yes" as we say, "Thanks be to God."

The third reading is taken from one of the four gospels. Because of the unique respect given to the gospel words of Jesus, it has long been the custom in the Church to stand in attentive reverence during the proclamation of the gospel.

Before proclaiming the gospel, the priest greets us with "The Lord be with you." As he announces the particular gospel of the day, he traces with his right thumb a series of three small crosses on his forehead, on his lips, and on his heart. Silently he prays that God will cleanse his mind and his heart so that his lips may proclaim the gospel worthily. In many places the congregation makes these small signs of the cross along with the priest. The gospel reading concludes with, "The gospel of the Lord." We respond, "Praise to you, Lord Jesus Christ." We thus proclaim our faith in the presence of Christ in the word. Then we sit for the homily.

The *homily* takes the word of God and brings it to our life today. Just as a large piece of bread must be broken to be eaten, a good homily "breaks open" the word of God in order that we might hear, understand, and act upon it.

On Sundays we then stand and together recite the Nicene Creed.

42

The creed is a statement of our faith in the word we have heard proclaimed in the Scripture and the homily. The creed reminds us of the faith we accepted at Baptism. As we make our profession of faith at Mass, we are reminded that each time we come to the Eucharist, we come through Baptism.

General Intercessions   The Liturgy of the Word comes to a close with what are called the general intercessions.

In the general intercessions, we pray that our Church and our world might come to look like the plan God has for us. Our petitions usually fall into four categories: the needs of the universal Church, all nations and their leaders, people in special need, and the needs of our local parish. As these petitions are announced, we all pray for these intentions in our hearts. Then we make our common response aloud: "Lord, hear our prayer."

☼ *What will you pray for so that your parish community will "reflect" the body of Christ proclaimed in the Scripture?*

Epiclesis

Consecration and Anamnesis

Doxology

Following the Liturgy of the Word, we move to the table of the Lord. In any meal celebration there are three movements: We bring the food to the table, say grace, and share the food. At Mass these actions are called the preparation of the gifts, the eucharistic prayer, and the communion rite.

Preparation of the Gifts Members of the community bring the bread and wine for the Eucharist to the priest at the altar. Then begins the preparation of gifts. The priest places the bread and wine on the table. He mixes water with wine and washes his hands. These gestures remind us of the Last Supper: Mixing water with the wine and washing hands were rituals the Jews followed at all meals in Jesus' time. The priest then invites us to pray that our sacrifice be acceptable to God. We respond "Amen" to the prayer over the gifts and stand to participate in the central prayer of the Mass.

The Eucharistic Prayer

The eucharistic prayer brings us to the very center of the Mass and to the heart of our Catholic faith. The structure of this prayer is that of a berakah.

The Dialogue The eucharistic prayer begins with a dialogue between the priest and the assembly: "The Lord be with you. . . ." The priest then asks if we are ready and willing to approach the table, to renew our baptismal commitment, to offer ourselves to God: "Lift up your hearts." And we say: "We lift them up to the Lord." The priest invites us to give thanks to the Lord our God. And we respond: "It is right to give him thanks and praise." (The word *eucharist* comes from the Greek, "to give thanks and praise.")

The Preface The priest begins the preface. Here *preface* retains its original meaning of speaking in the presence of God. We are brought into God's presence and speak directly to God, thanking him for his wonderful works. We join the choirs of angels, who praise God unendingly in the heavenly liturgy, saying:

> Holy, holy, holy Lord, God of power and might, heaven and earth are full of your glory.

Epiclesis The priest invokes the Father (epiclesis) to send the Holy Spirit to change our gifts of bread and wine into the Body and Blood of Christ. We also pray that we who take part in this Eucharist may become one body and one spirit. Only then can we experience the fullest presence of Christ.

Anamnesis The priest recalls the events of the Last Supper and the story of the institution of the Eucharist. (These words are called the "words of consecration.")

CATHOLIC ID

Do you know that we Catholics consider the Eucharist a sacrament of reconciliation? The Church tells us that when we receive the Eucharist worthily, our venial sins are forgiven. The Eucharist strengthens our love for God, self, and others, and this love wipes out sin. The Eucharist also preserves us from future sin. "The more we share the life of Christ and progress in his friendship, the more difficult it is to break away from him" (*Catechism*, 1395). Forgiveness of sin springs from the principal effect of the Eucharist in our lives: union with Christ.

43

- This tradition continues today. In some parishes it is customary to bring food for the poor to the altar at the same time that the gifts of bread and wine are carried up. This becomes a symbol of our unity with one another in the body of Christ.

- During the preparation of the gifts, the weekly collection is also taken up. In modern times most people are given money in exchange for the work of their hands and minds.

◆ Have the young people open their parish missalettes to the eucharistic prayer. Ask the students to focus on the appropriate photo at the top of pages 42 and 43 and then read quietly the prayers for the dialogue, preface, epiclesis, consecration, anamnesis, and doxology. Choose the first or second eucharistic prayer for this exercise.

◆ Have a volunteer summarize *Catholic ID* on page 43. Read together the words of the *Catechism*.

◆ Invite a volunteer to read *Catholic Teachings* on page 45. Explain that each diocese or individual parish has preparation seminars for those who wish to serve as eucharistic ministers.

Presentation (cont'd)

◆ Ask, "Why is it appropriate to pray the Our Father and extend the sign of peace before we receive the Body and Blood of Christ?" If students do not give the following responses, include them in your discussion:

• All during his public life, Jesus preached forgiveness and reconciliation. The Our Father summarizes Jesus' message.

• In order to be united with Jesus, we should be united with one another.

 Discuss some of the hymns or songs we sing at communion time. You may want to play a recording or read the lyrics of one that clearly explains that the Body and Blood of Christ unite us as one body in Christ. The following are suggestions: "At That First Eucharist" and "How Blest Are We" (found in many missalettes); "We Remember" by Marty Haugen, *With Open Hands*, GIA.

Have the young people write their reflections about the lyrics in their journals.

Conclusion ___ min.

◆ If time allows, have the young people form small groups to discuss *Things to Share*.

Assessment: Have the young people work in pairs to complete *Chapter 5 Assessment*.

He then speaks to us, inviting us to "proclaim the mystery of faith." A short and familiar acclamation is:

> Christ has died,
> Christ is risen,
> Christ will come again.

The priest continues to recall with us (anamnesis) the wonderful deeds which saved us: the passion, death, and resurrection of Christ.

Epiclesis for Unity The grateful memory of God's salvation leads us to make the second half of our petition—our primary petition (epiclesis) at every Eucharist—the petition for unity. We look forward to that glorious feast of never-ending joy in heaven and join our voices with those of all the saints who have gone before us as the priest raises the bread and wine and offers a doxology, a prayer of glory to God in the name of Christ:

> Through him,
> with him,
> in him,
> in the unity of the Holy Spirit,
> all glory and honor is yours,
> almighty Father,
> for ever and ever.

Our "Amen" to this prayer acclaims our assent and participation in the entire eucharistic prayer.

 Look back at the parts of the eucharistic prayer on these pages. What do you think we are saying "yes" to in each of the parts?

The Communion Rite

Now, we prepare to eat and drink at the Lord's table by praying together the Lord's Prayer: "Give us this day our daily bread; and forgive us our trespasses as we forgive those who trespass against us."

Communion is the sign and source of our reconciliation and union with God and with one another. Therefore, we make a gesture of union and forgiveness with those around us and offer them a sign of peace.

The priest then shows us the Bread and Cup and invites us to come to the table:

> This is the Lamb of God. . . .
> Happy are those who are called to his supper.

Here we are once more reminded that the Mass is both a sacrifice and a meal. We come forward to eat and drink the Body and Blood of Christ. We approach the minister, who gives us the eucharistic Bread with the words "The body of Christ." We respond "Amen." We then go to the minister with the Cup who offers it to us with the words "The blood of Christ," to which we again profess our "Amen."

During this procession we usually sing a hymn which unites our voices, thoughts, and spirits, even as the Body and Blood of Christ unites us as one body in Christ. Then we pray silently in our hearts, asking for all that this sacrament promises. The priest unites our prayers in the prayer after Communion, to which we respond "Amen."

Commissioning

Finally we prepare to go back to that world in which we work and play, study and live. The burdens we have laid down at the door of the church for this Eucharist we now take up again. But now we bear them with the strength received from this Eucharist and this community. The priest again says "The Lord be with you," this ritual phrase serving now as a farewell.

We bow our heads to receive a blessing. As the priest blesses us in the name of the Trinity, we make the sign of the cross as we did at the beginning of the Mass. The priest or deacon then dismisses the assembly: "Go in peace to love and serve the Lord." And we give our liturgical "yes" as we say "Thanks be to God."

 *Reflect for a moment. Decide on one way you will go forth from the Eucharist to be "bread" for someone.*

Answers for Chapter 5 Assessment

1. b	**2.** f	**3.** h	**4.** i	**5.** c
6. a	**7.** d	**8.** e	**9.** g	**10.** See page 44.

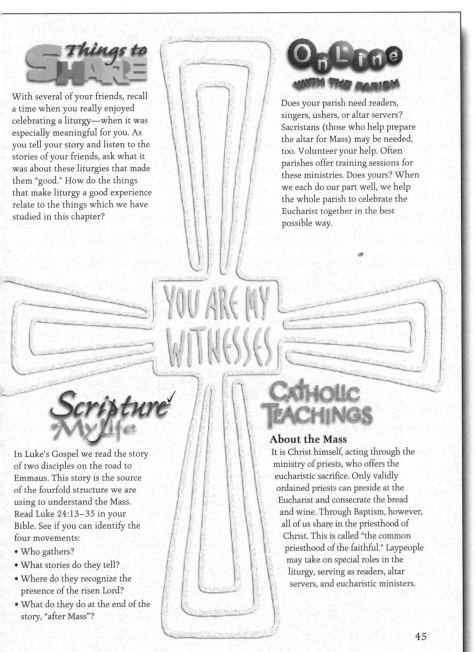

Things to SHARE

With several of your friends, recall a time when you really enjoyed celebrating a liturgy—when it was especially meaningful for you. As you tell your story and listen to the stories of your friends, ask what it was about these liturgies that made them "good." How do the things that make liturgy a good experience relate to the things which we have studied in this chapter?

OnLine WITH THE PARISH

Does your parish need readers, singers, ushers, or altar servers? Sacristans (those who help prepare the altar for Mass) may be needed, too. Volunteer your help. Often parishes offer training sessions for these ministries. Does yours? When we each do our part well, we help the whole parish to celebrate the Eucharist together in the best possible way.

Scripture My Life

In Luke's Gospel we read the story of two disciples on the road to Emmaus. This story is the source of the fourfold structure we are using to understand the Mass. Read Luke 24:13–35 in your Bible. See if you can identify the four movements:

• Who gathers?
• What stories do they tell?
• Where do they recognize the presence of the risen Lord?
• What do they do at the end of the story, "after Mass"?

Catholic Teachings

About the Mass
It is Christ himself, acting through the ministry of priests, who offers the eucharistic sacrifice. Only validly ordained priests can preside at the Eucharist and consecrate the bread and wine. Through Baptism, however, all of us share in the priesthood of Christ. This is called "the common priesthood of the faithful." Laypeople may take on special roles in the liturgy, serving as readers, altar servers, and eucharistic ministers.

45

Conclusion (cont'd)

FORUM Assignment

✔ Read pages 46–51. Underline in pencil the statements that express six key ideas.

✔ Complete the handout *For Granted*.

Closing Prayer: Reflect on the thought provokers on page 44. Then have a representative from each prayer-writing group read the petition written for the general intercessions. (See page 42.) Encourage volunteers to offer additional petitions. Direct all the young people to respond to each petition with the words "Lord, hear our prayer."

Evaluation: Have the young people explored the fourfold structure of the Mass? Do the young people see the need for their full participation in the celebration?

FOR CHAPTER 6

• copies of handout *Sealed in the Spirit*, page 46C
• copies of *Chapter 6 Assessment*, page 53A
• copies of *Highlights for Home*, page 53B
• drawing of a sunrise

Assessment

Choose the correct letter for the term that completes each statement.

- **a.** general intercessions
- **b.** preface
- **c.** homily
- **d.** Liturgy of the Eucharist
- **e.** gospel
- **f.** words of consecration
- **g.** creed
- **h.** Introductory Rites
- **i.** first reading

1 We sing "Holy, holy, holy Lord," during the _____.

2 In the _____ the priest recalls the events of the Last Supper and the story of the institution of the Eucharist.

3 The _____ are intended to gather us together into a worshiping assembly.

4 The _____ is ordinarily taken from the Old Testament.

5 The _____ takes the word of God and brings it to our life today.

6 In the _____ we pray for the needs of the universal Church, all nations and their leaders, people in special need, and the needs of our local parish.

7 The _____ consists of three parts: the preparation of the gifts, the eucharistic prayer, and the communion rite.

8 During the proclamation of the _____ , we stand in attentive reverence.

9 The _____ is a statement of our faith in the word we have heard proclaimed in the Scripture and homily.

10 Explain briefly what happens during the commissioning part of Mass.

_____
_____
_____
_____
_____
_____
_____
_____

© William H. Sadlier, Inc. Permission to duplicate is granted to the users of the *Faith and Witness* Program.

CHAPTER 5: Celebrating Eucharist

Highlights for Home

Focus on Faith

Today many families regret that a busy schedule sometimes prevents a family meal but are creative in scheduling a weekly "family night" instead. The sacrificial meal of the Eucharist is the family meal of the Church. We gather together as baptized brothers and sisters, as followers of Jesus Christ. We celebrate his death, his resurrection, and his presence with us in the sacrament. The outward structure of this eucharistic meal is the same as for any family meal: (1) We gather (the Introductory Rites). (2) We talk and tell stories (the Liturgy of the Word). (3) We bring food to the table, ask God's blessing, and share the food (the Liturgy of the Eucharist). (4) We end the meal (the commissioning).

This chapter reintroduces our young people to the celebration of the Eucharist in a deep and detailed way. Most have been celebrating and receiving the Body and Blood of Christ for many years. Now, from the perspective of belonging, they are able to reflect on their own experience of Eucharist as they explore the celebration of the holy sacrifice of the Mass.

Conversation Starters

. . . . a few ideas to talk about together . . . .

◆ When do you look forward to the celebration of the Eucharist and appreciate it most? Advent? Christmas? Easter? a special day when a family member is involved?

◆ Do you look forward to the Sunday celebration of the Eucharist? How do you prepare for it? How do you participate in it?

Feature Focus

Scripture & My Life on page 45 explains how the fourfold structure of the Eucharist is related to the story of the two disciples on the way to Emmaus. Try reading the Scripture passage suggested (Luke 24:13–35). Answer the questions with the passage in mind. Then see whether you can apply the questions to a contemporary celebration of the Eucharist. The risen Lord is just as present in the Eucharist today as he was at Emmaus!

Reflection

The opening pages of this chapter present Caravaggio's *Supper at Emmaus.* The scene is early evening, in a wayside inn, as Jesus blesses, breaks, and then gives the bread to his disciples. Up to this point Jesus had been an anonymous wayfarer, someone who had been with them on the road and had been cordially invited to supper. But at the moment of recognition, at the breaking of the bread, Jesus was revealed to them as their friend and Savior.

Picture yourself in this scene. Jesus has been with you all along the road. He has taught you from the Scriptures and from your own experience of life. Now he is about to offer you the greatest gift of all: himself, his life. How will you respond?

Adult Focus

In recent years a new way of preparing adults and young people for the sacraments of initiation (Baptism, Confirmation, and Eucharist) has been adopted by the Church. You may have experienced this new way implemented in your own parish. It is called the *Rite of Christian Initiation of Adults (RCIA)*.

This chapter introduces our young people to the RCIA as a means of their learning more about the sacraments of initiation. The chapter explains that this new method of instruction and gradual incorporation into the Church is not really new; rather, it is very old. The liturgical rites we celebrate as part of the RCIA today have their origins in the practices of the early Christians.

The important process we share with the early Christians is the lifelong process of conversion. Begun at Baptism, our conversion continues in our Christian lives today. Confirmation strengthens and affirms this process as we are sealed in the Spirit. The Eucharist, as it unites us to Christ and to one another in his body, nourishes us in this lifelong journey to God.

Catechism Focus

The themes of this chapter correspond to paragraphs 1214–1215, 1226–1241, 1243–1274, 1285–1289, and 1293–1305 of the *Catechism*.

Enrichment Activities

In Support

Write a group note of encouragement to the catechumens of your parish who are preparing for the sacraments of initiation or to the candidates who are preparing for Confirmation. Offer prayers of support, and thank the groups for their example in turning toward a life that is filled with the Holy Spirit.

Sacraments of Initiation Triptych

Have the young people work in small groups to make large triptychs (artwork presented in three panels or sections side by side).

Explain that on each panel the group should symbolize in words and/or illustration the meaning and significance of one of the sacraments of initiation. Display the triptychs in the church vestibule or parish hall to remind the parish community that conversion is "an uninterrupted task for the whole Church" (*Catechism*, 1428).

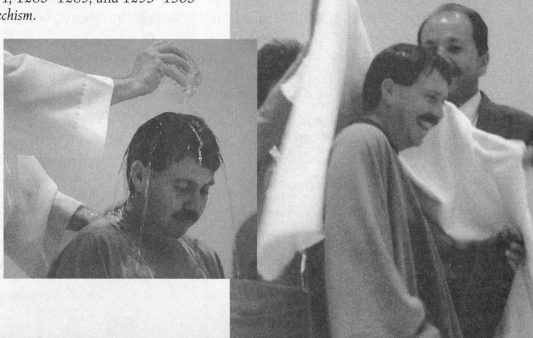

C
H
A
P
T
E
R
6

Teaching Resources

Overview

To deepen understanding of and appreciation for the sacraments of initiation: Baptism, Confirmation, and Eucharist.

Opening Prayer Ideas

Look at the photo on pages 46 and 47. Pray together Psalm 42:2–6.

or

Listen to a recording of a song based on baptismal or Confirmation themes: water, light, life, witness.

Materials

- Bibles, journals, and highlighters
- sunrise drawing

REPRODUCIBLE MASTERS
- *Sealed in the Spirit*, page 46C
- *Chapter 6 Assessment*, page 53A
- *Highlights for Home*, page 53B

Liturgy and Worship Journal:
For Chapter 6, use pages 24–27.

Supplemental Resources

VIDEOS
- *Confirmation: Commitment to Life*
- *What Catholics Believe About*
  —*Baptism*
  —*Confirmation*
  —*RCIA*

Videos with Values
1944 Innerbelt Drive
St. Louis, MO 63114–5718

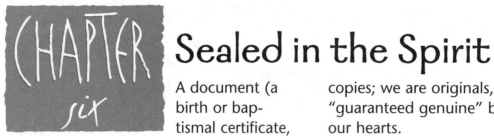

CHAPTER six

Sealed in the Spirit

A document (a birth or baptismal certificate, for example) is made authentic by being stamped with a seal. The seal is a small device that is used to press or emboss a design into a piece of paper. This embossed design cannot be copied or forged. It certifies that this particular document is an original.

Because we are sealed with the Spirit in the sacraments of Baptism and Confirmation, we are authenticated as Christians. For God "has also put his seal upon us and given the Spirit in our hearts" (2 Corinthians 1:22). We are not merely copies; we are originals, authentic, "guaranteed genuine" by the Spirit in our hearts.

In the space below design a "seal of authenticity" that expresses your life as a genuine Christian. Try to symbolize the work of the Holy Spirit in your life. Don't be afraid to be original!

The Sacraments of Initiation

I am the light of the world. Whoever follows me will not walk in darkness, but will have the light of life.
John 8:12

Objective: To deepen understanding of and appreciation for the sacraments of initiation: Baptism, Confirmation, and Eucharist.

Introduction ___ min.

Opening Prayer: Before the session begins, draw on the board or on posterboard an illustration of a sunrise like the one shown on page 48. Explain to the young people that when we celebrate the sacraments of Baptism, Confirmation, and Eucharist, we signify our willingness to turn from selfishness and sin to walk in the light of Jesus and with the Holy Spirit's guidance.

Then invite the young people to stand and face in the opposite direction from the sunrise drawing. Ask them to turn slightly in a clockwise direction toward the "light" after each response to the questions you will read. (After responding to the third question,

they should be facing the sunrise drawing.) Then say, "Let us take the time to renew our determination to renounce sin and selfishness. These questions were first asked of our parents and godparents at Baptism. Respond to each question with the words 'I do.'"

• Do you reject sin to live in the freedom of God's children?

• Do you reject the glamour of evil and refuse to be mastered by sin?

• Do you reject Satan, father of sin and prince of darkness?

Invite the young people to gather near the sunrise drawing. Have a volunteer read Jesus' words from page 47 (John 8:12). Then ask all to reflect quietly as you read the exhortation that the celebrant proclaims to the newly baptized:

You have been enlightened by Christ. Walk always as children of the light, and keep the flame of faith alive in your hearts.

Forum: Remind the young people that Eucharist is a sacrament of initiation. Invite each person to exchange papers with a partner. Then have the pairs take turns being chaplain and speaker, acting out the scripts they wrote on the handout *For Granted*.

Presentation ___ min.

Have the young people read the introductory questions quietly. Ask them to write their responses in their journals.

Note: Be sure the young people appreciate the ancient and constant tradition of the Church of baptizing infants. The *Catechism* has a beautiful and concise section on the Baptism of infants in paragraphs 1250 to 1252.

◆ Ask the young people, "What did Paul have to turn away from before becoming a great missionary?" (*persecuting Christians*) Then together do a dramatic reading of the account of Saul's conversion and Baptism (Acts 9:1–19).

Explain that after Paul was baptized, he helped others to abandon selfish ways and turn toward the life of grace.

◆ Share with the young people the story of the life-long process of conversion of Saint Elizabeth Ann Seton.

Think about one new beginning you might already have made in your life. Was it hard? Did you have help? Has it made your life better? What beginnings are you looking forward to?

Beginnings

How do you begin to become a Catholic? This probably doesn't seem to be a very important question if you already are a Catholic! Many of us were baptized when we were infants and have been Catholics ever since. In fact, since the earliest times, Baptism has been administered to infants and children. This continues today. But even so, the question of becoming Catholic is very important. That is because the *process* by which an unbaptized person becomes a Catholic is like a map that helps us understand how to follow Jesus.

The Church realizes that people coming to the Catholic faith as adults need a different kind of preparation, the kind that the early Church gave to the first converts from paganism. This preparation is called the *Rite of Christian Initiation of Adults* (*RCIA*). Through the liturgies and prayers it provides, the RCIA prepares adults and young people to become members of the Catholic Church. Sometimes this preparation can last one or two years. New Catholics

are initiated into the Church by receiving the three *sacraments of initiation*—Baptism, Confirmation, and Eucharist—all at once, usually at the Easter Vigil. So understanding the RCIA is a good way to understand the three sacraments of initiation.

Eucharist is closely connected to Baptism and Confirmation. Every time we come to the Eucharist, we come "through Baptism." (This is why we dip our fingers into the baptismal water and make the sign of the cross when we enter a church.) At each Eucharist we renew the promises of our Baptism: the promises to renounce evil and to follow Christ.

In order to understand our baptismal promises, we first need to learn about conversion. *Conversion* is the process of coming to believe that Jesus Christ is the Savior of the world. The word literally means "turning around, going in the other direction."

If conversion is a turning around, what do we *turn from*? What do we *turn toward*? Saint Paul tells us

48

we are to *turn from* the flesh, all that is selfish, all that seeks "me first" without considering what God wants, all that is sinful. We are to *turn toward* the spiritual, all that is life-giving and selfless, all that is generous, all that is filled with the Holy Spirit. Conversion is a lifelong task. Baptism is our first "turning," or act of conversion, but this process continues throughout our lives. It is made possible by the paschal mystery of Jesus Christ.

Becoming a Catholic

When an unbaptized person wants to become a Catholic or to see what the Catholic Church is all about, he or she usually seeks out a parish and participates in a series of inquiry evenings or information sessions. In some cases, moved by the grace of the Holy Spirit, the person might decide to take the first formal steps toward becoming a Catholic. This is called becoming a catechumen, or entering the catechumenate. The catechumenate

has four parts: instruction, moral conversion, worship, and ministry.

The root meaning of *catechumenate* is instruction. *Instruction* is the first step, an important part of the catechumenate. A person who wants to become a Catholic will naturally want to know what Catholics know. Above all, a catechumen must know Jesus and his Church.

The second step along the journey is "changing one's way of life," or *moral conversion*. As we come to know Jesus, we will want to act like Jesus. We will want to convert, "to turn around" and follow Jesus.

Worship is the third step along the way. Part of becoming a Catholic is worshiping together with Catholics, praying in a Catholic way. Catechumens will usually participate in Sunday Mass. They will leave after the homily in order to continue their reflection on the word of God while the baptized community celebrates the Eucharist.

49

◆ Explain to the young people that both Saint Paul's and Saint Elizabeth Seton's conversions brought about many important developments in the Church. Saint Paul became a great missionary, and Saint Elizabeth Seton founded a religious community of women, the Sisters of Charity. Today the sisters continue Elizabeth's ministry in schools, hospitals, and other charitable institutions. Ask the following questions:

• How can we follow these saints' example?

• Who, by his or her example, helps us to realize that conversion is a lifelong task?

◆ List the four steps of the catechumenate on the board: *instruction, moral conversion, worship, ministry*. Invite the young people to formulate a question for each step. For example: "What do I have to know to be a Catholic?" "How should I live as a Catholic?" "How do I worship as a Catholic?" "What is ministry for a Catholic?"

Ask two volunteers to role-play a conversation in which they use the questions on the board. One volunteer asks about becoming a Catholic; the other responds with appropriate answers.

FYI Elizabeth Seton was an exemplary member of the Episcopalian Church in New York City. When her husband died of tuberculosis at the beginning of a trip to Italy, Elizabeth and her daughter were welcomed into the home of their Catholic friends, the Filicchi family.

This family's faith and Catholic devotion to the Blessed Sacrament awakened Elizabeth's interest in the Catholic Church. After she returned home to New York, she studied Catholic doctrine and prayed for almost a year about the decision to convert. Elizabeth was received into the Catholic Church in March, 1805.

Presentation (cont'd)

◆ Challenge the young people to find evidence of the catechumenate's four steps in their own lives. Stress that the steps are part of preparation for the sacraments of initiation but that they are also the work of a lifetime. List the responses on the board.

◆ Ask, "Who has participated in the Easter Vigil?" Invite volunteers to relate their experiences. Help them to focus their response by asking questions such as these: "What do you remember most—the new fire, the paschal candle, the Baptism?" "Did you have friends or relatives among the newly initiated members of the Church?"

Explain that participating in the Easter Vigil is not obligatory. Ask, "Why, then, do Catholics take the time to do so?" Discuss this question with the group as a whole. Then, have the students work in small groups to plan brief radio or TV spots inviting Catholics to participate in the Easter Vigil. The theme of "welcoming new Catholics" as a reason for coming should receive special emphasis.

◆ Remind the young people that water and the words "I baptize you in the name of the Father and of the Son and of the Holy Spirit" are the signs of the sacrament.

Rite of Acceptance into the Order of Catechumens: presenting the gospels

Until they are baptized, catechumens are not able to participate fully in the Eucharist.

The fourth step is *ministry*. Those who know Jesus will want to tell others about Jesus. They will want to share their faith and serve others in his name.

Have you ever felt called to conversion, to changing your way of life? What did you do about it?

Initiation

There comes a day when a catechumen decides to ask for the sacraments of initiation: Baptism, Confirmation, and Eucharist. Because the catechumen chooses or elects the Church and the Church chooses or elects the individual, the catechumens are now called the elect. The *Rite of Election* takes place on the first Sunday of Lent.

The season of Lent is a season of spiritual retreat during which the

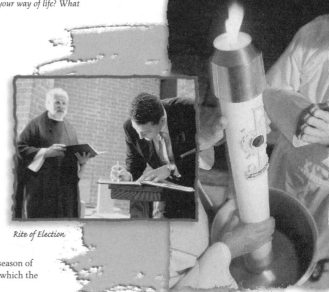

Rite of Election

Easter Vigil

catechumens prepare for their reception of Baptism, Confirmation, and Eucharist at the Easter Vigil. It is a time for those who are already baptized to encourage the catechumens, and to pray with them. At the Easter Vigil, the Saturday night before Easter, all that the catechumens have been preparing for comes together.

A *vigil* is a time to wait and watch. The liturgy begins after nightfall. We gather around the Easter fire and listen to Scriptures that call to mind the wonder of our salvation. We shout forth our alleluia, which is fresh and new because we have not used it during the forty days of Lent. And we hear in the gospel the proclamation that Jesus has risen from the dead.

Then the elect come forward. They go down into the baptismal water, down into the tomb with Jesus: They are baptized. They emerge from the baptismal pool dripping wet with new life. The newly baptized are then clothed with a white

50

garment, symbolizing that they have "clothed [themselves] with Christ" (Galatians 3:27). They are given candles lit from the Easter candle. Then they are anointed with oil: They are confirmed.

The vigil comes to its climax with the celebration of the Eucharist. The newly initiated join us for the first time at the table of the Lord.

Baptism

In the New Testament Christian initiation is described by means of many symbols and images. Baptism is "being born again." In this sacrament we come forth from the waters of Baptism and are born into God's family. We are filled with the Spirit of love, welcomed by the Christian community, and receive the family name "Christian." We start afresh. All our sins—original sin and all personal sins—are taken away.

Baptism is also a "dying." In Baptism we go down into the tomb, and are buried with Christ. We die to selfishness and sin so that the Spirit of Christ might be born in us.

Baptism is "seeing things in a new light." We emerge from the waters of Baptism and see things with God's eyes. We see a world in which we are no longer alone, a world in which we are connected with every other creature. We see a world in which we are loved and given power by the Spirit of God.

Baptism is "being adopted into a new family," the family of God. As family members we are brothers and sisters of Jesus Christ. We inherit everything that God has given to his Son, especially the great gift of eternal life.

Through these baptismal images the Church teaches that "Baptism is the basis of the whole Christian life, the gateway to life in the Spirit . . . and the door which gives access to the other sacraments" (*Catechism*, 1213). Through Baptism we are made members of Christ and members of his body, the Church. We are in Christ and Christ is in us. His work, his mission in the world, is now our own.

 Which image of Baptism has greatest meaning for you? Why?

Celebrating Baptism

We have learned that the principal prayer of each sacrament is often expressed as a prayer of blessing (berakah): (1) We call God by name, "Father." (2) We gratefully remember what God has done for us. (3) We invoke the Holy Spirit.

At Baptism the blessing of the water takes this form. The priest moves to the water and calls upon God. He prays that the Father will give us grace through the sign of the gift of water. As the prayer continues, we remember (anamnesis) God's saving acts, especially those involving water. We pray that all who are buried with Christ in Baptism may rise with him to new life.

The candidates are plunged into this water three times (or water is poured over their heads three times), and the priest baptizes them in the name of the Father, and of the Son, and of the Holy Spirit. The newly baptized come up from the water risen with Christ and all is now new.

51

◆ Ask the young people to recall, from their own experiences, the life-giving (*cool shower on a hot day*) and death-dealing (*a devastating flood*) properties of water. You may want to chart their responses on the board under the headings "Life" and "Death."

As a group, compose a "sentence poem" using the words and phrases from the chart. The following is an example:

> Baptism leads from death to life.
> Baptism is a shower of refreshing water.
> Baptism is tomb and womb and eternal life.

Ask the students to copy the sentence poem in their journals. Encourage them to feel free to reorder the sentences or to add more if they like.

◆ Direct attention to *Catholic Teachings* on page 53. Ask volunteers to summarize the meaning of *Baptism of blood* and *Baptism of desire.*

Presentation (cont'd)

Note: You may want to review the effects of original sin that are presented on page 25: weakness of will, tendency to sin, suffering, and death.

◆ Ask the students to recall the four parts of the catechumenate. (*instruction, moral conversion, worship, ministry*) Stress that Confirmation is a sacrament of initiation and that *initiation* means "beginning." What we began in Baptism, we continue in Confirmation. We continue to live the Christian life in these four ways.

◆ Direct attention to the photos on page 52. Explain that the anointing with oil and the words "Be sealed with the Gift of the Holy Spirit" are the essential signs of the sacrament.

Point out the presence of the sponsor in the photo at the left. Note that the sponsor literally "stands behind" the one being confirmed and has a hand on the candidate's shoulder. Ask, "What do you think this body language means?" (*spiritual support, help, prayers, guidance in life*) Explain that the Church encourages candidates for Confirmation to choose their godparents (sponsors at Baptism) as sponsors.

Assessment: If you are administering *Chapter 6 Assessment*, page 53A, allow about ten minutes for the young people to complete the test.

Confirmation

At the Easter Vigil the sacraments of initiation are celebrated together in one liturgy. The meaning of each of the three sacraments is found in the meaning of the other two and in the meaning of the whole ceremony. Catholics who were baptized as infants receive Confirmation later, usually at a time when they can understand what the sacrament means.

We do not find many writings about Confirmation dating from the early days of the Church because it was thought of as part of Baptism. When they spoke of Baptism, the early Christians meant Baptism-Confirmation.

Baptism washes away sin and frees us from original sin. *Original sin* was the rejection of God by our first parents, resulting in the loss of sanctifying grace. With their sin, Adam and Eve deprived themselves and all their descendants of the original state of grace given by God. Because of original sin, we need to be saved by Jesus and restored to God's grace.

Baptism washes away original sin and fills us with God's own life through the power of the Holy Spirit. This is what we call *sanctifying grace*. In God, the source of all holiness, we share in holiness. Confirmation seals us with the Spirit, strengthening the grace of Baptism. Baptism changes us so radically

CATHOLIC ID The ordinary minister of Baptism is a bishop, priest, or deacon. But did you know that in case of necessity, anyone can baptize? In an emergency a person baptizes by pouring water over the head of the one to be baptized while saying, "I baptize you in the name of the Father, and of the Son, and of the Holy Spirit."

that we can never be "unbaptized." Baptism makes us members of Christ's body, and this can never be undone. It is an indelible spiritual mark, or character, that cannot be taken away.

Confirmation strengthens and continues our Baptism. We receive the Holy Spirit in a special way. We are incorporated more firmly into Christ. Like Baptism, Confirmation marks us with an indelible character. The sacrament never needs to be repeated—nor can it be.

Celebrating Confirmation

A good way to understand Confirmation is to look at the way the Church celebrates it. First, the bishop or the delegated priest extends his hands over you (the typical gesture of invoking the Holy Spirit). Then, as he lays his hand on your head, he anoints your forehead with oil (remember that the name *Christ* means the "anointed one") and says, "Be sealed with the Gift of the Holy Spirit."

In Confirmation we are anointed with oil. It is a sign of consecration. We are anointed in order to share more fully in the mission of Jesus Christ. We are anointed as a sign that we have the seal of the Holy Spirit. Now we belong totally to Christ; we are enrolled in his service forever.

52

Answers for Chapter 6 Assessment
1. d **2.** b **3.** a **4.** d **5.** a
6. b **7.** b **8.** d **9.** b **10.** See page 52.

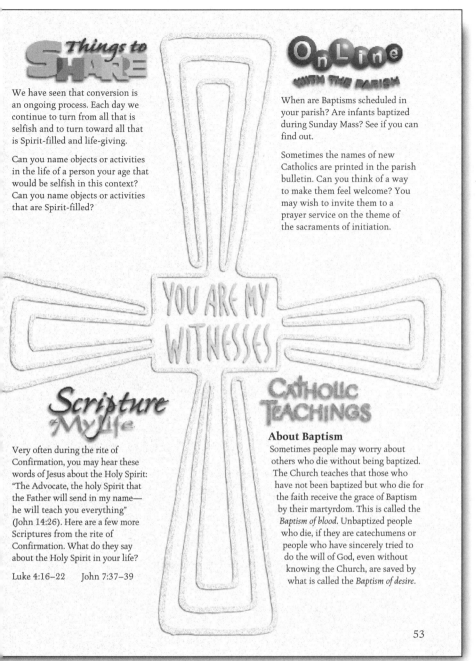

Things to SHARE

We have seen that conversion is an ongoing process. Each day we continue to turn from all that is selfish and to turn toward all that is Spirit-filled and life-giving.

Can you name objects or activities in the life of a person your age that would be selfish in this context? Can you name objects or activities that are Spirit-filled?

OnLine *with the Parish*

When are Baptisms scheduled in your parish? Are infants baptized during Sunday Mass? See if you can find out.

Sometimes the names of new Catholics are printed in the parish bulletin. Can you think of a way to make them feel welcome? You may wish to invite them to a prayer service on the theme of the sacraments of initiation.

YOU ARE MY WITNESSES

Scripture *My Life*

Very often during the rite of Confirmation, you may hear these words of Jesus about the Holy Spirit: "The Advocate, the holy Spirit that the Father will send in my name—he will teach you everything" (John 14:26). Here are a few more Scriptures from the rite of Confirmation. What do they say about the Holy Spirit in your life?

Luke 4:16–22   John 7:37–39

CATHOLIC TEACHINGS

About Baptism

Sometimes people may worry about others who die without being baptized. The Church teaches that those who have not been baptized but who die for the faith receive the grace of Baptism by their martyrdom. This is called the *Baptism of blood.* Unbaptized people who die, if they are catechumens or people who have sincerely tried to do the will of God, even without knowing the Church, are saved by what is called the *Baptism of desire.*

53

Conclusion ___ min.

Have a volunteer read *Things to Share.* Discuss briefly and then have the young people write their personal responses in their journals.

FORUM Assignment

✔ Read pages 54–61. Underline in pencil the statements that express five key ideas.

✔ Complete the "seal of authenticity" on the handout *Sealed in the Spirit.* Read the introductory question for Chapter 7 on page 56. Ask at least three people for their responses.

Closing Prayer: Direct attention to *Scripture & My Life* on page 53. Have the young people reflect on what the two Confirmation Scripture passages say to them about the Holy Spirit. Then distribute the handout *Sealed in the Spirit.* Invite the young people to begin their designs.

Evaluation: Have the young people discovered the importance and significance of the sacraments of initiation? Do they understand the relationship between Baptism and Confirmation?

FOR CHAPTER 7

- copies of handout *Standing Faithfully*, page 54C
- copies of *Chapter 7 Assessment*, page 61A
- copies of *Highlights for Home*, page 61B

Assessment

1 The sacraments of initiation are
  a. Baptism and Reconciliation.
  b. Baptism, Confirmation, and Reconciliation.
  c. Reconciliation and Eucharist.
  d. Baptism, Confirmation, and Eucharist.

2 Conversion
  a. only happens before Baptism.
  b. is a lifelong task.
  c. means "to plunge."
  d. means "a time to watch and wait."

3 The first step of the catechumenate is
  a. instruction.
  b. moral conversion.
  c. worship.
  d. ministry.

4 At the Easter Vigil the newly baptized
  a. must leave church after the homily.
  b. begin religious instruction.
  c. do not receive the Eucharist.
  d. are also confirmed.

5 _____ is the gateway to the Christian life.
  a. Baptism
  b. Eucharist
  c. Reconciliation
  d. Confirmation

6 Those who have not been baptized but who die for the faith receive
  a. Baptism by water.
  b. Baptism of blood.
  c. Baptism of desire.
  d. all of the above

7 At Confirmation the bishop
  a. pours water over a person.
  b. anoints a person's forehead with oil.
  c. only gives the homily.
  d. only asks questions of those to be confirmed.

8 The second step of the catechumenate concerns
  a. religious instruction.
  b. ministry.
  c. worship.
  d. moral conversion.

9 In _____ we are made members of Christ's body, the Church.
  a. the RCIA
  b. Baptism
  c. Confirmation
  d. the Rite of Election

10 Explain the symbolism of anointing with oil at Confirmation. Write your response on the reverse side of this page.

Highlights for Home

Focus on Faith

In recent years the Rite of Christian Initiation of Adults (RCIA) has been adopted as a way of preparing adults and young people for Baptism and full communion with the Church. You may have noticed this rite in your own parish, especially during Lent and its culminating point, the Easter Vigil.

This chapter uses the RCIA as a jumping-off point to a deeper understanding of Baptism and Confirmation. Baptism is the beginning of our conversion, our turning toward the life of the Spirit. Confirmation strengthens, affirms, and deepens that conversion. The four points given to the RCIA candidates as points of preparation are areas of lifelong growth for all of us: instruction, moral conversion, worship, and ministry.

During Lent we have the opportunity to support our parish's catechumens and candidates in prayer as they prepare to receive Baptism, Confirmation, and Eucharist at the Easter Vigil. We welcome, promise our prayerful support, and realize how grateful we are for the gift of our Catholic faith.

Conversation Starters

. . . . a few ideas to talk about together . . . .

◆ Have I ever felt "called to conversion" in some way? What was it like? Did I feel good about making a new beginning? Did it have a long-term effect on my life?

◆ Has anyone asked me to change lately? How did I feel? How did I respond?

◆ How do I see Baptism, Confirmation, and Eucharist as a call to follow Christ?

Feature Focus

Scripture & My Life on page 53 reminds us of the presence of the Holy Spirit in our lives. The first Scripture reference, Luke 4:16–22, recounts the incident in which Jesus read from the scroll in the synagogue and proclaimed, "The Spirit of the Lord is upon me." In the second, John 7:37–39, Jesus compares the Spirit to a river of living water within the believer. How is the Spirit upon you? In what direction is the river of living water, the Spirit, carrying you?

Reflection

The opening photograph on pages 46 and 47 shows a procession of young people, their hopeful faces illuminated by the candles they carry. Echoing Saint Ignatius of Antioch, they seem to be saying, "We are Easter people." What does it mean to be Easter people?

Easter is a time of new birth. The waters of Baptism are the womb of the Church. The Spanish phrase *dar a luz* ("to give birth") can be literally translated, "to give a light." New birth, new life, is new light. Baptism brings the new light of Christian life into the world.

My light is needed, too. Where? When?

OUR HOUSE OF PRAYER

Adult Focus

The ancient Hebrews were nomads. They had no fixed dwellings. They moved across the land, following their flocks and using tents for shelter. The ark of the covenant was sheltered in a tent. When Solomon built a Temple, another level of civilization was established. The Temple became the center of worship in Judaism.

Like the Temple, our churches are centers of worship. We gather in our churches in the name of Jesus to "continually offer God a sacrifice of praise" (Hebrews 13:15). Our church buildings symbolize what we live for in the present and long for in the future: the presence of God among us.

This chapter explores the significance of a parish church building as a gathering place for the celebration of the Eucharist and as a symbol of the body of Christ, which we, as the Church, are called to be. The artistic and architectural demands of such a building are explained, especially as Catholics seek a balance among the three elements of "seeing, hearing, and doing" in worship.

Catechism Focus

The themes of this chapter correspond to paragraphs 1179–1186 and 1197–1199 of the *Catechism.*

Enrichment Activities

Guest Speaker/Church Tour

You may want to arrange a church tour guided by a priest, deacon, or staff member of your parish. It might be helpful to make a copy of this chapter for the tour guide, highlighting the discussion of those parts of the church in which your group has expressed a special interest. Be sure to include the sacristy on your tour, with a look at vestments made and worn for special feasts and seasons.

Computer Connection

As a midsemester review, have the young people use a crossword software program, such as *WordCross*®, to develop a crossword puzzle. Have the young people form small groups to develop lists of words or terms and corresponding clues used in Chapters 1 through 7. Then explain to the groups that they can design their own puzzle step-by-step or let the computer automatically make a variety of puzzles from the same word list. Have the groups enter the word list and clues into the computer. Then have them print and exchange the puzzles.

Teaching Resources

Overview

To appreciate the parish church as a sign of Christ's presence among his people and as a symbol of Catholic life and worship.

Opening Prayer Ideas

Look at the photo collage on pages 54 and 55. Then pray together Ephesians 2:19–22. As you pray, think of your own parish church.

or

Express your thanksgiving for the house of God by prayerfully reading Psalm 27A.

Materials

- Bibles, journals, and highlighters

Liturgy and Worship Journal:

For Chapter 7, use pages 28–31.

REPRODUCIBLE MASTERS
- *Standing Faithfully*, page 54C
- *Chapter 7 Assessment*, page 61A
- *Highlights for Home*, page 61B

Supplemental Resources

VIDEOS
- *St. Etheldreda's: A Silent Witness* (Story of Britain's oldest Catholic Church)
- *Seven Cities of God* (Story of Father Junipero Serra's founding of missions)

Ignatius Press
P.O. Box 1339
Ft. Collins, CO 80522

Standing Faithfully

Read the prayer below. Then write your responses to each question.

The Brick

The bricklayer laid a brick on the bed of cement.
Then, with a precise stroke of his trowel, spread another layer
And, without a by-your-leave, laid another brick.
Then foundations grew visibly,
The building rose, tall and strong, to shelter men.

I thought, Lord, of that poor brick buried in the darkness at
  the base of the big building.
No one sees it, but it accomplishes its task, and the
other bricks
  need it.
Lord, what difference whether I am on the rooftop or in the
  foundations of your building, as long as I stand faithfully
  at the right place?

—Michel Quoist

Reflection

◆ I am a brick, a "living stone" in the Church. How do I feel about my position in the body of Christ? in my parish?

◆ Do I ever feel buried in darkness? When? Why?

◆ Do I ever feel recognized for what I am or do? When?

◆ When do I feel needed in my family, school, or parish? among my friends?

◆ Do I feel that I am in the right place for now? Why? Why not?

Our House of Prayer

LORD, I love the house where you dwell,
the tenting-place of your glory.
Psalm 26:8

Objective: To appreciate the parish church as a sign of Christ's presence among his people and as a symbol of Catholic life and worship.

Introduction ___ min.

Opening Prayer: Invite the young people to look at the photo collage on pages 54 and 55. Proclaim together Psalm 26:8.

Read each of the following prayer beginnings. Ask the young people to write their own conclusions in their journals.

• Jesus, when I see church steeples or domes,

• Jesus, when I look at the crosses against the blue sky,

• Jesus, when I hear the bells ringing,

• Jesus, when I feel the glow and warmth of the lights and candles,

• Jesus, when I see the pillars and arches,

• Jesus, when I gather with the parish community,

Chapter Warm-up: Have the young people imagine a world that has no churches, temples, synagogues, or mosques. Ask, "What do you think society would be like if there were no buildings in which to worship or if people were kept from gathering in churches to pray?" Allow a few minutes for the young people to describe this world.

Forum: Have the young people form small groups. Have the members share the seals they have designed on the handout *Sealed in the Spirit*. Then each group should share the responses they received in regard to the question asked in the introductory paragraph on page 56.

Each group should then use these responses to prepare a persuasive statement to dispute people who claim, "We don't need a church. We can worship God anywhere." Have a group representative then share the statement with all.

Presentation ___ min.

◆ Emphasize that during Jesus' public ministry, he gave witness by praying with the Jewish community in the Temple in Jerusalem and by reading Scriptures and praying in village synagogues.

◆ Point out that the disciples of Jesus did not need symbols of him because he was with them physically. Direct attention to "The House of God" on page 57. Ask, "What does our parish church signify to us now?"

◆ Discuss the following questions:

• How would you react if public worship was forbidden in this country?

• How can you show appreciation for having a church building within which to worship and having the freedom to worship there?

• What happens when dictators close churches and forbid people to gather to celebrate the sacraments?

◆ Direct attention to the photo on page 56. Explain that it shows the gathering of the worshiping community in the Basilica of Our Lady of Guadalupe in Mexico City. Then share the story of Father Miguel Pro.

You might sometimes hear people say, "I don't need a church. I can worship God anywhere." It is true that God can be found and worshiped anywhere. Why is a sacred place, a church, so important to us?

A Temple of Living Stones

Jesus himself needed and respected sacred space. He often found his own sacred space in "a deserted place" (Mark 1:35) where he prayed quietly alone. But he also gathered in places of worship with others. At the age of twelve, he went on pilgrimage with his parents to the Temple in Jerusalem (Luke 2:41). As an adult he prayed in the synagogue on the Sabbath "according to his custom" (Luke 4:16) and at least once even took a leading part in worship by reading the Scriptures (Luke 4:17). He often taught in the Temple and was concerned that the Temple truly be a house of prayer, not a marketplace (Luke 19:45–46).

Jesus taught something new about worship. Once a Samaritan woman asked him where it was best to worship—on the mountain where her ancestors had prayed or in Jerusalem. Jesus replied, "The hour is coming when you will worship the Father neither on this mountain nor in Jerusalem. . . . God is Spirit, and those who worship him must worship in Spirit and truth" (John 4:21–24).

What does this mean? It means that we now worship God in the Spirit and truth of Jesus, the Son of God. Although we do need places to worship, Jesus tells us that he himself is the primary place, the temple where God dwells. Through the sacraments of initiation, we are incorporated into this new temple, this body of Christ. We are now the sign and sacrament of God's presence on earth.

56

Our worship of God in the body of Christ, in the Spirit and truth of Jesus, "is not tied exclusively to any one place. The whole earth is sacred" (*Catechism*, 1179). In this sense it is true that we do not need church buildings. But this is not the whole story.

After Jesus ascended into heaven, his disciples would gather on the first day of the week to keep his message alive and to celebrate his risen presence in the Eucharist. They needed a *place* to do this: a place to come together, to tell their stories, and to share their meal.

At first the early Christians met in one another's homes. Later, when assemblies grew larger and worship in public became more acceptable, they used Roman basilicas for their gatherings. A *basilica* was not a temple or a place of worship; rather, it was a building designed for public meetings and other business. Even later, when Christians began to design and build their own churches, they used the familiar basilica form as a model, often adapting it to the shape of a cross.

The House of God

Our parish church, the place where we gather to worship, is a visible sign of our faith. It is the place where God dwells, the tenting place of his eucharistic presence. It is not only a house for us, for the Church, but also God's house. "Behold, God's dwelling is with the human race. He will dwell with them and they will be his people and God himself will always be with them" (Revelation 21:3).

A Place of Celebration

Our parish church serves multiple purposes, but the most important is the celebration of the Eucharist. How does the church building itself help us to celebrate the Eucharist?

Gathering The church is the place where we gather together for worship. This fact makes the design of a church different from the design of a sports stadium or a movie theater, for example. Most large public spaces have a stage where the action takes place and an area set aside for the spectators or audience. In church there is no stage because at Mass there is no audience. We are all *doers*, and the entire assembly area is the stage.

From wherever we stand in the assembly area, our attention is drawn to three important objects: the presider's chair, the lectern, and the altar. The presider's chair is positioned so that the priest is seen to be both a member of the assembly and the leader of the assembly. In the principal church of a diocese, the chair (*cathedra* in Latin) for the bishop gives its name to the entire building, the *cathedral*.

Chancery Chapel, Diocese of Victoria (Texas)

57

◆ Ask a volunteer to summarize *Catholic Teachings* on page 61. Have the young people highlight the last two sentences. Explain that the doors of a church are symbols of Jesus Christ. In the Prayer of Blessing of new church doors, the celebration emphasizes this symbolism:

> He is the Good Shepherd;
> he is the door through which
>   those who follow him
> enter and are safe, go in and
>   go out,
> and find pasture.

Tell the young people that in the late Middle Ages and during the Renaissance, the Church commissioned famous sculptors to design doors for churches and baptistries. Explain that Lorenzo Ghiberti (1378–1455) depicted the life of Christ and the four evangelists on the doors of the cathedral baptistry in Florence, Italy.

FYI Father Miguel Pro was a Mexican Jesuit priest who was ordained in Belgium in 1925. Upon his return to Mexico City in 1926, he found that religious persecution in Mexico had increased and that public worship was forbidden. But this did not stop Father Pro from bringing the word of God and the sacraments to the people. He celebrated Mass in their homes, traveling secretly and often in disguise.

One day in November 1927, he was seized by the police. He was executed ten days later.

Presentation (cont'd)

◆ Have volunteers explain the symbolism and use of the presider's chair, the lectern, and the altar.

Emphasize that because the altar represents Christ, we give it special reverence. Remind the students that the priest shows reverence to the altar at the beginning and at the end of the Eucharist. Ask, "Why is the altar anointed with oil?" (*because it is a symbol of Christ, the Anointed One*) Explain that when an altar is anointed, the bishop stands before it and says:

> We now anoint this altar.
> May God in his power
>   make it holy,
> a visible sign of the
>   mystery of Christ,
> who offered himself for
>   the life of the world.

◆ Ask, "What things in the parish church remind us of our Baptism?" (*the baptismal font or pool, the blessed water, the paschal candle because of its association with the Baptisms at Easter and the candle we all receive at Baptism as a symbol of the light of Christ*)

◆ Have a volunteer explain what the ambry is and what it contains. Have another volunteer explain what the three kinds of oil are and how each kind is used in the celebration of the sacraments.

◆ Ask, "Why is the reconciliation chapel often located near the baptismal area?" (*If we are not faithful to our baptismal promises, we need the sacrament of Reconciliation.*)

St. Mary's Cathedral, San Francisco

Storytelling   The church must be designed for the proclamation of God's word. We must be able to hear and see well. Good acoustics (sound quality) and sight lines are very important for this function.

The readings are proclaimed from the *lectern*, or *ambo*, a reading stand upon which the lectionary is placed and from which we proclaim the word of God.

Meal Sharing   As the liturgical action moves from storytelling to the sharing of our meal, our attention moves from the lectern to the altar. The altar is not an ordinary table. On the *altar* the sacrifice of the cross is made present under the sacramental signs. The altar is also the table of the Lord, to which we are all invited.

The altar, which is anointed with oil when a church is dedicated, also represents Christ, the Anointed One. As a sign of love for Christ, the priest greets the altar with an act of reverence at the beginning and end of the Eucharist.

In the thirteenth century Catholics did not receive Holy Communion frequently. Instead, looking at the sacred Host after the consecration became the high point of the Mass. So Catholics began to kneel during the eucharistic prayer. As the practice of kneeling was extended, kneeling benches were added.

Commissioning   Following Communion we are dismissed and commissioned to take the gospel message from the church to our daily lives in the world. What happens in the church must be connected to our lives outside the church. This connection is made clearer when the design and furnishings of the church building are related to the community it serves.

58

A Place of Worship

Because the sacrament of Baptism is the spiritual door to the Church, the baptismal font or baptismal pool is located near the front door whenever possible. In fact one early Church custom was to build the baptismal pool completely outside the church, in a separate building near the entrance. This building was called the *baptistry*. It signified the absolute need for Baptism before celebrating the Eucharist with the assembly. Today as we enter the doors of the church, we dip our fingers into blessed water and make the sign of the cross, that sign in which we were baptized. Each time we gather as the body of Christ for Eucharist, we continue and renew the celebration of our Baptism.

In this baptismal area you will also see a niche in the wall or a little chest called the *ambry*. It contains three vessels of oil: the oil of catechumens, which is used to bless and strengthen those preparing for baptism; the oil of the sick, with which the priest strengthens and heals those who are ill; and the sacred chrism, which is used in celebrating the sacraments of Baptism, Confirmation, and Holy Orders. The word *Christ* means "anointed one." So being anointed with oil is a sign of the special and strengthening presence of Christ, the Anointed One.

The reconciliation chapel, a small space designed for the celebration of the sacrament of Reconciliation (confession), is located in the baptismal area whenever possible. This reflects the historical connection between the sacraments of Baptism and Reconciliation.

Point out the altar, the presider's chair, and the lectern or ambo.

Another important area of a Catholic church is the place set aside for the tabernacle. Sometimes this is a side chapel; sometimes it is a prominent place in the sanctuary. The *tabernacle* is the place in which the Eucharist is kept, or reserved. The word comes from the Latin for "tent" or "little house."

Christ becomes present at the Eucharist in several ways. At different times during the eucharistic celebration, our attention is directed to these different ways in which Christ is really present: He is present in the gathered assembly and in the person of the priest. He is present in the Scriptures. He is present most especially under the forms of bread and wine. And as we are commissioned to go out into the world, we find Christ present there also.

Christ is also present in the *Blessed Sacrament*, that is, in the Eucharist reserved in the tabernacle. The Blessed Sacrament is reserved in this way so that the eucharistic Bread may be taken to those who are sick and to those who are dying. In addition the tabernacle has become the focus for the adoration of Christ under the eucharistic species. Catholics have a long tradition of praying before the tabernacle.

A lamp or candle burning before the tabernacle indicates to Catholics that the consecrated Bread is present there. Candles will also be found in other devotional areas and in the assembly area of the Church. At every Mass candles are lit. Once they were used primarily to give light for reading the Scriptures and celebrating the sacred action. Candles have lost much of their practical function, yet their symbolic purpose remains: The beautiful quality of candlelight reminds us of Christ, the Light of the World. As a candle consumes itself in the service of the liturgy, so must we spend ourselves in the service of God and of others.

Find time this week to make a visit to the Blessed Sacrament. In your prayer tell Jesus anything that is on your mind or in your heart.

Seeing, Hearing, Doing

Like our homes, church buildings can tell us so much just by the way they look. In some older churches, for example, you may find many paintings, statues, mosaics, and perhaps even several altars. Modern churches do not have these. Why are there such differences?

In the early days of the liturgy, when Latin was the spoken language of the congregation, both the ear and the eye had something to do. The ear listened to the meaning of the words, and the eye followed the sacred action. As Latin became less and less understood by the people in the congregation, their ears had less to do. So churches began to be more elaborately decorated to become feasts for the eyes.

In the early Middle Ages, a greater stress began to be placed on the sacrificial dimension of the Eucharist, and Holy Communion was received only by the clergy. Therefore the altar was moved farther away from the faithful and was placed against the wall.

From early times this wall had been decorated with a painting of the cross, the Lamb of God, or Christ in glory. These paintings now began to be placed on the altar itself.

59

◆ Ask, "How is Christ present in the Eucharist?" List the young people's responses on the board. Then have a volunteer explain the two reasons we reserve the Blessed Sacrament in the tabernacle.

◆ Direct the students' attention to the **thought provoker** on page 59. Adapt this suggestion to your group's situation. You may want to suggest a visit to the prayer corner as an alternative or as an additional quiet time for prayer.

◆ If you chose to share the *FYI* with your group, ask, "How do images beautify and enhance our worship?" "What would our churches be like without images?" (*statues, pictures, icons, stained-glass windows*)

FYI In the early days of the Church, some Church leaders felt that pictures (called *icons*) should not be allowed in churches. "God is spirit," they reasoned, "and should not be portrayed in any way." They were called *iconoclasts* (image breakers). Other Church leaders reasoned that because God became Man in Jesus, the use of pictures and statues was allowed and even encouraged. It took the Second Council of Nicaea (A.D. 787), to resolve this issue in favor of icons.

Presentation (cont'd)

◆ Draw attention to *Catholic ID* on page 60 for a discussion of vestments. Explain that the color of the vestments changes with the seasons. Ask the group to recall the colors of the liturgical seasons from their own observation. A complete explanation can be found on page 75 (Chapter 9).

◆ Have the young people write their responses to the **thought provoker** on page 60.

Conclusion ___ min.

Have a volunteer read *Scripture & My Life.* Have the young people write their response to the question in their journals.

Assessment: You are now half way through the semester course. If you wish to administer the Midsemester Assessment (pages 124–125) at this time, allow about twenty minutes for its completion.

If you are administering *Chapter 7 Assessment*, page 61A, allow the young people ten minutes to complete the test.

 The vestments worn by the priest at the liturgy have their roots in the earliest years of the Church. Originally they came from the way that ordinary people dressed. Today their function has changed. As powerful visible parts of our liturgy, they help us to celebrate the sacred mysteries of the Church. Like everything connected with the liturgy, vestments should be beautiful and well made because they are part of our worship of God.

The altar was filled with statues or paintings: first the crucifixion, then the patron saint of the parish or town. Later other saints were added.

After the Second Vatican Council (1962–65), the bishops determined that the liturgy would once again be celebrated in our own languages. Once again we can understand Sacred Scripture and the prayers at Mass. As our ears became active again, we discovered that sometimes too many decorations in the church could distract us from concentrating on what we were hearing! Today we Catholics are looking for a balance of seeing, hearing, and doing.

Does this mean that newer churches are better than the older ones? Does this mean that churches should have no decoration at all? No, absolutely not. We will not strengthen the ear by starving the eye. No one wants to remove statues and decorations from our churches simply to get rid of them. Statues and beautiful objects of art, banners, and flowers will always be an important part of the environment for our worship.

Many churches have stained-glass windows. In former times the pictures formed by the stained glass, in addition to bathing the assembly area with beautiful light, illustrated Bible stories for those who could not read. But stained-glass windows are not merely history lessons. Their artistic beauty reveals to us something of the beauty of God.

Around the walls of many churches, you will find the stations of the cross. This is a set of pictures,

60

statues, or even simple crosses (numbered from one to fourteen) which mark incidents in the last journey of Jesus to the cross.

This form of devotional prayer became popular in the late Middle Ages. The desire of Christians to follow in the footsteps of Jesus on his way to the cross had led to a long tradition of pilgrimage to the Holy Land. Those who could not afford the expense of the long and dangerous trip to Jerusalem could, by praying the way of the cross, participate in the passion of Jesus in their own villages. Catholics still pray the stations of the cross today, especially during Lent. We go to each station and meditate on an event of the passion. However, the church is primarily a place for our liturgical worship. Personal devotions, such as the stations of the cross, should not distract from the principal purpose of the assembly area.

There is a great variety in the way Catholic churches are decorated. Some are simple, others more elaborate. When we visit the home of friends, we know that the warmth, hospitality, and friendship we experience there are more important than the cost or style of the furniture. In the same way, in a Catholic church the principal beauty is found in the hospitality of our assembly, our devotion to the Eucharist, and the love we carry forth to our brothers and sisters.

 *Describe those things in your parish church that help you to pray.*

Answers for Chapter 7 Assessment

1. c	2. d	3. b	4. a	5. a
6. a	7. d	8. b	9. c	10. Accept reasonable responses.

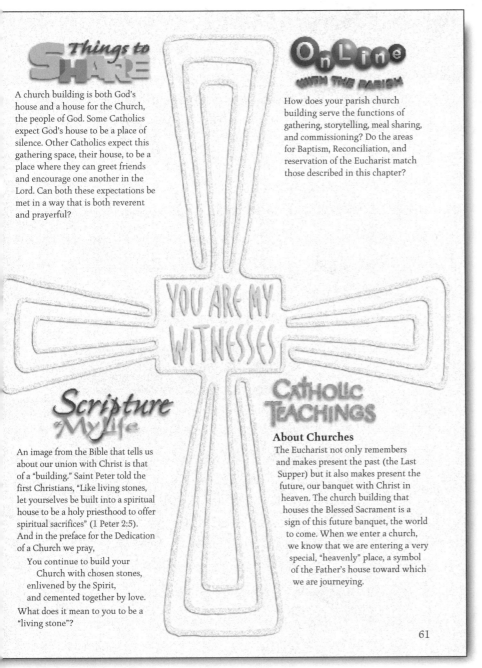

YOU ARE MY WITNESSES

Things to SHARE

A church building is both God's house and a house for the Church, the people of God. Some Catholics expect God's house to be a place of silence. Other Catholics expect this gathering space, their house, to be a place where they can greet friends and encourage one another in the Lord. Can both these expectations be met in a way that is both reverent and prayerful?

On Line WITH THE PARISH

How does your parish church building serve the functions of gathering, storytelling, meal sharing, and commissioning? Do the areas for Baptism, Reconciliation, and reservation of the Eucharist match those described in this chapter?

Scripture of My Life

An image from the Bible that tells us about our union with Christ is that of a "building." Saint Peter told the first Christians, "Like living stones, let yourselves be built into a spiritual house to be a holy priesthood to offer spiritual sacrifices" (1 Peter 2:5). And in the preface for the Dedication of a Church we pray,

You continue to build your
   Church with chosen stones,
enlivened by the Spirit,
and cemented together by love.

What does it mean to you to be a "living stone"?

Catholic Teachings

About Churches
The Eucharist not only remembers and makes present the past (the Last Supper) but it also makes present the future, our banquet with Christ in heaven. The church building that houses the Blessed Sacrament is a sign of this future banquet, the world to come. When we enter a church, we know that we are entering a very special, "heavenly" place, a symbol of the Father's house toward which we are journeying.

61

Conclusion (cont'd)

◆ Discuss the questions posed in *Things to Share* and *On Line with the Parish.*

◆ Distribute the handout *Standing Faithfully.* Explain that the young people may use the prayer and questions for personal prayer during the week.

FORUM Assignment

✔ Read pages 62–69. Underline in pencil the statements that express six key ideas.

✔ Make up a "Dream Sunday" schedule. Indicate what you would do from the time you wake up until you turn in at night. Indicate where you would like to be. Just be sure your "Dream Sunday" pleases both you and Jesus.

Closing Prayer: Have a prepared volunteer read the prayer "The Brick" on the handout sheet. Then together read Ephesians 2:19–22. Proclaim with the group the following words:

We are living stones, built upon Christ,
who is God's chosen cornerstone.

Evaluation: Do the young people appreciate their parish church as a beautiful symbol of faith? as the gathering place of the community around the Eucharist and the other sacraments? as the house of God? Do they understand what the principal beauty of the Catholic Church is?

FOR CHAPTER 8

• copies of handout *Quite a Character,* page 62C
• copies of *Chapter 8 Assessment,* page 69A
• copies of *Highlights for Home,* page 69B
• three-dimensional objects for human-camera activity (See page 64.)
• thematic music for Lent-Easter

Assessment

1 A reading stand upon which the lectionary is placed is the
a. basilica.
b. ambry.
c. lectern.
d. tabernacle.

2 The ____ is the place in which the Eucharist is kept, or reserved.
a. basilica
b. ambry
c. ambo
d. tabernacle

3 The ambry, the chest containing three vessels of oil, is usually located
a. on the altar.
b. in the baptismal area.
c. near the presider's chair.
d. in the reconciliation chapel.

4 The parish church is primarily a place for our
a. liturgical worship.
b. private meditations.
c. visits to the Blessed Sacrament.
d. celebration of Reconciliation.

5 ____ we gather as the body of Christ for the Eucharist, we continue and renew the celebration of our Baptism.
a. On Sundays when
b. Only on Easter when
c. Only in Lent when
d. Only when the bishop is the celebrant,

6 A ____ was a building designed for public meetings in which Christians met for worship.
a. basilica
b. ambry
c. lectern
d. tabernacle

7 In a Catholic church the principal beauty is found in
a. hospitality.
b. devotion to the Eucharist.
c. the love we share.
d. all of the above

8 The priests began wearing vestments at the liturgy in the
a. Middle Ages.
b. Church's early years.
c. seventeenth century.
d. after the Second Vatican Council.

9 The word *Christ* means
a. "light."
b. "temple."
c. "anointed one."
d. "sacred."

10 Why do we need churches?

_____
_____
_____
_____
_____
_____
_____

CHAPTER 7

Highlights for Home

Focus on Faith

In one city where Catholic roots are strong, people often identify their neighborhood by naming their parish: "I live in Our Lady of Refuge." "I live in St. Philip's." The parish is our spiritual home, and the parish church symbolizes what "dwelling with God" means. The parish church is the place in which we share the family meal, the Eucharist. There we are fed with the Bread of Life, and there the Blessed Sacrament is reserved in the tabernacle.

As you share this chapter on the church building with your son or daughter, help them to realize that no matter what the style of the parish church, the true beauty of the church consists in the hospitality of the parishioners, their devotion to the Eucharist, and their sharing of love.

Conversation Starters

. . . . a few ideas to talk about together. . . .

◆ What do you particularly appreciate about your parish church? Do you have a favorite window, statue, or picture?

◆ How does the atmosphere of the church affect you when you pray alone? during a sacramental celebration?

Feature Focus

The *Scripture & My Life* feature on page 61 presents two sources for consideration: the Scripture passage from 1 Peter 2:5, in which we are called "living stones," and the preface for the dedication of a church. The verse from 1 Peter is "let yourselves be built." It seems to suggest that we have a choice. We *allow* ourselves to become a real part of this structure. The dedication preface hints at the only way this can be done: We must be "cemented together by love." Christian love is like cement—strong, binding, and lasting!

Reflection

Take a few moments to look at the collage of churches on pages 54 and 55. The variety of architectural styles illustrates that the Church takes all that is human and uses it for the service of God. Picture your own parish church. Place it, just for now, at the top of a high mountain. You see it from a distance and begin to walk the road toward it as you pray the following words:

Send your light and fidelity,
  that they may be my guide
And bring me to your holy mountain,
  to the place of your dwelling,
That I may come to the altar of God,
  to God, my joy, my delight.

Psalm 42(43): III, 3–4

SEASONS OF PRAISE

Adult Focus

"Seasons of Praise" invites us to recall the ways in which the prayer life of the Church is intimately connected with the cycle of nature: coming to life, flowering, dying, and rising once again. The major liturgical seasons of Lent-Easter, Advent-Christmas, and the periods of Ordinary Time provide an opportunity for us to grow in our understanding of the paschal mystery of Christ and the ways in which God is present in our lives.

In this chapter the young people are encouraged to explore the seasons of the Church year in which the Church unfolds the entire mystery of Christ from his incarnation until his ascension, Pentecost, and the anticipation of his return in glory. It is a mystery so rich that no one single prayer or liturgical celebration can ever completely express it. They will discover the grace and mystery of God's time of salvation in which the saving acts of his Son continue to happen in their lives today.

Catechism Focus

The theme of Chapter 8 corresponds to paragraphs 638–640, 1163–1171, 1361–1366, 2180–2188 of the *Catechism*.

Enrichment Activities

Medleys of the Seasons

The young people might enjoy putting together taped medleys of secular and spiritual songs on the following themes: nature's seasons, the seasons of our lives, the seasons of the Church year. Appropriate selections might include "Winter Grace" (from the album of that name, by David Haas and Jeanne Cotter, GIA); "All My Life's a Circle" by Harry Chapin; and "Summertime Blues" by Eddie Cochran.

Making Growth Charts

Using newsprint or long strips of wallpaper, have partners work together to make a teen-year variation on the growth charts by which children measure their changing height. Have them mark off their present height. In the space between that mark and the bottom, have them record and illustrate their growth as Catholics (Baptism, First Eucharist, Confirmation, participation in retreats, ministries).

A Personal Church Season Calendar

Have the young people refer to the explanation of the Church seasons on page 126. Invite them to make their own Church year calendars. They may wish to include illustrations or photos of symbols that help them understand the meaning of these seasons.

Teaching Resources

Overview

To explore the meaning of the Lord's Day; to appreciate the ways in which the liturgical year helps us to enter into the paschal mystery.

Opening Prayer Ideas

Write a prayer about being in touch with God through nature.

or

Pray Psalm 111:1–5. Reflect on its "clues" about ways to keep the Lord's Day holy.

Materials

 Liturgy and Worship Journal:
For Chapter 8, use pages 32–35.

- Bibles, journals, and highlighters
- objects for camera activity (See page 64.)
- background music
- drawing paper, markers

REPRODUCIBLE MASTERS
- *Quite a Character*, page 62C
- *Chapter 8 Assessment*, page 69A
- *Highlights for Home*, page 69B

Supplemental Resources

VIDEOS
Seasons of Life
Sheed & Ward
P.O. Box 419492
Kansas City, MO 64141

Lent: A Time of Renewal
St. Anthony Messenger Press
1615 Republic Street
Cincinnati, OH 45210

CHAPTER eight

Quite a Character

Some young people model themselves after a favorite professional athlete or popular musician. As people grow older, their tastes and values change. However, the most important thing about any young person never changes. He or she was marked at Baptism with the "character" of Jesus. The way we reflect that character is unique to each of us. Take the following *Quite a Character* test to see how you are doing in your life right now.

Choose a number between 1 and 5 to indicate how strongly you are reflecting each Jesus quality (5 = highest level, 1 = lowest level).

Jesus' Character Traits in Me	My Level of Reflection 1 2 3 4 5
Faithful to God's will	
Faithful to prayer/worship	
Compassionate to those in need	
Openness in sharing faith	
Forgiving toward others	
Healthy self-love	
Healthy friendships	
My total score =	

Add your total score. Decide for yourself how well you are reflecting Jesus' character traits. Choose one trait you will exercise this week. Describe how you will do that.

Every day I will bless you;
I will praise your name forever.

Psalm 145:2

Seasons of Praise

Objectives: To explore the meaning of the Lord's Day; to appreciate the ways in which the liturgical year helps us to enter into the paschal mystery.

Introduction ___ min.

Opening Prayer: Proclaim together Psalm 145:2 on page 63. Then invite responses to the photographic collage on pages 62 and 63. Ask, for example, "Do you have a favorite season? What is it? Why is it your favorite?" "What do the changing seasons tell us about life? about God?" Read the following lines of Thomas Moore's prayer poem "God's Presence in Nature." Encourage a sharing of ideas about the reflections of God they find in nature.

> Thou art, O God, the life and light
>   Of all this wondrous world we see,
> Its glory by day, its smile by night,
>   Are but reflections caught from Thee.
> Where'er we turn, Thy glories shine,
> And all things fair and bright are Thine!

Forum: Choose a host to conduct a TV talk show on the theme "Dream Sundays." Have the host invite participants to share their schedules and explain why they think their choices would also please Jesus. Members of the audience may question or comment on any of the dreams that are being shared. The host summarizes the kinds of activities, places, and companions chosen. If time allows, he or she might write on the board categories of activities, such as prayer or worship, entertainment, resting or relaxing, music or sports, "hanging out" with friends, visiting the sick or elderly, and getting in touch with nature.

Presentation ___ min.

◆ Have someone read aloud the opening question on page 64. Invite reflection on the seasons of the young people's lives. Ask, "Which part of the cycle of life—coming to life, growing, flowering, dying, being born again—are you in now?" Explain that the cycle may refer to our entire lives from birth to physical death to cycles we go through repeatedly as we grow and change.

◆ Have the young people form small groups. Give each group a three-dimensional object to observe in detail, for example, an ornate crucifix, a statue, a decorative vase, a flower arrangement. Direct the group leaders to place the object in the center of a table. Explain that each person should imagine that she or he is a camera and should sit at a different angle to and a different distance from the object. He or she may not move, nor may the object be moved. Have each person close one eye and "take a 60 second exposure" of the object, focusing on every detail that can be seen from that one point of view. When the minute is up, the leader writes a three-dimensional description of the object based on what each "camera" saw. Then invite one or more of the group leaders to present their three-dimensional portraits.

Point out to the young people that our celebration of the liturgical year enables us to "walk around," or get different angles on, the mystery of Christ from his incarnation to his return in glory.

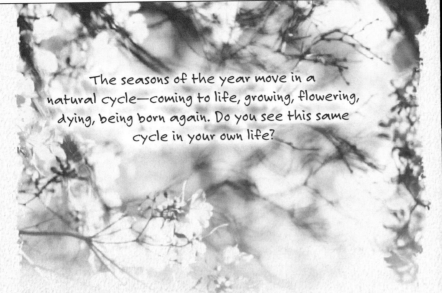

The seasons of the year move in a natural cycle—coming to life, growing, flowering, dying, being born again. Do you see this same cycle in your own life?

The Liturgical Seasons

Our life of prayer in the Church follows the same beautiful cycle of coming to life, growing, flowering, dying, being born again. Just as the seasons give variety to nature, the seasons of the liturgical year (the Church's year) give variety to the liturgy. Our life of prayer has its seasons also.

The two principal seasons of the liturgical year are formed around the two great feasts of Easter and Christmas. First we will explore the season of Easter and its preparation period, Lent. Then we will look at the season of Christmas and its preparation time, Advent. Finally we will explore Ordinary Time, the period between the Lent-Easter season and the Advent-Christmas season.

We can see a certain parallel with the birth, life, death cycle of the natural year. We can think of two great moments, birth and death, separated by the ongoing experiences of growing and changing. The Church year, then, has two main seasons, Lent-Easter and Advent-Christmas, separated by two seasons of Ordinary Time.

The seasons of the Church year do not exist simply for the sake of variety or change; they serve a much deeper purpose. As we have learned, each time we celebrate the liturgy, we celebrate the paschal mystery of Christ. In the liturgical year, the Church unfolds the entire mystery of Christ. This mystery is so complex and rich in meaning that no one single prayer or liturgical celebration can ever express it adequately.

The liturgical year helps us to "walk around" the paschal mystery. During the course of a year, we view it from different angles, in different lights. Within the cycle of a year, the Church unfolds the whole mystery of Christ, from his incarnation and birth until his ascension, the day of Pentecost, and the expectation of his return in glory.

The liturgy enables us to pass from our past-present-future concept of time into God's time of salvation, so that the grace and mystery of the event remembered are in some way made present. When we hear the passion of Christ proclaimed on Good Friday and sing "Were You There When They Crucified My Lord?" the answer is *yes*! You were there! You are there now! You do not have to feel disappointed that all the wonderful events of our faith happened long before you were born. These wonderful events of Christianity are happening now, *today*.

64

Before we look at the various seasons of the liturgical year, we will look at the word that gives us the key to understanding why we have a liturgical year in the first place. That word is *today*. A prayer from the psalm that we often find in the liturgy is:

Oh, that today you would hear his voice:
Do not harden your hearts. . . .
Psalm 95:7–8

The liturgical year, with its various feasts and seasons, helps us to keep our hearts open *each day* to the voice of God in our lives and in our world.

The Lord's Day

When most Catholics think of the major feasts of the liturgical year, they usually think of Christmas and Easter. But the *original* Christian feast day is Sunday. Sunday is the key to the whole liturgical year.

At the time of Jesus, Sunday was called "the first day of the week." The other days were simply numbered in order: the second day, the third day, and so on. The only day given a special name was the seventh day, the Sabbath. Each of the four gospels mentions explicitly that the resurrection of Jesus took place on "the first day of the week"— that is, Sunday.

The Christian celebration of Sunday has a different focus from the Jewish sabbath. Jews rest on the sabbath because God rested on the seventh day: "God blessed the seventh day and made it holy, because on it he rested from all the work he had done in creation" (Genesis 2:3). The Christian Sunday is primarily a day to assemble for worship. At first the Christian Sunday was a workday like the other days of the week; only later did it take on the Jewish characteristic of a day of rest.

65

◆ Invite volunteers to serve as a trio or quartet of liturgical singers. If possible, play a recording of the African American spiritual "Were You There." Then have a volunteer in the back of the room hold up cue cards with the following "Were You there" questions to be said or sung by the group. Direct the young people to reflect quietly about their response to each question.

• Were you there when Jesus Christ was born?

• Were you there when Jesus was baptized?

• Were you there when they shared the Last Supper?

• Were you there when they crucified my Lord?

• Were you there when he rose from the dead?

◆ Conduct a three-minute brainstorming session in which you challenge the young people to come up with as many meaningful ways as they can think of to complete the statement: "Sunday is _____." (Among those to be included from the text are: *the key to the liturgical year, the Lord's Day, a day to gather for worship, the day of Christ's resurrection*.) Have two volunteer recorders alternately write the responses on the board as quickly as possible.

Presentation (cont'd)

◆ Have a volunteer summarize *Catholic Teachings* on page 69. Emphasize that although some people have to work on Sundays, God wants all of us to find a way to be with him in prayer and leisure for whatever time is available to us.

◆ Have volunteers share the statements they underlined on pages 64 through 68. Ask all to highlight the main ideas highlighted on the reduced pupil pages.

Note: The following activity is optional.

◆ For this activity have the young people work alone or with a partner. Play thematic music quietly in the background while the young people work. The title song and "The Seed That Falls on Good Ground" from the album *By Cross and Water Signed* by M.D. Ridge (OCP) would be appropriate.

Making Lenten Pictographs

A pictograph uses symbols to communicate a message. Design a pictograph using symbols, numbers, and a few key words to communicate the following messages:

• Baptism is the key to Lent.

• Lent can be seen as a forty-day retreat or faith journey.

• Baptism marks us forever with the "character" of Jesus.

• During Lent the Spirit tells us, "Give it up! Move on!"

Encourage everyone to review pages 66 and 67 before making their pictographs. Distribute markers and long strips of drawing paper. Display the completed pictographs.

The Sunday assembly for Eucharist is at the very heart of the meaning of Sunday. As we sit at the eucharistic table—with Jesus, with the disciples, with all those who believed in the resurrection throughout ages past, and with all those who will believe in ages to come—past, present, and future become one. We come to the table of the One who died in the past and taste the future banquet of heaven. We sing of our confidence in life:

Dying you destroyed our death,
rising you restored our life.

We sing of our freedom:

Lord, by your cross and resurrection
you have set us free.

 In which eucharistic acclamation do we proclaim our faith that Christ will come again?

Day of Resurrection

What we think about Sunday depends on what we think about the resurrection. Do you believe in the resurrection? If you are a Christian, you will surely answer yes to that question. But what if we ask, "Do you believe in the resurrection not only as a historical event but also as happening *now*?"

What does it mean to believe that the resurrection is now? Consider this: Have you ever watched a movie that you have seen before? In spite of all the twists and turns of plot, you already know that everything turns out all right in the end. In the same way, the resurrection tells us that everything will turn out more than "all right" for us. The resurrection tells us that sorrow will be overwhelmed by joy, loss by victory, and death by new life. This is the role the resurrection of Jesus plays in our daily lives.

66

There are times when life can be discouraging and the world disappointing. There are times when we look around us and see so much pain and violence that we are tempted to wonder: Is death winning the battle? But in the midst of all that is evil in the world, the resurrection is God's great cry of triumph. The resurrection is our proof that life has a happy ending. The risen Jesus is our proof that loving and forgiving one another even as God loves and forgives us is a road that leads, not to death, but to life. The resurrection lets us know that God is in charge. Sin and evil will never win in the end. God's love and life will triumph.

The Lenten Retreat

Lent is the time of preparation for the celebration of Easter. It begins on Ash Wednesday and extends to Holy Thursday. Lent is like a retreat. It is a time of prayer, fasting, and almsgiving (which means sharing what we have with the poor).

When you hear the word *Lent*, what picture comes to mind? Penance, purple, fish, ashes, fasting, sacrifice, giving up movies? These are the images many Catholics associate with Lent. But your idea of Lent will be closer to the Church's meaning of the season if the first thing that comes to your mind is an image of new life—of Baptism. Baptism provides the key to Lent.

We have seen that in the fourth and fifth centuries, the Church developed liturgies to assist people who wanted to become Christians. The final forty days of this faith journey, the final "forty-day retreat" before Baptism, became what we now call Lent. Lent is the time for the catechumens to continue their preparation for Baptism, Confirmation, and Eucharist. It is a time for those of us who are already baptized to reaffirm what this sacrament means in our lives today.

For some Christians, Baptism is an event that happened long ago and does not have much impact on what they do today. But Baptism, as we have seen, changes us so radically that we are different, "marked" forever. Baptism gives us the spiritual mark that we call *character*. We are "characterized" by the life of Jesus that we find in the gospels. Once we are baptized, the promises of our Baptism should influence our decisions for the rest of our lives.

When we understand Baptism as the focus of Lent, the things we choose to give up can be more clearly understood. Our Lenten sacrifices are not a negative giving up of something. Rather, they direct us to a positive goal, joyful union with God.

Dying and Rising

Baptism is both a dying and a rising. Saint Paul says, "If, then, we have died with Christ, we believe that we shall also live with him" (Romans 6:8). The penitential aspect of Lent, the "giving something up" part, is related to the dying aspect of Baptism. But the "dying" is not an end in itself. We need to keep our eyes fixed on the "rising" that Baptism offers us.

But death, in whatever form it comes, is never easy. Sometimes we resist change in our lives, even change for the better. Jesus promises us that life will spring out of death: "Unless a grain of wheat falls to the ground and dies, it remains just a grain of wheat; but if it dies, it produces much fruit" (John 12:24). The intention of the farmer is not to kill the seed. Yet in order to grow, the seed must change its life-form. It cannot remain the same old seed!

Here is another example. When you were in the first grade, you were at the bottom of the heap; everybody else was older and seemed stronger and smarter. But now, just when it seems that you are at the top, you have to start over again in high school.

What if you would decide that you want to stay where you are, where you are comfortable? You would probably be told, "Give it up! Move on!"

Sometimes we get attached to something that keeps us from moving on. We can get caught at a particular stage of growth in our Christian lives. But during Lent we may hear the voice of the Spirit tell us, "Give it up! Move on!"

For most of us, moving on involves letting go of something *good* in order to get *an even greater good*. It means planting small seeds and looking forward to a good harvest.

Is there something now that keeps you from moving on in your faith? Write about it in your journal.

CATHOLIC ID

The laws of fast and abstinence call us to reflection, sorrow for sin, and a more serious approach to Christian life.

In the United States, Catholics who have completed their fourteenth year are bound by the law of abstinence on Ash Wednesday and all Fridays during Lent. Abstinence means that on these days we do not eat meat. Ash Wednesday and Good Friday are also days on which Catholics over eighteen are bound to fast (that is, to eat only one full meal).

67

◆ Print the terms *Lent* and *Triduum* on the board. Call for definitions of these key words. Explain that the former is from the Middle English word *lenten,* meaning "spring."

◆ Have a volunteer summarize *Catholic ID* on page 67. Then ask another person to clarify the difference between fasting and abstinence.

◆ Discuss the 🖐 **thought provoker** on page 66.

🖐 Have a volunteer read aloud the **thought provoker** on page 67. Have the young people write their responses in their journals.

FYI In the Middle Ages when most people were unable to read, the Church often used music and drama to explain the liturgical "moment." For example, in Lent the joyful Alleluia was never heard. In some places to dramatize its absence the word was printed on a ball and thrown out the Church door on Ash Wednesday, the first day of Lent! At the Easter vigil the Alleluia was greeted with the extended ringing of bells every time it was sung.

Presentation (cont'd)

◆ Duplicate or put on the board the following chart:

The Triduum

The Holy Day   The Ritual

Have the young people work with partners to fill in their charts using the information on page 68. (The completed charts should show: *the Holy Thursday ritual is the Mass of the Lord's Supper, which includes the washing of the feet; the Good Friday liturgy, which includes the reading of the Passion and adoration of the cross; the Easter Vigil liturgy, which includes blessing the new fire, lighting the paschal candle, singing Alleluias and the Easter Proclamation, and initiation of catechumens.*) Emphasize that we prepare for all three by fasting, praying, and reflecting on the meaning of the Triduum.

◆ Use the 🌤 **thought provoker** on page 68 to initiate planning for a group celebration of the Triduum.

◆ Encourage the young people to share *Highlights for Home* and discuss the questions in *Things to Share* with their families.

The Triduum

Did you know that the oldest Christian feast is Sunday? Jesus rose on the Sunday after the Passover, and, remembering this, Christians began to celebrate the Sunday closest to the Jewish Passover with special solemnity. This "Christian Passover" became what we now call Easter.

The Christian Passover soon became the special time to celebrate the sacrament of Baptism, the sacrament of our passing over from death to life in Christ. As the rites and celebrations surrounding Christian initiation grew and developed, the Christian community found that one twenty-four-hour day was simply not enough time to experience the mystery, and the celebration was extended to three days. Today we call this celebration the *Triduum*, from the Latin word meaning "three days."

The three-day observance begins with the Mass of the Lord's Supper in the evening on Holy Thursday and ends with evening prayer on Easter Sunday. The solemn liturgies of the Triduum are the most important liturgies of the Church year. The washing of the feet after the gospel of Holy Thursday is followed by the reading of the Passion and the adoration of the cross on Good Friday. At the Easter Vigil, the darkness and grief of Good Friday is broken by the blessing of the new fire and the paschal candle, the singing of the Easter Proclamation, the first sounds of the "Alleluia," and the sacramental initiation of the catechumens.

These are ceremonies we can experience at no other time during the year. They teach us the meaning of Christ's life, death, and resurrection, not in words alone, but in symbols and rituals: in fire, in water, in darkness, in light, in walking, in kneeling, in standing again.

It takes a special kind of attention and alertness to enter into these mysteries. How can we come to these events fully aware and prepared? The Church recommends that we fast, especially on Good Friday and, where possible, Holy Saturday as well. This fasting is very different from dieting. The purpose of fasting is not to lose weight; its purpose is to gain insight into the mysteries of the Triduum. It is a fast of awareness. It creates a hunger that can be satisfied only by the best of foods: our Easter Eucharist, which we share with those who join us at our eucharistic table for the very first time.

Catholics eighteen years of age and under are not obliged to fast, but even younger Catholics can prepare, through prayer and simple acts of love and selflessness, to celebrate the Triduum with an open heart and a clear mind.

🌤 *As a group, plan ways you will prepare during Lent this year to celebrate the Triduum together in your parish.*

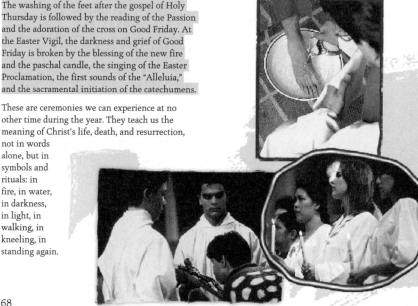

68

Answers for Chapter 8 Assessment				
1. d	**2.** c	**3.** d	**4.** a	**5.** a
6. d	**7.** a	**8.** b	**9.** d	**10.** Accept reasonable responses.

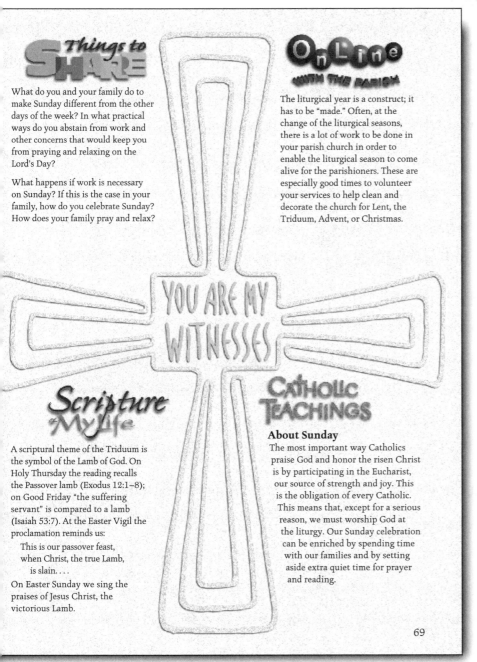

Things to SHARE

What do you and your family do to make Sunday different from the other days of the week? In what practical ways do you abstain from work and other concerns that would keep you from praying and relaxing on the Lord's Day?

What happens if work is necessary on Sunday? If this is the case in your family, how do you celebrate Sunday? How does your family pray and relax?

OnLine *with the parish*

The liturgical year is a construct; it has to be "made." Often, at the change of the liturgical seasons, there is a lot of work to be done in your parish church in order to enable the liturgical season to come alive for the parishioners. These are especially good times to volunteer your services to help clean and decorate the church for Lent, the Triduum, Advent, or Christmas.

Scripture *of My Life*

A scriptural theme of the Triduum is the symbol of the Lamb of God. On Holy Thursday the reading recalls the Passover lamb (Exodus 12:1–8); on Good Friday "the suffering servant" is compared to a lamb (Isaiah 53:7). At the Easter Vigil the proclamation reminds us:

> This is our passover feast, when Christ, the true Lamb, is slain. . . .

On Easter Sunday we sing the praises of Jesus Christ, the victorious Lamb.

Catholic Teachings

About Sunday

The most important way Catholics praise God and honor the risen Christ is by participating in the Eucharist, our source of strength and joy. This is the obligation of every Catholic. This means that, except for a serious reason, we must worship God at the liturgy. Our Sunday celebration can be enriched by spending time with our families and by setting aside extra quiet time for prayer and reading.

69

Conclusion ___ min.

FORUM Assignment

✔ Read pages 70–77. Underline in pencil the statements that express six key ideas.

✔ Choose one of the four gospels and scan the stories of Jesus that take place "in between" his birth, death, and resurrection. Choose one story that appeals to you. Be prepared to tell the story and share what it reveals to you about Jesus in "ordinary time."

Closing Prayer: Distribute the handout *Quite a Character.* Allow a few minutes for the young people to complete the test. Encourage respect for an individual's privacy. Then invite the young people to look at the photo collage on pages 62 and 63. Proclaim together Psalm 145:2 on page 63.

Evaluation: Do the young people understand the meaning of the liturgical year, the Lord's Day, and the Triduum? Do they appreciate the baptismal focus of Lent?

FOR CHAPTER 9

- copies of handout *Holy Spirit, Is That You?* page 70C
- copies of *Chapter 9 Assessment*, page 77A
- copies of *Highlights for Home*, page 77B
- recording of Pete Seeger's folk song "Turn, Turn, Turn"
- drawing paper, posterboard, markers, scissors, glue
- magazines and newspaper

Assessment

 1 The liturgical year
a. unfolds the mystery of Christ.
b. follows a cycle of birth, life, and death.
c. has ten main seasons.
d. both a and b

 2 When we celebrate in memory of Jesus,
a. we live in the past.
b. we live in the future.
c. he is present to us today.
d. none of the above

3 Sunday is
a. the original Christian feast.
b. the Lord's Day.
c. the day of Christ's resurrection.
d. all of the above

 4 For Christians Sunday is
a. primarily a day of worship.
b. primarily a day of fasting.
c. primarily a day of rest.
d. just like the Jewish Sabbath.

 5 The resurrection of Jesus
a. is our proof that life has a happy ending.
b. has no meaning for us.
c. should not be celebrated every year.
d. meant sin had triumphed.

 6 Lent is a time for
a. remembering our Baptism.
b. praying, fasting, giving alms.
c. letting go of some things.
d. all of the above

 7 By our Baptism we are
a. marked with the character of Jesus.
b. not changed.
c. freed from making sacrifices.
d. denied free will.

 8 Triduum refers to
a. three days before Christmas.
b. three-day celebration of the paschal mystery.
c. a town in ancient Rome.
d. days at the beginning of Lent.

 9 Celebrating the Triduum
a. involves symbols and rituals.
b. recalls Christ's death and resurrection.
c. begins on Holy Thursday.
d. all of the above

10 How can we best prepare for Easter?

_____
_____
_____
_____

Highlights for Home

Focus on Faith

In a Christmas sermon (1625), the English poet John Donne observed "Now God comes to thee, not as in the dawning of day, not as in the bud of the spring, but as the sun at noon to illustrate all shadows . . . all occasions invite his mercies, and all times are his seasons." When we as Catholics actively connect with the Church's liturgical year, we experience the truth of "all times are his seasons."

Each liturgical season (Advent-Christmas, Lent-Easter, Ordinary Time) links us with the unfolding mysteries of Christ's life. Each Sunday calls us to be present once again at the key event in salvation history: the resurrection of Jesus from the dead. The Lord's Day reminds us that he has overcome death—and so will we.

Family life is deeply enriched when we focus on and participate fully in the Church year.

Conversation Starters

. . . . a few ideas to talk about together . . . .

◆ What is our favorite part of the liturgical year? Why?

◆ How might we make our Sundays a more joyful, peaceful, or loving celebration of Christ's resurrection?

◆ What forms of fasting might we pledge ourselves to during Lent or at other times when we want to gain spiritual insight?

Feature Focus

The *Catholic Teachings* feature on page 69 focuses on our obligation to participate in the liturgy on Sundays. The Eucharist is the heart of our Catholic faith. When we go forth from the Mass to live the Eucharist, we may spend the Lord's Day in restful leisure, visit the sick, share time with family members, or spend quiet time in the presence of Jesus in meditative prayer or spiritual reading.

Reflection

Ask yourself, "What season of the Church year are we celebrating right now?" "How can we make this time a season of praise in our lives?"

Ask the Holy Spirit to help you be present to Jesus during this particular season. Sit in silence. When you are ready, pray Psalm 145:2:

Every day I will bless you;
I will praise your name forever.

YEAR OF GLORY

Adult Focus

During the "great fifty days" of the Easter season, we welcome with the risen Lord the neophytes (newly initiated Christians) into the family of faith. This period of mystagogy (learning about and reflecting on the paschal mystery) deepens our commitment to Christ and his Church. In stories from the Acts of the Apostles, we hear once again how the early disciples followed Jesus' example of healing, teaching, and evangelizing. And we are reminded that their stories are to be repeated in our lives.

The triumphal Easter season culminates in Pentecost with our celebration of the coming of the Holy Spirit. The liturgy makes Pentecost present to us now, and we grow in our understanding of the Holy Spirit's work in our lives today not only through the liturgy but also through reflection on the Scriptures and our own lives and experiences.

During the Advent and Christmas seasons, we express our longing for the coming of Christ and the fulfillment of God's kingdom in our midst. Ordinary Time celebrates the mystery of Christ not in one specific aspect, such as his birth or resurrection, but in all its aspects. It also encourages us to make the most of our "ordinary time" to grow spiritually and become faithful disciples of Jesus Christ.

Catechism Focus

The theme of Chapter 9 corresponds to paragraphs 731–737, 1095, 1163, and 1168-1171 of the *Catechism*.

Enrichment Activities

Interviewing Neophytes

The young people might enjoy interviewing several neophytes from their own or other parishes. Suggest that they use audiotape or videotape to record the neophytes' responses to questions about their experiences of the catechumenate, the Easter Vigil, and mystagogy. They might also ask what attracted the neophytes to the Church, how they interacted with their sponsors, and what they now enjoy most about being Catholics.

Collecting Angel Stories

Most teens are very interested in the role angels play in our lives. They might be encouraged to put together a collection of angel stories taken from the Scriptures (such as Luke 1:26–38; Matthew 2:13–15, Acts 12: 1–11), from literature (*A Month by Month Guide to Entertaining Angels* by Father Mark Boyer, ACTA Publications; *A Dictionary of Angels* by Gustav Davidson), and from the media (*Touched by an Angel*).

Teaching Resources

Overview

To explore the meaning of Pentecost and the gift of the Holy Spirit; to understand that Advent and Christmas express our longing for God's reign.

Opening Prayer Ideas

Pray antiphonally Ecclesiastes 3:1–8. Write a refrain for the song "Turn, Turn, Turn."

or

Make a drawing that illustrates Psalm 119:105. Let it be your prayer for Ordinary Time.

Materials

- recording of Pete Seeger's folk song "Turn, Turn, Turn."
- drawing paper, posterboard, markers, scissors, glue
- magazines and newspapers

 Liturgy and Worship Journal:
For Chapter 9, use pages 36–39.

REPRODUCIBLE MASTERS
- *Holy Spirit, Is That You?*, page 70C
- *Chapter 9 Assessment*, page 77A
- *Highlights for Home*, page 77B

Supplemental Resources

VIDEOS
By Way of the Heart: The Sacredness of the Ordinary
Paulist Press
997 Macarthur Blvd.
Mahwah, NJ 07430

Seasons of Life
Sheed & Ward
P.O. Box 419492
Kansas City, MO 64141

Holy Spirit, Is That You?

The Holy Spirit probably won't make an appearance as "tongues of fire" or "a driving wind" in your everyday life. But the Spirit is present—guiding, inspiring, and breathing life into you as a follower of Jesus. Give examples of how the Spirit has come to you in the following ways.

In the presence of a person . . .

In a scientific or natural wonder . . .

In a song or a poem . . .

In a prayer . . .

In a story . . .

In these other ways:

A Year of Glory

Praise the LORD, all you nations!
Give glory, all you peoples!
The LORD'S love for us is strong;
the LORD is faithful forever.
Hallelujah!
Psalm 117

Objective: To explore the meaning of Pentecost and the gift of the Holy Spirit; to understand that Advent and Christmas express our longing for God's reign.

Introduction ___ min.

Opening Prayer: If possible, play any recording of Pete Seeger's folk song "Turn, Turn, Turn." It has been recorded by several artists and is widely available. Ask the young people to form two groups. Have them alternate in praying aloud Ecclesiastes 3:1–8.

Explain that the liturgical year gives us the opportunity to turn to Jesus in every season. Pray the following litany, asking the group to respond to each petition saying "Jesus, you are the reason we celebrate this season."

• During the Advent season, when we are thinking about the gifts we will receive at Christmas, help us not to strain family relationships during this hectic time. Help us to turn to you in prayer, Jesus.

• During Christmas, when we want to party constantly with our friends, help us to spend quality time with both family and friends and to rejoice as we turn to you.

• During Ordinary Time, when life may seem boring or routine, help us to make it interesting by finding ways to help others. Help us to turn to you in gratitude and pray.

• During Lent, help us to live our baptismal promises by remembering the poor, the hungry, and the homeless in prayer and action. As we encounter your sufferings in others, help us to turn to you.

• During the Easter season, we tend to think about the new clothes we want to buy. Help us to rejoice in our new life in you and to remember this greatest of gifts as we turn to you.

• During Ordinary Time after Pentecost Sunday, when we are bogged down with end-of-school activities and excited about summer plans, help us to find the Holy Spirit in our everyday lives and to turn to you in prayer.

Forum: Distribute Bibles and have the group gather in a storytelling circle. Two student hosts alternate in calling on participants to share their chosen stories of Jesus in "ordinary time." Whenever questions arise about the meaning or context of the stories, the young people may use their Bibles to clarify these concerns. The hosts might also record on the board names of stories chosen by the group, as well as the number of times certain stories are chosen. (This information may be used in planning prayer services, retreats, or gospel reflections.)

Presentation ___ min.

◆ Invite responses to the photograph on pages 70 and 71. What message does it communicate? What feelings does it evoke about Jesus?

◆ Read together the song lyrics at the top of page 72. Explain that these words are based on the writing of an author who lived three centuries before Jesus. Ecclesiastes was pessimistic about the ability of human beings to act at the right time to achieve God's purposes. He had not heard the good news, so he could not share our privilege of celebrating the triumph of Jesus over sin and death. He missed out on the beauty of the liturgical year and the opportunity to grow in holiness by uniting ourselves with Jesus in every season.

◆ Have volunteers review pages 72 and 73. Then have the young people highlight the main ideas on these reduced pupil pages.

"There is a season, turn, turn, turn . . . And a time for every purpose under heaven."©

(Song lyrics adapted from Ecclesiastes 3:1)

How do these words suggest that we live in a world of time, of change, of new beginnings?

The Great Fifty Days

We human beings don't usually like sudden changes. We like predictable changes. We like to know ahead of time that a change is coming so that we can prepare for it. The seasons of the Church year are seasons of change, seasons of preparation, and seasons of new beginnings.

At the heart of our Christian life is the belief that God has radically changed the universe through the paschal mystery of Jesus. We call this radical change *salvation*. It is the focus of our Easter celebration.

72

Easter is "the Feast of feasts,' the 'Solemnity of solemnities'" (*Catechism*, 1169). Easter is so important that we cannot even begin to celebrate it adequately in one day. It takes a "week of weeks." It takes fifty days, a *Pentecost* (from the Greek word meaning "fifty"). *Each day* of these fifty days is Easter.

At the Easter Vigil we received new members into our community through the sacraments of initiation. During their time of preparation, the catechumens learned about the sacraments "from outside," as it were. Now, as *neophytes* (newly initiated Christians), they experience the sacraments of Baptism and Eucharist "from within" the community.

For the neophytes (and for us as well) this fifty-day season of Easter is the time of mystagogy. *Mystagogy* is a time for learning about and reflecting on the mysteries of faith. The Easter season is a time for the community and the neophytes to grow in their understanding of the paschal mystery. It is a time to make the paschal mystery part of our lives through meditation on the gospel, sharing in the Eucharist, and doing good works.

The newly baptized have not only "put on Christ"; they have also put on his body, the Church. They have joined a new family. And they (and we) take time during these fifty days to learn who that family, that Church, is. We find the picture of the birth and early growth of the Church in the Acts of the Apostles.

The Story Continues

The Acts of the Apostles forms one story with the Gospel of Luke. If you compare the way the two parts of this story (Luke 1:1–4 and Acts 1:1–2) begin, it is clear that Luke/Acts is meant to be read as a unit. Luke/Acts is a very special form of writing. The author wants to show three things: (1) the life and deeds of Jesus, (2) how his life and deeds were continued in the lives and deeds of the first disciples, and (3) how his life and deeds are to be continued by us in the Church today.

In Luke's Gospel we see Jesus healing the sick; in Acts we see Peter doing the same. In the gospel we see Jesus brought before the high priest to be interrogated; in Acts we see the same thing

happening to Peter. The death of Stephen, the first martyr, parallels the death of Jesus. Stephen prays, "Lord, do not hold this sin against them" (Acts 7:60) as Jesus had prayed "Father, forgive them, they know not what they do" (Luke 23:34).

Why did Luke write in this way? He wanted to show us that what Jesus did during his lifetime, the first disciples also did during theirs, and we—today's disciples—are to do during ours! As we hear readings from the Acts of the Apostles proclaimed at each Mass during the great fifty days, we might ask ourselves these questions: "Is this our Church family today?" "Are we a healing Church?" "Are we a forgiving Church?" The stories in Acts are not simply stories of long-ago people and places. They are *our* stories, *our* pictures. The challenge of the great fifty days of Easter is to continue the story of Luke/Acts today, in our Church and in our lives.

Filled with the Spirit

On the final day of our fifty-day celebration of Easter, we celebrate Pentecost. As with each feast and each liturgical season of the year, its meaning is best understood by looking at the Scripture readings. The readings for Pentecost speak of the sending of the Holy Spirit. The word *spirit* is a translation of the Hebrew word *ruah*, which means "breath," "air," or "wind."

In the second reading for Pentecost, we read about the descent of the Holy Spirit upon the disciples: As they were gathered together, they heard a noise like a strong wind (*ruah*). "Then there appeared to them tongues as of fire. . . . And they were all filled with the holy Spirit and began to speak in different tongues, as the Spirit enabled them to proclaim" (Acts 2:3–4). Right away we begin to see the gifts and graces of the Spirit at work in the Church.

In the gospel for Pentecost, we read John's account of Jesus giving the Holy Spirit. On the evening of the first day of the week, "Jesus came and stood in their midst and said to them, 'Peace be with you. . . . As the Father has sent me, so I send you.' And . . . he breathed [*ruah*] on them and said to them, 'Receive the holy Spirit'" (John 20:19–22). Sins are to be forgiven! The gifts of peace and reconciliation are given to the Church.

73

◆ Print the terms *neophyte* and *mystagogy* on the board. Call first on students whose names begin with *n* or *m* to define the terms. (*Neophytes are newly initiated Christians who have experienced Baptism, Confirmation, and Eucharist at the Easter Vigil. Mystagogy is a time of learning about and reflecting on the mysteries of Catholic faith. It begins during the fifty-day Easter season, when the neophytes deepen their understanding of the paschal mystery.*)

◆ Have a volunteer summarize the explanation of our liturgical celebration of Pentecost. Ask another volunteer to summarize *Scripture & My Life* on page 77.

To help the young people remember the seven gifts of the Holy Spirit, have them draw a circular chart, divided into seven segments, in their journals. Direct them to inscribe the name of one of the gifts on each segment. Then read the names of the seven gifts aloud together. Then have the young people write how these gifts help them to follow the Spirit's lead.

FYI Pope John XXIII was seventy-seven years old when he became the leader of the Roman Catholic Church. He was talking with a good friend about ways the Church should respond to the many problems that were afflicting the world. Suddenly, out of the blue, he knew the answer. "My soul was illumined by a great idea," he said. That great idea was the Second Vatican Council, which brought about positive changes in the Church and the world. As soon as the idea came to him, Pope John felt "a profound sense of joy and hope." He knew he was following the Holy Spirit's lead.

Presentation (cont'd)

Note: The following activity is optional.

◆ Have the young people form small groups of "Spirit Communicators." Distribute large sheets of drawing paper or half sheets of posterboard, markers, scissors, glue, and Catholic and secular magazines and newspapers. Invite each group to produce a visual aid that illustrates the three primary sources of our understanding of the work of the Holy Spirit.

Encourage the young people to incorporate in their collages or other artwork symbols of the Pentecost Spirit such as breath, air, wind, and fire. While they are working, you may want to play thematic music such as "Lord, Send Out Your Spirit" by Jeanne Cotter from the album *How Excellent: Songs for Teens*, vol. 1 (GIA).

Have the young people display and comment on their completed work.

◆ Discuss the ☀ **thought provoker** on page 74. Invite the young people to write their responses in the space provided on page 74.

◆ Ask a volunteer to read aloud the prophecy from Isaiah 11:6. Then tell the following true story:

In County Louth, Ireland, there is a beautiful seventeen-foot-high cross. It was carved in the tenth century by an unknown artist. Among the inscriptions on the cross is Isaiah 11:6. However, the artist did not choose to carve a lamb or a leopard to illustrate Isaiah's prophecy of peace and universal tolerance. He carved instead two contented cats. One cat is being hugged by a mouse. The other has three little birds perched on its paw.

The liturgy combines these accounts in order that we might reflect and ask ourselves: "How does the Holy Spirit act in the Church today?" "How does the Spirit come to me?" The liturgy makes Pentecost present to us now, today.

Our understanding of the work of the Holy Spirit today comes from three sources. The first is the witness of the Scriptures, which we have briefly explored. The second is the public prayer of the Church, the liturgy. The third is our own lives and experience.

Let us consider the prayer of the Church. In Eucharistic Prayer IV we speak directly to God and recall Jesus' sending us the Holy Spirit:

And that we might live no longer for ourselves but for him,
he sent the Holy Spirit from you, Father,
as his first gift to those who believe,
to complete his work on earth
and bring us the fullness of grace.

What can we learn from this prayer? First we learn that the Holy Spirit is not the possession of an exceptional few. The Holy Spirit is given to *every* Christian, to all who believe.

The gift of the Holy Spirit is a gift of *mission*. When Jesus gave the Holy Spirit, he told the disciples, "As the Father has sent me, so I send you" (John 20:21). What the Father gave Jesus to do, the risen Lord commissions us to continue. This is the message of Pentecost. This is the work of the Holy Spirit. This is the work of a lifetime.

The Holy Spirit works with each one of us for the good of all. How is the Spirit breathing life into you?

74

Madonna of the Chair, Raphael, 1514

Advent and Christmas

During Advent we go back to the beginning. We do not forget that we are celebrating the same Jesus who died and rose for us but we remember also that he chose to share ordinary human life with us. He chose to become one of us and to experience life as we do: its joys, sorrows, disappointments, hopes.

Advent is a time of joyful expectation. What do we expect, and why are we joyful? The answer to these questions is given in the Scriptures proposed for the season.

From the First Sunday of Advent until December 16, the readings express the hope and longing for that day when the plan of God will be completed. We dream of how things ought to be and long for the day when Christ will come again in glory. From December 17 to December 24, the readings direct our attention to the birth of Jesus.

The prophet Isaiah sets the tone for Advent. He voices the hope and longing of God's people, wandering far away from home, in exile in a foreign land. They want to return home. They dream of the day when God's rule will prevail and wars will end. God's people long for the time when all hatred and prejudice will cease, when the streets will be safe and children will not live in fear.

How and when will this all come about? We do not know. Asked by the Pharisees when God's reign would come, Jesus replied, "Behold, the kingdom of God is among you" (Luke 17:21).

How can the kingdom be among us when the world is so full of sin and violence? To see the kingdom, we need a special kind of light: faith. The light of Advent (as symbolized in the Advent wreath and in all the other beautiful lights we see at this time of year) little by little replaces the darkness of doubt and discouragement. By the light of faith, we see the kingdom.

Christmas, then, is a celebration of light— the light of Christ, the Word made flesh. In the birth of Jesus, the invisible God becomes visible. In the life of Jesus, we see God's plan for the world unfold. This plan is revealed gently and quietly, even as God gently and quietly appeared among us in the stable at Bethlehem.

In our lives, too, God's plan is usually revealed gently and quietly: in a quiet moment of prayer, in the stillness after the loss of a friend, in those minutes at night before we fall asleep. Little by little we are to grow into the likeness of Christ.

Christmas is the season when we pray fervently for the final revelation of God's mysterious plan. We pray for an end to war, hunger, and injustice. We pray, *Marana tha!* "Come, Lord Jesus!"

White, red, green, violet—what do these liturgical colors mean? Red (the color of fire) symbolizes the Holy Spirit, and is used on Pentecost and for the sacrament of Confirmation. Red (the color of blood) is also used on days when we celebrate the passion of Jesus (for example, on Passion Sunday and Good Friday) and on days when we celebrate the feasts of martyrs. White, the color of joy and victory, is used for the other feasts of the Lord, Mary, and the other saints. White is also used for the seasons of Easter and Christmas. Violet is used for the seasons of Lent and Advent. Green, the color of life and hope, is used during Ordinary Time.

Have you ever noticed how often at Mass we pray for the coming of Christ? Can you recall a few examples?

Ordinary Time

What is Ordinary Time? If we take *ordinary* to mean "usual, average, of inferior quality or second-rate," it will be hard to get excited about Ordinary Time. However, these days are not ordinary in that sense. *Ordinary* here means "not seasonal." *Ordinary Time* is the time that lies outside the seasons of Lent-Easter and Advent-Christmas. In Ordinary Time, the Church celebrates the mystery of Christ not in one specific aspect but in all its aspects.

During the *seasons* of the Church year, the readings from Scripture are chosen according to the theme of the season: Lent, Baptism; Easter, resurrection; the great fifty days of Easter, Acts of the Apostles; Advent, Isaiah and joyful expectation; Christmas, God's taking flesh. During Ordinary Time the readings are not chosen according to a theme. Rather, in Ordinary Time we read from the various books of the Bible from beginning to end in a continuous fashion. This is the key to understanding Ordinary Time.

In Ordinary Time we concentrate for an entire year on the life and work of Jesus Christ as proclaimed in one of the Gospels, either Matthew,

75

Have the young people form small groups to discuss ways artists might illustrate Isaiah 11:6 for today's world. Ask each group to choose one illustration to describe for the other groups.

You may want to have the young people listen to one or more of the songs from the album *Prophets of Hope* by Trisha Watts (OCP).

◆ Distribute missalettes to help the young people respond to the **thought provoker** on page 75. Some examples are the memorial acclamations; Our Father; Holy, Holy, Holy; and Advent prayers and hymns.

◆ Have a volunteer review *Catholic ID*. Some may want to make charts of the liturgical year using seasonal colors. Display the charts for other groups in the parish.

◆ Do a two-minute brainstorming session in which students supply as many accurate completions of the following statement as they can: "Ordinary Time in the Church year is _____." (*outside the seasons of Advent-Christmas and Lent-Easter; a time for non-thematic Scripture readings; a time to get to know Jesus better through gospel readings from Mark, Matthew and Luke; not an inferior or second-rate time of the year*)

Presentation (cont'd)

◆ Have the young people highlight the main ideas highlighted on reduced pupil pages 74 through 76.

◆ Read together Mark 4:4–20 as suggested in the  **thought provoker.** Suggest that the young people write their responses in their journals.

◆ Have a volunteer summarize *Catholic Teachings* on page 77. Tell the young people that Gallup polls indicate that seventy-five percent of teens in America believe in angels. Many enjoy popular TV shows and movies about angels. If time allows, invite students to share their ideas or stories about angels who protect and guide us. Clarify any mistaken ideas. (For example, people do not become angels when they die.)

Conclusion ___ min.

◆ Have a volunteer read *On Line With the Parish.* If possible, have a representative of the parish liturgy committee present to encourage the young people to participate in these Advent activities.

Assessment: If you plan to administer *Chapter 9 Assessment*, page 77A, allow about ten minutes for its completion.

Mark, or Luke. (John's Gospel is read principally during the liturgical seasons.) As we meet Christ in the Scriptures, we come to know him better. Knowledge of the Scriptures is knowledge of Christ.

Ordinary Time enables us to hear the whole gospel—not just the "big stories" of birth, death, and resurrection, but all the "in between" stories, parables, and teachings. Our Christian life is not just Christmas and Easter. It is all the days in between, the ordinary days. And perhaps that is what makes it difficult.

The hardest part of following Jesus is simply that, for the most part, it is so terribly ordinary! Getting up every morning and going to school, treating others with respect and fairness, doing homework and chores every night, practicing a musical instrument day after day, showing up for sports practice night after night—these things seem so ordinary, so routine, and possibly even boring. However, we know that the truly valuable things in our lives are achieved just that way: little by little, day after day.

For the most part God is not revealed in the spectacular or the sensational. Rather, the miracle of the kingdom is found in our daily efforts and everyday growth. We take up our cross daily and allow God's Spirit to help us grow gradually into the likeness of Jesus.

Read Mark 4:4–20, the parable of the sower. Think of God's word "sown" in your heart. What kind of soil has it fallen on?

76

Answers for Chapter 9 Assessment

1. b   **2.** b   **3.** a   **4.** b   **5.** d
6. c   **7.** b   **8.** c   **9.** a   **10.** See pages 75–76.

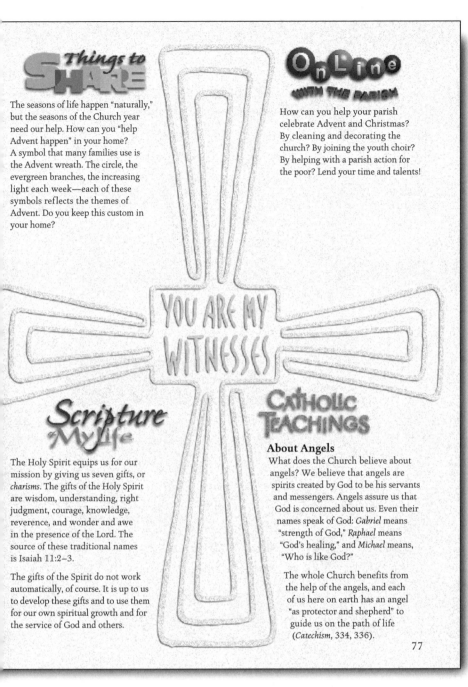

Things to SHARE

The seasons of life happen "naturally," but the seasons of the Church year need our help. How can you "help Advent happen" in your home? A symbol that many families use is the Advent wreath. The circle, the evergreen branches, the increasing light each week—each of these symbols reflects the themes of Advent. Do you keep this custom in your home?

OnLine WITH THE PARISH

How can you help your parish celebrate Advent and Christmas? By cleaning and decorating the church? By joining the youth choir? By helping with a parish action for the poor? Lend your time and talents!

Scripture of My Life

The Holy Spirit equips us for our mission by giving us seven gifts, or *charisms*. The gifts of the Holy Spirit are wisdom, understanding, right judgment, courage, knowledge, reverence, and wonder and awe in the presence of the Lord. The source of these traditional names is Isaiah 11:2–3.

The gifts of the Spirit do not work automatically, of course. It is up to us to develop these gifts and to use them for our own spiritual growth and for the service of God and others.

CATHOLIC TEACHINGS

About Angels

What does the Church believe about angels? We believe that angels are spirits created by God to be his servants and messengers. Angels assure us that God is concerned about us. Even their names speak of God: *Gabriel* means "strength of God," *Raphael* means "God's healing," and *Michael* means, "Who is like God?"

The whole Church benefits from the help of the angels, and each of us here on earth has an angel "as protector and shepherd" to guide us on the path of life (*Catechism*, 334, 336).

77

Conclusion (cont'd)

◆ Encourage the young people to share *Highlights for Home* and the custom of the Advent wreath with their families. This custom is described in *Things to Share* on page 77.

FORUM Assignment

✔ Read pages 78–85. Underline in pencil the statements that express six key ideas.

✔ Complete the handout *Holy Spirit, Is That You?* Add the heading "In peace and reconciliation." Explain the ways on the reverse side of the handout.

Closing Prayer: Have Psalm 117 printed on a poster displayed behind the prayer table. Invite the young people to gather in a semicircle in front of the table. Ask the young people to raise their arms in a victory gesture like that of the risen Jesus in the photo on pages 70 and 71. Then direct them to pray the psalm in "victory voices."

Evaluation: Do the young people understand the meaning of the Easter, Advent-Christmas seasons and Ordinary Time? Are they aware of the Holy Spirit's presence in their lives and their need to come to know Jesus better during their own "ordinary times"?

FOR CHAPTER 10

- copies of handout *Oh, What a Web!*, page 78C
- *Chapter 10 Assessment*, page 85A
- *Highlights for Home*, page 85B

Assessment

 1 The "great fifty days" is
a. Ordinary Time.
b. the Easter season.
c. Advent.
d. Lent.

 2 Mystagogy is
a. a time of reflecting on Advent.
b. a time for the neophytes to learn more about the Church.
c. the season of Easter.
d. the Lenten retreat.

 3 The prophet _____ sets the tone for Advent.
a. Isaiah
b. Hosea
c. Ezekiel
d. Daniel

 4 At Pentecost we celebrate
a. the birth of Jesus.
b. the descent of the Spirit.
c. the birth of the Spirit.
d. Saint Peter's birthday.

 5 We understand the Spirit's work
a. through the Scriptures.
b. through the liturgy.
c. through our own experiences.
d. all of the above

 6 During Advent we
a. prepare for Easter.
b. celebrate Christmas.
c. long for Christ's coming.
d. focus on the cross.

 7 Christmas celebrates
a. the risen Christ.
b. the Word made flesh.
c. the paschal mystery.
d. the Eucharist.

 8 The Church teaches that angels
a. have wings.
b. are human.
c. protect and guide us.
d. wear white robes.

 9 Ordinary Time means
a. not seasonal.
b. second-rate time.
c. the season after Advent.
d. the season after Lent.

10 Describe the purpose of Ordinary Time.

_____
_____
_____
_____
_____
_____

Highlights for Home

Focus on Faith

In *The Spiritual Life of Children*, Robert Coles interviews a fourth-grader who wonders how "the Holy Ghost comes down." The boy recalls how a bird had once flown up close to him and then flew off. He wonders if the bird might have had a message for him. He consults an uncle who is a priest. The boy reports, "He told me never to forget that God has his own way of reminding us of him—that he's around!"

One of the ways God has of reminding us Catholics of the Holy Spirit's presence is the liturgical year. Not only at Pentecost but throughout the Church year, the Holy Spirit "comes down" to inspire and guide the disciples of Jesus. Ordinary Time (outside the seasons of Lent-Easter and Advent-Christmas) offers us the opportunity each year to grow in our knowledge of and love for Jesus as we reflect on the Gospels of Matthew, Mark, and Luke. By attending to the Scriptures, the liturgy, and our prayer life, we come to understand how the Holy Spirit works in us.

Conversation Starters

. . . . a few ideas to talk about together . . . .

◆ How might we make the neophytes in our parish feel more at home in our faith community?

◆ What can I do to become more aware of the Holy Spirit's presence in my ordinary life?

◆ How will we pray and work for the coming of God's kingdom?

Feature Focus

The *Catholic Teachings* feature on page 77 focuses on the meaning and significance of angels in our lives. Catholics believe that angels are God's servants and messengers. Out of love for us, God has given each person an angel whose mission is to protect, shepherd, and guide us in this life.

Reflection

Among the Church's treasures is a beautiful prayer to the Holy Spirit composed in the thirteenth century by an unknown writer. In a restful place, slowly pray the following verses. Then close your eyes and feel the breath of the Holy Spirit.

Come, Father of the poor
Come, giver of all gifts
Come, light of every heart.

Give goodness its reward
Give safe journey through death
Give joy that has no end.
(Amen, Holy Spirit. Amen.)

THE SACRAMENT OF RECONCILIATION

Adult Focus

In Mark's Gospel (Mark 2:1–12) there is a dramatic account of a paralyzed man being lowered by his friends through a roof to be laid at the feet of Jesus. What did the paralytic want of Jesus? Healing. What is the first thing Jesus said to him? "Child, your sins are forgiven." The greatest evil, the greatest sickness, the greatest paralysis we can have in our lives is sin. God's forgiveness, then, is the first and greatest gift Jesus gives the paralyzed man—and us.

One of the most profound ills of our age, which our young people face daily, is the denial of sin. If there is no sin, there is no need of forgiveness, conversion, or reconciliation. Therefore, we must provide opportunities for our young people to experience their need for God's forgiving and unconditional love. They need moments when they recognize that if they first reach out and touch "the hem of his garment" in prayer they will be healed, moments when they are encouraged to turn from sin and turn for home where a loving father awaits them.

This chapter explores the sacrament of Reconciliation, Jesus' gift of healing to his Church. It is a sacrament that restores and supports the life of our souls. It is a sacrament that continually turns us towards home and the welcoming love of the Father.

Catechism Focus

The theme of this chapter corresponds with paragraphs 1422–1497 of the *Catechism*.

Enrichment Activities

Computer Connection

Have the group use a word-processing software program, such as *The Writing Center*™, to compose a newsmagazine article recapping an imaginary interview with the lost son, his father, his brother, and a neighbor attending the celebration of his return (Luke 15:11–32). Have the young people form news teams. To conduct the interviews, one team member should ask questions from a prepared script for each of the characters. The characters may wear costumes and be photographed when interviewed. The photos can be scanned into the final articles when the teams take their work to the computer. If the teams are using *The Writing Center*™, have them set up their articles to appear in a two-or-three column layout and include the scanned-in photos. Have the news teams print and present the news articles to the entire group.

A Story of Forgiving Love

If possible, show the segment from the video *Jesus of Nazareth* in which Jesus tells the parable of the lost son. It appears on the second of the three tapes, right after the miraculous catch of fish. The film beautifully blends Peter's resentment of the still unconverted Matthew, the tax collector, with Jesus' gentle and wry telling of how God extends forgiveness.

This three-tape video is an invaluable addition to any religion library.

Teaching Resources

Overview

To discover that through the sacrament of Reconciliation our relationship with God and with the Church is restored.

Opening Prayer Ideas

Pray together the Our Father. Have volunteers suggest gestures to express each petition.

or

Invite volunteers to role-play the parable of the lost son (Luke 15:11–31).

Materials

- Bibles, journals, and highlighters

REPRODUCIBLE MASTERS
- *Oh, What a Web!*, page 78C
- *Chapter 10 Assessment*, page 85A
- *Highlights for Home*, page 85B

Liturgy and Worship Journal:
For Chapter 10, use pages 36–39.

Supplemental Resources

VIDEOS
Pardon and Peace: Sacrament of Reconciliation
Franciscan Communications/
St. Anthony Messenger Press
http://www.american
catholic.org

Jesus of Nazareth
Ignatius Press
P.O. Box 1339
Ft. Collins, CO 80522

CHAPTER ten

Oh, What a Web!

Oh, what a tangled web we weave,
When first we practice to deceive!

from "Lochinvar" by Sir Walter Scott

Sometimes people get caught up in the web of selfishness and sin. Before we celebrate the sacrament of Reconciliation, we are asked to take some time to unravel the selfish situations in which we and others have become involved. We do this by examining our conscience.

Look at the photograph of the spider's web on this page. Imagine you are the spider who has had a change of heart. You begin to unravel the web strand by strand. On the reverse side of this page, write questions young people might ask themselves to help identify selfish entanglements. The following examples will help you get started.

Love of God

◆ Do I use God's name with profanity or with respect?

Love of Neighbor

◆ Have I gossiped about someone or spread false rumors?

Love of Self

◆ Have I given in to peer pressure and done something I know is wrong? Have I done this just to be popular?

The Sacrament of Reconciliation

Lord, you are kind and forgiving,
most loving to all who call on you.
Psalm 86:5

Objective: To discover that through the sacrament of Reconciliation our relationship with God and with the Church is restored.

Introduction ___ min.

Opening Prayer: Invite the young people to look at the photo of the river on pages 78 and 79. Read together Psalm 86:5 on page 79. Then have the group continue to look at the photo as you read aloud the following verses that are taken from the Celtic Blessing of Peace-Healing.

• Deep peace, a quiet rain to you;
• Deep peace, an ebbing wave to you!
• Deep peace, pure red of the flame to you.
• Deep peace, pure green of the grass to you.
• Deep peace, pure brown of the earth to you.

• Deep peace, pure blue of the sky to you.
• Deep peace of the quiet earth to you,
• Deep peace of the sleeping stones to you,
• Deep peace of the Son of Peace to you,
• Deep peace, deep peace!

At the end of the blessing, invite the young people to exchange a sign of peace.

Chapter Warm-up: Ask, "Of what sacrament does the symbol of water remind us?" (*Baptism*) Ask, "What does the symbol of water have to do with the sacrament of Reconciliation?" (*Water is a sign of cleansing, and Reconciliation gives us the opportunity to become "clean" again; Reconciliation also gives us the opportunity to confess that we have not kept the promises we made at Baptism, and to be forgiven.*) Explain that we will learn more about the Baptism-Reconciliation connection during this session.

Forum: Have the young people form small groups to discuss what they have written about their awareness of the Holy Spirit's presence. Have a representative from each group report all the responses written for "In peace and reconciliation." Emphasize with the group that the Holy Spirit has continually guided the Church in its understanding of the sacrament of Reconciliation throughout history.

Presentation ___ min.

◆ Direct attention to the forgiveness story at the top of page 80. Discuss the two questions following the story. Stress the importance of forgiveness with another example from the teaching of Pope John Paul II:

> The former country of Yugoslavia had been divided by a devastating war between two groups of people, the Croats and the Serbs. Sarajevo was the capital city, and it suffered severely during this war. This ancient, beautiful city was divided by ethnic hatred. Former neighbors and friends became enemies. Many innocent people were killed. Children playing in parks were shot at because they were on the "wrong side" of an ethnic divide. When the war ended, Pope John Paul visited Sarajevo and begged the people to rebuild their city on "the courage of forgiveness."

Remind the group that the pope is passing on the teaching of Jesus and not just his own opinion. Ask the following questions:

• What do you think the pope meant by "the courage of forgiveness"?

• Why does forgiveness take courage?

Some people were shocked when they learned that Pope John Paul II had gone to the jail cell of the man who tried to assassinate him. They were even more shocked when they found out that the pope forgave the man. Why do you think the pope did this? Are forgiveness and mercy so important in our lives?

Christ and the Samaritan Woman at the Well, Paolo Veronese, sixteenth century

Rich in Mercy

When the writers of Sacred Scripture wanted to describe their experience of God's love and mercy, they used some very dramatic imagery. When God forgives and removes our sins, he is described as putting them "as far as the east is from the west" (Psalm 103:12). Our God is truly a God of compassion!

Jesus wanted us to experience this forgiveness of God even more in our lives. Only God can forgive sins, and this is why Jesus, God's only Son, came among us. He wanted to free us from sin, to heal our wounded and broken natures. Who else but Jesus told the stories of the lost sheep and the prodigal son (Luke 15:1–7, 11–32)? He wanted us to know how much God loves us.

After Christ's resurrection the early Church community recognized what he had done for them. By offering his life for us on the cross, Jesus had redeemed us. He had reconciled us to God and to one another. This means that in Christ we were brought back again into friendship with God. We first share in this reconciliation and forgiveness at Baptism. But what about the sins we commit after Baptism?

We need to be healed over and over again. We need to turn to Jesus, who is the sacrament of God's

80

forgiveness. How do we do this? Jesus entrusted his Church with the mission of healing and forgiveness, especially in the sacraments. In the Eucharist we share in Christ's Body and Blood, given for us and shed for the forgiveness of sins. In the Eucharist we realize and share in the peace Christ gave to us.

Jesus did not stop there, however. He gave his apostles and their successors the power to forgive sins. On Easter night Jesus appeared to his apostles and breathed on them. He said, "Receive the holy Spirit. Whose sins you forgive are forgiven them, and whose sins you retain are retained" (John 20:22–23). This same Holy Spirit makes our hearts ready to receive God's forgiveness. And we do this in a most wonderful way in a special sacrament.

Actually we may know this sacrament by many names. It is called the *sacrament of Reconciliation* because through it our relationship to God and to the community of the Church is restored. This sacrament is also called the sacrament of *Penance*. Penance celebrates our continuing conversion, our turning from selfishness and sin to the spirit of love and generosity. The word *penance* can also mean that part of the sacrament in which the priest asks us to say certain prayers or to perform some other action to help atone for our sins.

For many years most Catholics called the sacrament *Confession. Confession*, however, names only one part of the sacrament and not the most important part at that. *Reconciliation* names what is most important, what Jesus does. Sinners are brought back to God and to the community. They are reconciled.

The sacrament of Reconciliation is a beautiful celebration of love and forgiveness. The sacrament is never meant to make us feel false guilt or to become overly concerned with sin. Nor is the sacrament meant to make us blame ourselves for things beyond our control. The Church teaches us that it is meant for healing what is broken, for setting free that which

is bound up. In addition this sacrament is not just intended for the times when we commit serious, or mortal, sin. Whenever we confess our venial sins, we are strengthened and grow in God's grace.

Let's look more closely at the celebration of Reconciliation in the life of the Church.

A Reconciling Church
Over the centuries the way the sacrament of Reconciliation was celebrated changed and developed. The basic elements of the sacrament, however, remain. There must be a conversion, a turning, to God; a confession of sins to a priest; a penance to show sorrow for sin and a decision to avoid sin; a reconciliation to God and to anyone harmed by sin; and forgiveness of sin.

In our parishes today we go to confession face-to-face with a priest or from behind a screen. Often communal penance celebrations are held, always accompanied by individual confessions to a priest. The sacrament of Reconciliation is a sacrament of healing, a sacrament of joy and peace. In it our sins are forgiven and we are restored to friendship with God, with others, and with ourselves.

81

◆ Draw attention to *Catholic Teachings* on page 85. If you wish, share the information on mortal sin detailed in the *FYI*. A detailed explanation of mortal and venial sin may be found in Chapter 4 of *Morality: A Course on Catholic Living,* William H. Sadlier's *Faith and Witness* program.

◆ Ask the young people to share the main ideas that they have underlined. Have them highlight the statements highlighted on reduced pages 80 through 85.

◆ Distribute the handout *Oh, What a Web!* Allow about ten minutes for the young people to discuss the questions they might add. Suggest that the Ten Commandments and the Beatitudes are helpful guides. Ask each group to appoint a recording secretary to list what the group thinks are the five most significant questions for each panel. After calling the groups together, ask the secretaries to read the questions. Appoint a committee to put all the questions together into a small booklet. Keep the booklet in the prayer corner for future reference.

FYI The Church teaches that venial sin is evil and should be avoided because it weakens our life with God.

For a sin to be mortal, the Church teaches that three conditions must be met:

• It must involve a grave and serious matter.

• We must have full knowledge that what we are doing is mortally sinful.

• We must freely and fully consent to it.

Presentation (cont'd)

◆ Remind the young people of the four parts of the celebration of the Eucharist. Ask, "How many parts does the sacrament of Reconciliation have?" (*four*) "What are these parts?" (*gathering, storytelling, sacramental action, commissioning*) Write these parts on the board, leaving room for more writing under each one. Ask the young people to fill in this chart with information about each part. For example:

gathering

minister of hospitality greets us

introductory rites:

hymn

liturgical greeting

prayer offered by priest

◆ Explain that within the communal rite of Reconciliation individual and private confession to a priest is always provided. Ask, "Why do you think this private and individual confession is included in the communal rite?"

◆ Ask for responses to the **thought provoker** on page 82. You may want to write the young people's responses on the board. Emphasize that it is the word of God that helps us to know our sinfulness, that helps us to develop a "sense of sin." You may want to stress that we sometimes need guidance on what a sin is and what it is not. Explain that sometimes we can get too worried about sin and become scrupulous or unnecessarily concerned about it. This is the opposite of what Reconciliation is intended to give us—the peace of Christ.

The Communal Rite

The Second Vatican Council revised the rites for Reconciliation to express more clearly what the sacrament really means and what it really does. These rites show that the sacrament is clearly a liturgical act. Like the Eucharist, Reconciliation celebrates the paschal mystery of Christ. Like the Eucharist, it consists of four parts: gathering, storytelling, the sacramental action, and commissioning.

There is no "one way" to celebrate this sacrament. Here is a general description of the *communal* celebration of the sacrament of Reconciliation.

Gathering The community gathers at the appointed time. There is a minister of hospitality at the door of the church to welcome us and to distribute any materials we may need to participate in the sacrament. The introductory rites usually include a hymn, a liturgical greeting, and a prayer by the priest to gather the assembly together.

Storytelling Once we are gathered, we tell the stories of God's love and mercy that are recorded in the Bible. In hearing these stories of God's love, we come to see how much we are loved and to realize how little we have loved in return. The difference between these two loves—*how much* God has loved us and *how little* we have loved him—is called the "sense of sin." This is an important part of the

82

sacramental process. It is the word of God that helps us to know our sinfulness.

Sin must be understood in relation to love. God has loved us so much, and we have so often failed to return that love. When we examine our lives in the light of the message of Jesus, we find that Jesus calls us to wholeness, to maturity. He came that we might have life and have it abundantly. For the Christian sin is not merely breaking the rules; it is the failure to grow. Sin is being today just as you were yesterday. Sin is the failure to respond to the love God has shown us in Christ Jesus.

After we have heard how much God loves us, we examine our lives to see how well we have loved God and our brothers and sisters in return. We examine our conscience in the light of the Scriptures. Together we express our sorrow in an Act of Contrition. Then we each confess our sins to a priest in private and hear the proclamation of God's forgiveness (absolution): "I *absolve* you."

 In what ways do the Scriptures help us prepare for Reconciliation?

The Sacramental Action This prayer of absolution is the central prayer and sign of the sacrament of Reconciliation.

As in all liturgical prayers, the prayer of absolution is directed to the Blessed Trinity. It also mentions the principal effects of the sacrament: forgiveness, pardon, and peace.

The prayer of absolution that we hear each time we celebrate the sacrament is this:

> God, the Father of mercies,
> through the death and resurrection of his Son
> has reconciled the world to himself
> and sent the Holy Spirit among us
> for the forgiveness of sins;
> through the ministry of the Church
> may God give you pardon and peace,
> and I absolve you from your sins
> in the name of the Father, and of the Son,†
> and of the Holy Spirit.

Our response is "Amen."

We have responded to the word of God by confessing our sins and receiving God's forgiveness. Now we celebrate this forgiveness, for it is God's response to *our* word. This part of the celebration might include a hymn, a proclamation of praise and thanksgiving for God's mercy, the Lord's Prayer, the kiss of peace, a song of thanksgiving, and a concluding prayer.

Commissioning The communal rite of Reconciliation concludes with prayers, blessings, and dismissal.

Conversion of Heart

Catholics celebrate Reconciliation even when they have less serious sins to confess. Why? Because this sacrament is a great help to what Jesus wants for all his followers: conversion of heart.

In the life of the Church, the primary moment of conversion is the moment of Baptism. Yet conversion is not limited to that moment. It is the work of a lifetime. As followers of Christ we are called to a continual conversion of heart. One big "turning toward" God at Baptism is not enough for a full Christian life. We must continually turn toward God, as a growing plant continually turns toward its source of light, growth, and energy.

Conversion is a grace of the Holy Spirit. Under the Spirit's guidance we are led to right thinking and good action. And with

The priest is strictly forbidden to use *in any way* anything he hears in the sacrament of Reconciliation. He can never, *never*, NEVER tell anyone what sin you confessed. If he does so, he himself commits a mortal sin. This obligation and promise is called the *seal of confession*. That is, the priest's lips are sealed, and he cannot reveal your sin or your identity.

the help of the Spirit, we find the honesty to admit our failings and the courage to promise to do better. The sacrament of Reconciliation keeps us on track in our own individual work of conversion. It helps us to stop and reflect on how far we have come, and it helps us to resolve to continue the journey.

When the Fathers of the Church explained Baptism, they imagined an individual in the midst of a shipwreck. How to be saved in the midst of a raging sea? Grab a plank! This first plank is the sacrament of Baptism. When they taught about the sacrament of Reconciliation, they called it "the second plank" (*Catechism*, 1446). As Christians we need both to keep us afloat.

83

◆ Have a volunteer read aloud the prayer of absolution on page 83. Encourage the young people to listen carefully to it. Ask, "What principal effects of the sacrament of Reconciliation are mentioned in this prayer?" (*forgiveness, pardon, peace*)

◆ Ask a volunteer to explain what *contrition* is. (*sorrow for having sinned, hatred of the sin committed, and a firm decision not to sin again*) Ask, "Why is the decision not to sin again a part of contrition?" (*Without this decision, we would not be taking our own actions or the sacrament of Reconciliation seriously.*) Explain that it is wrong to think of the sacrament of Reconciliation as a revolving door or a "license" to sin again. We may indeed sin again, but we cannot take sin lightly. We must do all we can to avoid it.

◆ Introduce the element of *confession* by asking, "Why do we confess our sins to a priest? Why don't we confess them privately to God?" (*Our sins are not private. They affect the whole body of Christ. The priest represents both Christ and his body, the Church.*)

◆ Ask a volunteer to explain *satisfaction*. Point out that the penance we are given in the sacrament helps to satisfy our human need for justice, to "make up for" what we have done wrong.

◆ Have a volunteer summarize *Catholic ID*. Ask, "Why would you think the seal of confession would be necessary?"

Presentation (cont'd)

◆ Draw attention to the  **thought provoker** on page 84. Explain that the essential sign of the sacrament is the absolution spoken by the priest.

◆ Draw attention to the stained-glass window on page 84. Explain that the hand is raised because, when a priest gives absolution, he raises his hand in a sign of blessing and prayer over the person to be absolved. As he does so, he prays the prayer of absolution given on page 83. When he comes to "of the Son" he makes the sign of the cross in blessing over the person absolved.

Conclusion ___ min.

◆ Discuss the questions in *Things to Share*. Ask, "Do you think that knowing the priest is bound by the seal of confession is an encouragement to individuals to speak freely in this sacrament?"

Assessment: If you are administering *Chapter 10 Assessment,* page 85A, allow about ten minutes for the students to complete the test.

The Individual Rite

The individual rite of Reconciliation is another way the Church gives us to celebrate this sacrament. There are two important elements to this rite.

The first element is human action: contrition, confession, and satisfaction (doing one's penance). The second element is God's action: the forgiveness of sins through the Church. Both our human actions and God's action are equally essential.

Contrition *Contrition* is sorrow for having sinned, hatred for the sin committed, and a firm decision not to sin again. Before Reconciliation we should take time to make an examination of conscience and to ask ourselves if we really are sorry for our selfish actions and wrong choices.

Confession Confessing our sins to a priest is an essential part of this sacrament because the priest forgives sin in the name of Jesus Christ and the Church. We are the Church, the body of Christ in the world. Sin affects the whole body of Christ. Just as in physical sickness, when one part is in pain, the whole body suffers. The priest represents Christ, so it is his task and joy to welcome sinners, as Jesus did, and to restore them to their rightful place in the body of Christ.

Sometimes people worry about what the priest thinks of them when they tell him their sins. They imagine that the priest sees them at their worst. Actually the very opposite is true. *Everybody* sins, but only *some* sinners are moved to

84

do penance. When you tell your sins to the priest and express your desire to repent, the priest sees you at your best. The priest sees you, not in your sinning, but in your repentance.

Satisfaction *Satisfaction* is simply repairing, in some way, the harm our sins have done. Returning or paying for stolen goods, for example, is one obvious way of making satisfaction for the sin of stealing.

This kind of satisfaction is usually included in the *penance* given. A penance can be prayer, an offering, works of mercy, service to a neighbor, voluntary self-denial, sacrifices, and most of all a patient acceptance of the ordinary circumstances of our lives.

Reconciliation Now we turn to God's action in the sacrament of Reconciliation: the forgiveness of sins. Through this forgiveness, as Pope John Paul II explained, we are reconciled with self, God, the entire Church, and "with all creation" (*Catechism,* 1469). Reconciliation is a sacrament of peace and comfort, a sacrament sealed in the conversational tones of a human voice: "I absolve you.... Go in the peace of Christ."

The symbol of the sacrament of Reconciliation is the symbol of language. How would you explain this statement?

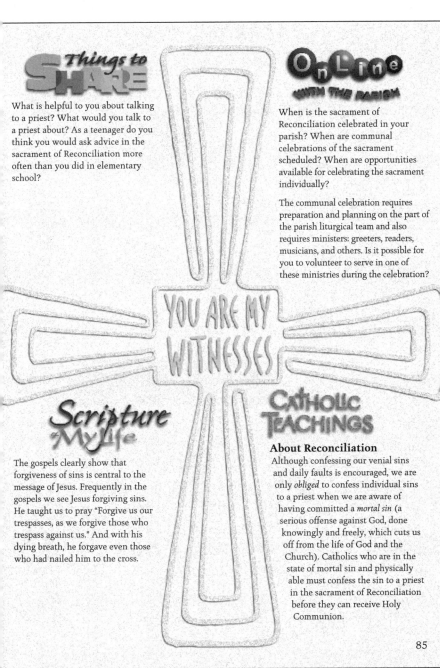

Things to SHARE

What is helpful to you about talking to a priest? What would you talk to a priest about? As a teenager do you think you would ask advice in the sacrament of Reconciliation more often than you did in elementary school?

OnLine WITH THE PARISH

When is the sacrament of Reconciliation celebrated in your parish? When are communal celebrations of the sacrament scheduled? When are opportunities available for celebrating the sacrament individually?

The communal celebration requires preparation and planning on the part of the parish liturgical team and also requires ministers: greeters, readers, musicians, and others. Is it possible for you to volunteer to serve in one of these ministries during the celebration?

Scripture My Life

The gospels clearly show that forgiveness of sins is central to the message of Jesus. Frequently in the gospels we see Jesus forgiving sins. He taught us to pray "Forgive us our trespasses, as we forgive those who trespass against us." And with his dying breath, he forgave even those who had nailed him to the cross.

Catholic Teachings

About Reconciliation

Although confessing our venial sins and daily faults is encouraged, we are only *obliged* to confess individual sins to a priest when we are aware of having committed a *mortal sin* (a serious offense against God, done knowingly and freely, which cuts us off from the life of God and the Church). Catholics who are in the state of mortal sin and physically able must confess the sin to a priest in the sacrament of Reconciliation before they can receive Holy Communion.

85

Conclusion (cont'd)

◆ Have a volunteer summarize *On Line with the Parish*. You may want to suggest that the young people plan a communal celebration for other youth groups within the parish.

FORUM Assignment

✔ Read pages 86–93. Underline in pencil the statements that express six key ideas.

✔ Write your questions, concerns, and fears about the existence of illness and pain in the world.

Closing Prayer: Have the group read together the exchange of Peter and Jesus about forgiving others (Matthew 18:21–22). Point out that Jesus was trying to teach his followers that their forgiveness must be without limit. Then pray or sing together the Our Father.

Evaluation: Do the young people understand the purpose of the sacrament of Reconciliation and its role in their lives of faith?

FOR CHAPTER 11

- copies of handout *A Spiritual Safety Net*, page 86C
- *Chapter 11 Assessment*, page 93A
- *Highlights for Home*, page 93B
- one of the videos listed in *Supplemental Resources*, page 86B (optional)

Assessment

1. _____ is sorrow for having sinned, hatred for the sin committed, and a firm decision not to sin again.
   a. Satisfaction
   b. Contrition
   c. Absolution
   d. Penance

2. When may a priest break the seal of confession?
   a. for a murder case
   b. for a serious crime
   c. never
   d. none of the above

3. Circle the *false* statement.
   a. Reconciliation is only intended for the times when we commit serious sins.
   b. Reconciliation is a sacrament of healing.
   c. The effects of Reconciliation are forgiveness and pardon.
   d. Reconciliation is clearly a liturgical act.

4. _____ is simply repairing, in some way, the harm our sins have done.
   a. Penance   c. Contrition
   b. Absolution   d. Satisfaction

5. By performing a _____ we help atone for our sins.
   a. penance   c. absolution
   b. satisfaction   d. contrition

6. Pardon, or being set free, from sin is called
   a. penance.
   b. confession.
   c. absolution.
   d. conversion.

7. Circle the true statement.
   a. Baptism means we will never sin again.
   b. Forgiveness meant nothing to Jesus.
   c. Sin affects the whole body of Christ.
   d. Conversion is something we do all on our own.

8. What is God's action in the sacrament of Reconciliation?
   a. contrition
   b. confession
   c. satisfaction
   d. the forgiveness of sins

9. The sign of the sacrament of Reconciliation is
   a. bread and wine.
   b. words of absolution.
   c. oil.
   d. water.

10. Name one important thing you have learned about the sacrament of Reconciliation. How has it helped you to appreciate this sacrament?

    _____
    _____
    _____

CHAPTER 10

CHAPTER 10: The Sacrament of Reconciliation

Highlights for Home

Focus on Faith

Jesus understood human life "from the inside out." In the Letter to the Hebrews, we read that "we do not have a high priest who is unable to sympathize with our weaknesses, but one who has similarly been tested in every way, yet without sin" (Hebrews 4:15). In Jesus is revealed the compassion of God. He often reassured sinners, "Your sins are forgiven. Go in peace."

In the sacrament of Reconciliation, we encounter Christ and are offered the same reassurance today. In our battle with the sins of everyday life—envy, jealousy, meanness of spirit, anger, pride— the sacrament of Reconciliation gives us another chance to turn to God in our need for continual conversion, to turn to God who heals our brokenness.

From the early Church to today, it is clear that forgiving and being forgiven are essential to Christian life. For Jesus himself taught us to pray: "Forgive us our trespasses as we forgive those who trespass against us."

Conversation Starters

. . . . a few ideas to talk about together . . . .

◆ What would you say is the attitude toward sin today in society as a whole? among your friends? in your family?

◆ How hard do you find it to admit when you are wrong? Can you recall a time when doing so helped heal a friendship?

◆ How can you grow in your appreciation of the sacrament of Reconciliation?

Feature Focus

The *Catholic ID* on page 83 reminds us of the obligation of the priest to honor the seal of confession. This obligation is a great reassurance to us, because we can be sure that everything we say to the priest is totally confidential. Protected by the seal of confession, Catholics through the ages have celebrated Reconciliation without fear of gossip or scandal.

Reflection

Take a quiet moment to look at the photograph on pages 78 and 79. The many colors interspersed with the water may remind you of the story of Noah, a story that began with a flood of water and ended with a rainbow: symbol of the covenant, symbol of reconciliation.

Imagine yourself sitting beside this quiet pond. How is the rainbow of your life reflected in the waters of Baptism? Are the colors fading a bit in the routine of daily life? Renew the covenant now. Pick up three stones from the beach. Pray, "God, forgive me" and throw a stone into the pond. Let forgiveness ripple through your life. Pray, "Help me to forgive others," and toss the next stone into the pond. Pray, "Help me to forgive myself," and plop the last stone in. Watch it disappear.

THE ANOINTING OF THE SICK

Adult Focus

The question "Why me?" in the face of illness and suffering may not be as self-pitying as it sounds. It is often more possible to tolerate difficult situations if we can sense deeper meaning behind them. Viktor Frankl was able to survive the devastation of a concentration camp by writing a book in his head. That book became the core of his philosophy and one of the most important written in the twentieth century: *Man's Search for Meaning*.

The search for meaning begins at an early age and never ends. As toddlers, our young people gazed at the green grass and the blue sky and asked, "Why?" Now they ask, "Why do people suffer?" "Why do people die?"

This chapter will not answer these questions. But it will introduce the young people to the great gift of the sacrament of the Anointing of the Sick, in which Jesus Christ, through his Church, strengthens and brings peace to the suffering. This sacrament is an instrument of healing of the soul and also of the body, if God so wills. At the last stages of life, this sacrament, together with Penance and Eucharist as Viaticum, prepares us for the final journey, the passage from death to eternal life.

Catechism Focus

The theme of this chapter corresponds to paragraphs 1500–1525 of the *Catechism*.

Enrichment Activities

Ministers to the Sick

You may want to ask someone in your parish who ministers to the sick to speak with your group. This person may be a eucharistic minister, or someone delegated by the parish to visit the sick in homes or in hospitals in order to maintain a link with the parish community. If you have a hospice for the dying in your community, invite one of the volunteers to share with your group the work of this special group. Have the young people prepare a list of questions to ask this minister or volunteer.

Praying with the Sick

Plan a prayer service to film and send on videotape to a nursing home or rehabilitation center. Encourage the young people to choose a joyful, upbeat theme. Responses should be simple so that those in the center may join you in praying. Consider using traditional hymns if you are going to send the video to a nursing home.

Teaching Resources

Overview

To deepen understanding of the sacrament of the Anointing of the Sick.

Opening Prayer Ideas

Look at the photo on pages 86 and 87. Open your Bibles to Psalm 23 and pray it together. **or** Pray in silence for all those who are sick. Remember those who are without friends or family to comfort or encourage them.

Materials

- Bibles, journals, and highlighters
- videos mentioned on page 88

Liturgy and Worship Journal:
For Chapter 11, use pages 44–47.

REPRODUCIBLE MASTERS
- *A Spiritual Safety Net,* page 86C
- *Chapter 11 Assessment,* page 93A
- *Highlights for Home,* page 93B

Supplemental Resources

PAMPHLETS
Catholic Youth Update
- "For Our Healing: The Sacrament of the Anointing of the Sick"
- "Jump-Starting Your Future: Getting Control of Your Habits"
- "When It's More Than Just the Blues: An Interview on Depression"

St. Anthony Messenger
1615 Republic Street
Cincinnati, OH 45210
See video suggestions in Presentation.

A Spiritual Safety Net

Just as people invest in medical insurance policies as economic safety nets in case of illness or medical emergencies, we should invest our time in planning a spiritual safety net for such a time. Read the questions below. Discuss the topics with your family and friends. Consider your plans for spiritual health an important safety net to have in place in healthy times as well as in times of illness.

1. In Sirach 6:16 we read that a loyal friend is a life-saving remedy. What qualities should a person have in order to be considered a life-saving remedy?_____

_____

_____

_____

_____

2. What spiritual attitudes or habits can you develop now to prepare you to do what God wants in both sickness and health?_____

_____

_____

_____

3. How will reflecting on the Scriptures help you flex spiritual muscle at all times? What are your favorite readings that comfort you when your spirit sags?_____

_____

_____

_____

_____

4. What can you do to develop a supportive atmosphere at home, in school, in your neighborhood? How can you tone things down when they reach a fever pitch? How can you pump supportive energy into attitudes weakened by indifference?_____

_____

_____

_____

_____

CHAPTER 11

The Anointing
of the Sick

Even when I walk through a dark valley,
  I fear no harm for you are at my side. . . .
You anoint my head with oil;
  my cup overflows.
Psalm 23:4–5

Objective: To deepen understanding of the sacrament of the Anointing of the Sick.

Introduction ___ min.

Opening Prayer: Have the young people look at the photo on pages 86 and 87 as you read Psalm 23:1– 4 from the Bible. Ask, "Why might we compare experiencing physical suffering with walking through a dark valley?" "How does knowing that Jesus is with us give us comfort and support?"

You may wish to share the following young person's prayer with the group:

Jesus, there were many times throughout your life when you experienced the same emotions I feel now. Often I forget the fact that you were once a young person like each of us. You worried about the problems facing society, even though they may have been different from the ones we face. You loved your family and friends. You laughed when something brought you joy. Many times you felt pity for those who were suffering, and you

even cried at Lazarus's tomb. When you were taken away by those who wanted to convict you, all your friends left you, and you were alone. It probably was difficult for you to explain to those around you that you were the son of God, and you felt discouraged.

Dear Jesus, help each of us to remember these things. Help us to understand and to have insight. Each of us is a special sign of God's love. Help us to see that in each of us, and never let us be afraid to show our emotions, especially the love that we have for you! Thanks for showing us that it is okay to feel the way we do!

Elizabeth
Holy Cross High School
Marine City, Michigan

Invite the young people to imagine that they are sitting or walking with Jesus in a quiet place. They are sharing with him their questions, concerns, and fears about the existence of illness and pain in the world. Have the young people write their reflections in their journals.

Forum: Discuss with the young people their thoughts and society's attitudes about suffering and illness. Remind the young people that pain, suffering, and death are the effects of original sin.

Have a prepared volunteer emphasize that it is everyone's responsibility to learn about our bodies so we can care for them and seek appropriate help when we experience pain. Have the volunteer explain that our studies will also help us dispel myths or false teachings about suffering and illness.

Presentation ___ min.

◆ Have the young people form small groups to discuss ways that we exercise our responsibilities for personal health and safety. Ask the young people to include the dangers of exercise addiction and couch potato-ism. Point out that we need to maintain a balance between exercise and relaxation.

◆ Discuss people who have given us good example in the face of suffering. You may wish to show one of the following videos:

• *Tyler, A Real Hero* is a film about a college athlete whose life was changed dramatically by a paralyzing accident.

• *Encounter with Garvan Byrne* is a film about a twelve-year-old boy who suffered from painful bone cancer. In the film he shares his insights about the meaning of life and his deep faith in Jesus.

Both videos are available from:
Ignatius Press
P.O. Box 1339
Ft. Collins, CO 80522

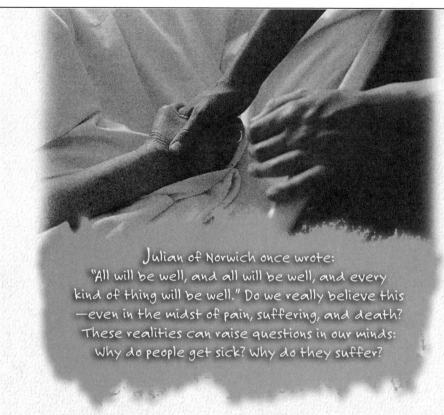

Julian of Norwich once wrote: "All will be well, and all will be well, and every kind of thing will be well." Do we really believe this —even in the midst of pain, suffering, and death? These realities can raise questions in our minds: Why do people get sick? Why do they suffer?

The Mystery of Suffering

People have asked questions like these since the beginning of time!

There is no easy answer to the mystery of suffering. It is one of those big questions whose answer is discovered bit by bit through our lived experience.

It is also a dangerous question because we can easily jump to overly simplified (and consequently, wrong) answers: "He got sick because he was bad." "She is ill because God wants her to suffer." It is very dangerous to think in this way, for such thinking leads to false conclusions about suffering and false conclusions about God.

We know that God created us out of love and that creation is holy and good. Suffering and illness do not exist because God wants them to exist. But if they do not come from him, where do they come from?

Sometimes, but not always, they come from our own ignorance and poor decisions. We have the responsibility to care for our bodies, to be attentive to proper nourishment, exercise, rest, and relaxation. Pain is often a message from the body telling us that something is wrong, that something needs to be corrected or cared for.

Human illness can urge us to learn more about the functions of the body through the study of chemistry, biology, physiology, and other sciences. In so doing, perhaps we can help others someday. Even more important, illness is a call to learn more about our inner selves, about life and its meaning.

88

We know that one of the hardest things about being sick is the sudden end to our ordinary activities at school, with friends, in sports, and so on. Much of the way we think about ourselves is tied up with what we can do. When our health is taken away, we find that we cannot do very much! Then we begin to wonder who we really are.

But faith gives us a new way of seeing illness. In God's eyes we are more than what we do, more than our accomplishments. The world often judges people by how much money they make, by how many things they have. Illness can remind us that God loves us for who we are, not for what we have or what we do.

Jesus and Healing

We know about God's love and concern for the sick because we can see it made visible in Jesus. On almost every page of the gospels, we see Jesus bringing health and wholeness to those who are ill and suffering.

Jesus Heals a Blind Man, Duccio di Buoninsegna, thirteenth century

89

Look, for example, at the first chapter of Mark's Gospel. After Jesus called the first disciples, he cured a man with an unclean spirit; then he cured Peter's mother-in-law, who was in bed with a fever. Mark continues: "When it was evening, after sunset, they brought to him all who were ill or possessed by demons. The whole town was gathered at the door. He cured many who were sick with various diseases, and he drove out many demons" (1:32–34).

Jesus has hardly begun his ministry, but already he is known as someone who heals the sick and cares for them. Jesus himself is a visible sign of God's desire for our health and wholeness. When we see Jesus as a sign of God's healing, we are well on our way to understanding the Church as a sign of healing. The Church exercises this ministry in many ways and celebrates it in the sacrament of the Anointing of the Sick.

Healing in the Early Church

Jesus' desire to heal the sick did not stop when he ascended into heaven. He had told his disciples to continue this work: "So. . . . they anointed with oil many who were sick and cured them" (Mark 6:12–13).

In the Letter of James, we read of the way in which one early Christian community continued this healing work of Jesus. "Is anyone among you sick? He should summon the presbyters of the church, and they should pray over him and anoint [him] with oil in the name of the Lord, and the prayer of faith will save the sick person, and the Lord will raise him up. If he has committed any sins, he will be forgiven" (James 5:14–15).

James tells us that prayer is necessary in every situation in our lives: when we are well, when we are sick, and at every moment in between. It is in this context of prayer that James tells us of his

◆ Have the young people read the healing of Peter's mother-in-law (Mark 1:29–31) and the healing of the paralytic (Mark 2: 1–12). If time allows, ask the young people to work in small groups to prepare eyewitness accounts of those whose lives were changed by Jesus' healing touch. Have one person in each group act as a reporter interviewing the eyewitnesses for a nightly news feature.

◆ Ask a volunteer to read aloud the passage from the Letter of James (James 5:13–15) on page 89. Stress that this is an early account of the community involved in prayer for healing. Suggest that volunteers look up and read these accounts of healing in the early Church: Acts 5:12–16; Acts 9:32–35; and Acts 14:8–10.

Ask, "Who is healing in these prayers?" (*Peter, Paul, and Barnabas*) Stress that the author of Acts wanted to emphasize that these leaders of the Church had received the power and authority of Jesus himself. This is when healing took place.

◆ Have the young people discuss the statements they underlined in this chapter. Then ask the group to highlight the key concepts highlighted on reduced pages 88 through 92.

Presentation (cont'd)

◆ Invite the groups to think of the ways we still use oil in the care of our bodies and as a healing ointment today. (*sunscreen, bath oil, ointment for sore muscles*) Emphasize that we still use oil to "heal and strengthen and preserve."

◆ Direct attention to *Scripture & My Life* on page 93. Ask volunteers to look up and read each of the Scripture passages listed there. Explain that the Church has always been concerned about the sick as we see in the Acts of the Apostles and the letter of James. Later, many monasteries set aside a section of the guest house as an infirmary for the sick of the area. These were the first hospitals.

◆ Have a volunteer summarize *Catholic ID* on page 90. Take this opportunity to acquaint the young people with the work of parish groups who help the sick. Perhaps the Saint Vincent de Paul Society collects blankets or brings food and clothing to the homebound. Other groups may sew or make bandages for the sick. There may be a phone network to support the sick in prayer, or a group of people who are involved in bringing meals to the sick and homebound.

◆ Ask a volunteer to summarize the history of the sacrament of healing under its various names.

One of the ways in which we Catholics show our concern for the sick is our practice of having priests, deacons, or eucharistic ministers bring Holy Communion to them in their homes or in the hospital. In this way they are united to the Lord in the sacrament of the Eucharist and also to the community of believers. In some parishes the eucharistic ministers come forward before the dismissal and are given the Eucharist to bring to the sick.

What are some other ways in which we show our concern for the sick?

community's practice of praying for the sick. The sick person calls for the priests. When they arrive, they pray. The phrase "pray over" the sick person suggests a laying on of hands, the ancient sign of blessing. They anoint the sick person with oil.

When priests and teachers later explained the meaning of the rites of anointing, they drew a parallel between physical healing by medical doctors and spiritual healing administered by the Church. Many good things can be learned from this analogy. But one bad effect it had was that the Church's anointing was put off as long as possible, just as going to the doctor was put off until the sick person was at death's door. The sacramental anointing (*unction* in Latin) came to be called *Extreme Unction*, the last anointing. The sacrament for the *sick* became a sacrament only for the *dying*. The priest's final absolution of our sins and this anointing at the time of death came to be called the *last rites*.

The focus of the sacrament then changed from physical healing to spiritual healing, to the forgiveness of sins. The public, liturgical rite of the early Church became a private ceremony. Often only the priest and the dying person were present. Extreme Unction had become more private than public, more fearful than joyful, and more dreaded than celebrated. For many Catholics, when the

90

priest arrived with the holy oil for the last rites, it was a sure sign of death.

However, following the liturgical reforms of the Second Vatican Council, Extreme Unction became once again the sacrament of the Anointing of the Sick as we know it today.

 Take a moment to think of those "among you" who are sick. Pray for them now.

The Second Vatican Council made three important changes in the rite of the sacrament.

First, it was important to teach that this sacrament is not just intended for the dying, that it is primarily a sacrament of healing for all Christians who are seriously ill. It can be received more than once—each time, in fact, that a Christian becomes seriously ill, and again if the illness worsens. So the Council suggested that we call this sacrament not Extreme Unction but the sacrament of the *Anointing of the Sick*.

Second, this sacrament of healing was restored to its liturgical setting. No longer was it to be considered a private action between the priest and the sick person. The community's role of prayerful support was restored, and the celebration of the Anointing of the Sick within the Eucharist was encouraged.

Third, the focus of the sacrament was directed once again toward *healing*. In anointing the hands of the sick, the priest leads the community in prayer. We pray that our sick brothers and sisters will be raised up to share in the life of the resurrected Jesus—both physically and spiritually.

Celebration of Anointing

The celebration of the sacrament may take place at a Sunday or weekday Mass in a parish church, in the home of the sick person, in the hospital, or in an emergency situation. Here is a general description of the way the sacrament is celebrated at the Sunday liturgy.

Gathering The parish Eucharist begins as usual. Sometimes the sick, along with the whole congregation, are blessed with baptismal water. In Baptism we died with Christ; the suffering that these sick persons are now experiencing is part of that dying.

Storytelling We then read from the Scriptures and hear how Christ has conquered suffering and death by his own death and resurrection.

The homily relates the readings to the Christian meaning of suffering. Those who are ill or suffering can freely and lovingly choose to unite their sufferings with the sufferings of Christ. Following the homily we join in a litany of intercession for the sick, for the parish, and for the needs of the world.

Imposition of Hands

Those to be anointed are invited to come forward. With silent and intense prayer to the Holy Spirit, the priest lays his hands on the head of each person. This is one of the key symbolic actions of the sacrament. The gesture indicates that this particular

person is the object of the Church's prayer. It is a sign of blessing. Most important, it was Jesus' own gesture of healing: "At sunset, all who had people sick with various diseases brought them to him. He laid his hands on each of them and cured them" (Luke 4:40).

Invocation The priest blesses God for the gift of oil. Olive oil reminds us of the suffering of Jesus in the Garden of Olives (Luke 22:39–46). The oil is blessed by the bishop of the diocese on Holy Thursday. It is this blessing that makes the oil sacramental.

Anointing with Oil Next we see the essential rite of the sacrament. The priest anoints each sick person with the oil. He makes the sign of the cross first on the person's forehead and then on the palm of each hand. He prays that God in his love and mercy will "raise" the sick person to health. We all respond, "Amen."

◆ Have the young people form small groups to be TV or radio-commentator teams. Ask them to explain to listeners or viewers each part of the Anointing of the Sick as it takes place at a Sunday liturgy. In their commentaries, they may also want to include a discussion of the changes in the celebration of the sacrament made after the Second Vatican Council.

◆ Call attention to the **thought provoker** on page 90. Take time to pray a short litany for the sick people known to your group. The response might be, "Lord, heal him (her) and bring him (her) peace."

You may want to pray the Final Prayer taken from the Liturgy of Anointing.

Father in heaven . . .
    grant [the sick we have prayed for] comfort in [their] suffering.
When they are afraid, give [them] courage,
when afflicted, give [them] patience,
when dejected, afford [them] hope,
and when alone, assure [them] of the support of your holy people.
We ask this through Christ our Lord. Amen.

◆ Have a volunteer summarize *Catholic Teachings* on page 93.

Just in case...
some pronunciation helps

Viaticum . . . . . . Vi-**ah**-tik-kum

Presentation (cont'd)

◆ Ask, "Who can receive anointing?" You may want to list the responses on the board.

◆ Ask the question posed in the 🔆 **thought provoker** on page 92. A few responses may be found in the last paragraph on this page.

Conclusion ___ min.

◆ Emphasize with the young people that through the sacrament of the Anointing of the Sick we are strengthened to unite ourselves more closely to the passion of Christ. Our suffering is transformed into and becomes a participation in the saving work of Christ. Help the young people realize that for those who suffer from terminal illness and will not recover this sacrament will help them give witness with dignity and peace.

Note: The Church's teaching about moral issues at times of sickness and death are addressed in Chapter 8 of *Morality: A Course on Catholic Living*, William H. Sadlier's *Faith and Witness* Program.

Assessment: If you are administering *Chapter 11 Assessment*, allow the young people to work in pairs.

An Exchange of Signs

The celebration of the sacrament of the Anointing of the Sick is a ritual moment that makes visible and present to the sick and to the whole community who we are as Church: a community of healing and support. That is why the whole parish community is invited to come together in prayerful support of those among us who are in special need.

The sick, in return, offer a sign to the community: In this sacrament they tell the community that they are prepared to offer their suffering, in union with Christ's, for the good of the whole Church and the salvation of the world.

This exchange of signs between the sick and the healthy members of the community is at the heart of the sacrament. The sick are assured in the ritual that their suffering is not useless, that it is a sharing in the saving work of Jesus. Their sins are forgiven. At the same time the Church asks the Lord to lighten their suffering, to give them peace and courage, and to save them.

Who can receive anointing? How sick does one have to be in order to be anointed? The Church tells us that the sacrament is for those whose health is seriously impaired by sickness or old age. One does *not* have to be in danger of death. The sacrament is most fruitful when the person being anointed is well enough to participate fully in it.

A person can be anointed before surgery when a serious illness or disability is the reason for the operation. In this case it is preferable to celebrate the sacrament even before the person goes to the hospital.

The sacrament is for all ages and all types of illness. Sick children who have sufficient use of

OI stands for Oleum Infirmorum (Latin for Oil of the Sick).

92

reason to be strengthened by the sacrament can be anointed. Persons with the disease of alcoholism or suffering from other addictions can be anointed, as can those who suffer from various mental disorders.

But the big question is, "Does it work?" Does the sick person experience healing? The answer is yes. The sacrament is the prayer of the Church, the body of Christ. Christ himself has assured us that whatever we ask the Father in his name will be granted.

In the sacrament we pray that the sick be healed in body, in soul, and in spirit. God knows more than we do what healing the sick person needs most: that a wound be healed, that a fear turn to confidence, that loneliness disappear, that bafflement in the face of all the whys—Why me? Why suffering? Why now?—may turn into understanding. Ultimately we pray that the sacrament of the Anointing of the Sick will give us a better understanding of the mystery of a loving God who raised his crucified Son, bearing his victorious wounds, to be with the Father in glory.

 Describe what you think is meant by spiritual healing.

Answers for Chapter 11 Assessment

1. b   **2.** b   **3.** d   **4.** c   **5.** a

6. d   **7.** b   **8.** a   **9.** d   **10.** See page 92.

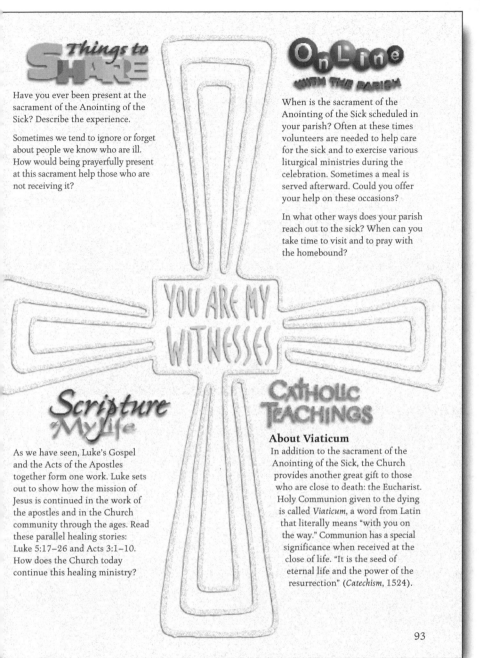

Things to SHARE

Have you ever been present at the sacrament of the Anointing of the Sick? Describe the experience.

Sometimes we tend to ignore or forget about people we know who are ill. How would being prayerfully present at this sacrament help those who are not receiving it?

OnLine WITH THE PARISH

When is the sacrament of the Anointing of the Sick scheduled in your parish? Often at these times volunteers are needed to help care for the sick and to exercise various liturgical ministries during the celebration. Sometimes a meal is served afterward. Could you offer your help on these occasions?

In what other ways does your parish reach out to the sick? When can you take time to visit and to pray with the homebound?

Scripture of My Life

As we have seen, Luke's Gospel and the Acts of the Apostles together form one work. Luke sets out to show how the mission of Jesus is continued in the work of the apostles and in the Church community through the ages. Read these parallel healing stories: Luke 5:17–26 and Acts 3:1–10. How does the Church today continue this healing ministry?

Catholic Teachings

About Viaticum
In addition to the sacrament of the Anointing of the Sick, the Church provides another great gift to those who are close to death: the Eucharist. Holy Communion given to the dying is called *Viaticum*, a word from Latin that literally means "with you on the way." Communion has a special significance when received at the close of life. "It is the seed of eternal life and the power of the resurrection" (*Catechism*, 1524).

YOU ARE MY WITNESSES

93

Conclusion (cont'd)

◆ Discuss the questions posed in *Things to Share* and *On Line with the Parish.*

FORUM Assignment

✔ Read pages 94–101. Underline in pencil the statements that express six key ideas.

✔ Complete the handout *A Spiritual Safety Net.* Be prepared to share your responses during next session's *Forum.*

Closing Prayer: Invite the young people to look again at the photos and artwork in the chapter. Then pray a spontaneous litany of petition. Ask the group to respond, "Jesus, bring your healing touch to our world" after each petition. You may wish to begin by praying the following:

• Jesus, help us to act in kindness and compassion when we hear a friend is ill.

• Jesus, help our health-care workers to act with compassion, not indifference.

Evaluation: Do the young people understand the Church as a community of healing and support for the sick? Do they understand the history of the sacrament of the Anointing of the Sick? Do they appreciate the sacrament as a sign of both physical and spiritual healing?

FOR CHAPTER 12

• copies of handout *Following in Christ's Footsteps,* page 94C
• *Chapter 12 Assessment,* page 101A
• *Highlights for Home,* page 101B
• net made by volunteers, and index cards
• invitations to seminarian or priest to speak with group

Assessment

1 Jesus' desire to heal the sick _____ when he ascended into heaven.
  a. stopped completely
  b. did not stop
  c. was of no concern to his disciples
  d. had no meaning

2 Illness should remind us that
  a. God is punishing us.
  b. God loves us for who we are.
  c. we are basically lazy.
  d. we are useless.

3 The name *Extreme Unction* means
  a. "anointing with oil."
  b. "physical healing."
  c. "spiritual healing."
  d. "the last anointing."

4 Most of the time during Extreme Unction _____ were present.
  a. relatives and friends
  b. the physician, the priest, and the patient
  c. only the priest and the dying person
  d. none of the above

5 During the liturgical celebration of Anointing, the priest anoints with oil _____ of the sick person.
  a. the forehead and each hand
  b. the hands, lips, and eyes
  c. the lips, eyes, and forehead
  d. the eyes, ears, and heart

6 The word *Viaticum* means
  a. "the last anointing."
  b. "Jesus' healing touch."
  c. "anointing with oil."
  d. "with you on the way."

7 Viaticum is _____ the dying.
  a. the sacrament of Reconciliation for
  b. Holy Communion given to
  c. the last anointing of
  d. the laying on of hands over

8 The Second Vatican Council suggested that the sacrament
  a. be called Anointing of the Sick.
  b. is intended for the dying.
  c. be considered a private action.
  d. include final absolution of our sins.

9 Healing in the early Church included
  a. anointing with oil.
  b. laying on of hands.
  c. forgiveness of sins.
  d. all of the above

10 Explain the meaning of the exchange of signs between the sick and the healthy members of the community during the Anointing of the Sick. Write your response on the reverse side of this page.

CHAPTER 11

Highlights for Home

Focus on Faith

Our bodies are fragile compositions which can break down and suffer—from diseases like cancer and heart disease to injuries from accidents. These more devastating assaults on our bodies test our endurance and our faith. In times like these we have the assurance that God is with us as comforter and healer. The Church is the visible sign of his presence.

In times of illness and suffering, the sacrament of the Anointing of the Sick offers hope and comfort, strength and courage. The sacrament was once reserved for the dying; now it is celebrated for the living. It can be received more than once, each time, in fact, that a Christian becomes seriously ill. And it is always directed toward *healing*. We pray with the Church that our sick brothers and sisters will be "raised up" to share in the life of the risen Jesus — both physically and spiritually.

Conversation Starters

. . . . a few ideas to talk about together . . . .

◆ Am I comfortable around sick people? How can I remember to think of them as part of the faith community?

◆ How do I support the sick members of my parish? In prayer? In celebrating the Sacrament of Anointing when my parish schedules it? With cards or phone calls?

Feature Focus

Scripture & My Life on page 93 reminds us that the healing ministry of the Church originated with Jesus, continued through the apostles, and now is an integral part of our mission today. You might want to consider the many ways the healing ministry of the Church touches your life and the life of the community around you. From large hospitals to mobile clinics, the Church tries to be a sign of healing for physical as well as spiritual ills.

Reflection

Take a moment to look at the photograph on pages 86 and 87. Then read the verse of Psalm 23 that it illustrates. This psalm is the well-known one which begins, "The LORD is my shepherd."

Have you ever heard the saying, "The only way out is through"? The key word is *through*. We will get through the dark valley because we are with the shepherd who is not walking far ahead of us, but, as the psalmist has written—at our side. Whenever we walk through the dark valley, we are not alone. Whatever the darkness—illness, lack of employment, a rift with a friend—we can trust that healing and a cup overflowing with mercy await us. "I can get through this, for you are at my side."

THE SACRAMENT OF HOLY ORDERS

Adult Focus

When Joseph Cardinal Bernardin died in 1997, he was remembered as a leader and teacher of gentleness and strength, a shepherd who sought justice at great cost to himself, a reconciler of opposing groups, and a wise mentor to his fellow priests. One person summed it up, saying, "He was a priest in the image of Christ."

This was a very appropriate description of Cardinal Bernardin; it is also close to being a definition of the priesthood itself. In the sacrament of Holy Orders, a man is called to share in a unique way Jesus' mission of "sanctifying, teaching, and building the Christian community." The ordained priest "becomes—in the Church and for the Church—a real, living, and faithful image of Christ, the priest" (*Directory on the Ministry and Life of Priests*, Vatican Congregation for the Clergy, 1994).

The ordained ministers of the Church are bishops, priests, and deacons. Bishops, who have the primary ministry to teach, govern, and sanctify, receive the fullness of the priesthood. They share their ministry with the priests and deacons whom they ordain by the laying on of hands. From the earliest days of the Church the ordained ministry has thus literally been handed on from the apostles, of whom our bishops today are the successors. It is through this succession that our faith has been preserved and strengthened through the centuries. Our young people need the security of knowing and appreciating that the Church is built on the solid rock of a faith consistently upheld by the teaching, governing, and sanctifying work of those ordained to be priests "in the image of Christ."

Catechism Focus

The themes of Chapter 12 correspond to paragraphs 1533–1536 and 1544–1588 of the *Catechism*.

Enrichment Activities

Write Requests

Several weeks before beginning this chapter, have the young people write to a variety of religious orders of priests, diocesan seminaries, and diocesan diaconate programs for vocational materials. Many addresses can be found in *The Official Catholic Directory*, available in most rectories.

Guest Speakers

Consider inviting a diocesan priest, a religious order priest, a seminarian, or a permanent deacon to speak to your group or to participate in a panel discussion. A good resource in regard to finding guest speakers is your diocesan director of vocations. Ask your pastor how you might contact him or her. Make a list of possible guests, and involve students in the process of planning and inviting. You may want to ask your guests to share videos of their ordinations.

Interviews

Have selected volunteers prepare and conduct, by regular mail or E-mail, interviews with priests or permanent deacons who serve as chaplains of the following: police or sheriff departments, hospitals or emergency services, professional sports teams, prisons, state or federal legislatures, or the armed services. You may want to invite these men to be guest speakers.

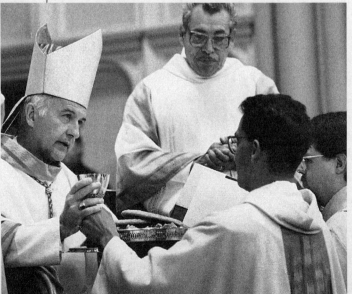

Teaching Resources

Overview

To increase awareness of Holy Orders as the sacrament through which the mission and authority Christ gave his apostles continues in the Church.

Opening Prayer Ideas

Pray together a shortened form of the Litany of the Saints on guide page 94–95.

or

Read together Acts 6:1–7 and share your reflections.

Materials

- Bibles, journals, and highlighters
- props or audiovisual equipment for guest speakers (optional)
- net made by volunteers, and index cards

REPRODUCIBLE MASTERS

- *Following in Christ's Footsteps*, page 94C
- *Chapter 12 Assessment*, page 101A
- *Highlights for Home*, page 101B

 Liturgy and Worship Journal:
For Chapter 12, use pages 48–51.

Supplemental Resources

VIDEOS

The Changing Sacraments "Clerical Clarence: Priesthood" St. Anthony Messenger/ Franciscan Communications http://www.american-catholic.org

Answering God's Call: The Experience of Priesthood Catholic Communication Campaign www.nccbuscc.org/ccc. or 1–800–235–8722

CHAPTER *twelve*

Following in Christ's Footsteps

You are a reporter for a weekly news show. Your producer has given you an assignment. She wants a fifteen-minute segment about the role of a priest. The producer wants to make sure you cover three important areas: ministry, divine worship, and authority. She wants a "human interest" angle, too—something personal about this particular priest. (For example, when did he realize that he was being called by God to become a priest, to follow in Christ's footsteps in a unique way?)

This sheet is your "prep sheet." For each category, prepare two or three questions to ask Father during your interview.

Ministry	Divine Worship
Authority	**Personal Information**

The Sacrament of Holy Orders

How beautiful upon the mountains
are the feet of him who brings glad tidings,
Announcing peace, bearing good news.
Isaiah 52:7

Objective: To increase awareness of Holy Orders as the sacrament through which the mission and authority Christ gave his apostles continues in the Church.

Introduction ___ min.

Opening Prayer: Invite the young people to look at the photograph on pages 94 and 95. Read together Isaiah 52:7. Remind the group that we are all called by our Baptism to announce peace and to bear good news to others. The priests of the Church are called to commit themselves to this work in a special way. This photograph shows an ordination ceremony at the moment when the Litany of the Saints is prayed over the candidates for the priesthood. At this moment, the entire Church in heaven and on earth is united in prayer for these men who have answered Christ's call to the ordained ministry. Pray the form of the following litany. Ask these saints to guide those who are now serving in the priesthood.

The response for each of the following petitions is, "Pray for us."

> Holy Mary, Mother of God,
> Saint Michael,
> Saint John the Baptist,
> Saint Joseph,
> Saint Peter and Saint Paul,
> Saint Stephen,
> Saint Francis Xavier,
> Saint John Vianney,
> All holy men and women,

Forum: Have a volunteer "television talk-show host" facilitate discussion of the questions on the handout *A Spiritual Safety Net*. Distribute index cards and have the young people write one or two actions that would help people to develop and promote a spiritually supportive environment at home, in the religious-education program, and in the parish. Then ask the volunteers who made the net to display it and attach the index cards to it. You may want to display the "Spiritual Safety Net" where it may be seen by other parish groups.

PRESENTATION

Presentation ___ min.

◆ Draw attention to the statement at the top of page 96 and the question following it. Write the word *essential* on the board and record responses under it. To stimulate more thought at both "macro" and "micro" levels, rephrase the statement to read, "The pope is essential to the life of the parish. Why?" Help the group to see the relationship between their answers to these questions and their answers to the original question.

◆ Play a game of "What Is the Question?" You may divide the group into two teams if you wish. Read the statements below, and ask the group members to come up with the correct question for the statement. Make up additional statements as time permits.

• They consecrate each Christian for the common priesthood of the faithful. (*What are the sacraments of Baptism and Confirmation?*)

• It is the sacrament through which the mission and authority Christ gave his apostles continues in the Church. (*What is Holy Orders?*)

• They are the episcopate, the presbyterate, and the diaconate. (*What are the three ranks of Holy Orders?*)

• This word means "priest." (*What is a presbyter?*)

• They are ministry, divine worship, and authority. (*What are the three essential ways a man shares in the priesthood of Christ?*)

The priesthood is essential to the life of the Church. Why do you think this is so?

The Call to Holy Orders

Did you know that each of us was called at Baptism to share in the priesthood of Christ? We share in his priesthood by living out our baptismal promises and by continuing Christ's work on earth. The sacraments of Baptism and Confirmation consecrate each Christian for the common priesthood of the faithful. We are not ordained ministers, but we are called to share the good news of Christ and to carry on his mission in the world.

Some, however, are called to share in Christ's priesthood in a unique way as his ordained ministers. In the sacrament of Holy Orders, men are consecrated for a special life of sacramental ministry to the body of Christ, the Church. What makes the ordained ministry different?

Holy Orders is the sacrament through which the mission and authority Christ gave his apostles continues in the Church. "The Church confers the sacrament of Holy Orders only on baptized men" (*Catechism*, 1598). The sacrament includes three ranks, or orders:

• the episcopate (bishops)
• the presbyterate (priests)
• the diaconate (deacons).

In this chapter we will look at each of these orders and examine the ways in which each is celebrated in the liturgy of the Church. In general, however, we can say that in Holy Orders a man shares in the priesthood in three essential ways: ministry, divine worship, and authority.

96

96

Ministry   Before Christ ascended into heaven, he gave his apostles this mandate:

> Go, therefore, and make disciples of all nations, baptizing them in the name of the Father, and of the Son, and of the holy Spirit, teaching them to observe all that I have commanded you. And behold, I am with you always, until the end of the age.
> Matthew 28:19–20

Those ordained to ministry today have the same mandate: to bring the gospel to all people and to baptize them in the name of the Trinity.

All ministry is service, and Jesus made it quite clear that his ministers were to be the servants of the Church. At the Last Supper he washed the feet of his apostles, symbolically demonstrating their call to service. He told them that he "did not come to be served but to serve" (Mark 10:45).

We read in the Acts of the Apostles that after Jesus Christ ascended to his Father and after the coming of the Holy Spirit, the apostles led the early Church in two ways:

- They traveled through the known world preaching the good news of salvation through Jesus Christ.
- They taught and passed on to the early followers of Jesus their lived memories of his words and actions, especially of his death and resurrection.

Divine Worship   The ordained ministers of the Church celebrate the Eucharist and the other sacraments with the people of God.

Priests share in Christ's priesthood to the highest degree in the Eucharist. In this divine worship they act in the person of Christ himself. They proclaim and offer to the Father Christ's paschal mystery, for "in the sacrifice of the Mass they make present again and apply, until the coming of the Lord, the unique sacrifice of the New Testament" — Christ himself (*Catechism*, 1566).

Authority   Ordained ministers share in the authority of Jesus Christ. In the gospel we see Jesus sending his disciples out to teach, to baptize, to heal, and to forgive with this authority.

After the resurrection the Church grew very rapidly as more and more people joined the Christian community. The apostles chose others to help them in their work of teaching and leading the Church in worship and service. The apostles laid their hands on them and prayed that the Holy Spirit would strengthen them. In time these successors of the apostles, as we will see, were called bishops. Bishops in turn ordained priests to help them in the work of ministry. The authority of bishops and priests comes, not from themselves, but from Jesus Christ.

Holy Orders confers an indelible mark. As in the sacraments of Baptism and Confirmation, this unique sharing in the priesthood of Christ is given only once; it cannot be repeated. One who is ordained is ordained forever.

The Apostolic Call

Jesus knew that he could not do his work for the kingdom alone. He needed helpers to carry out his mission of preaching God's love, healing the sick, and reconciling sinners. In the Gospel of Luke, we read that before choosing his apostles, Jesus "departed to the mountain to pray, and he spent the night in prayer to God. When day came, he called his disciples to himself, and from them he chose Twelve, whom he also named apostles" (Luke 6:12–13).

After the resurrection these apostles, as we know from the accounts given in the Acts of the Apostles, did carry out the work of Jesus. They were the first missionaries. They founded and guided local churches. When the need arose, they met together to consider the best decision to make for the life and growth of the Church.

In time the apostles ordained others to follow in their footsteps. From one generation to the next, new apostolic leaders have been called and ordained to service in the Church. Our bishops today are successors to the apostles, for they share to the fullest extent in the grace of Holy Orders. Bishops teach, govern, and sanctify with the authority of Christ. In his local church the bishop is the chief teacher, the chief governor, and the chief priest.

The bishop is also responsible, under the leadership of the bishop of Rome, the pope, and together with all the other bishops, for the teaching, governance, and sanctification of the entire Church throughout the world. Bishops often meet together to discuss current issues facing the Church and the world.

97

◆ You may want to expand upon the meaning of *presbyterate* by supplying this historical context: When a local Church was founded, it was usually founded by an apostle or a leader, like Paul, who was called an *apostle* even though he was not one of the original Twelve. Once the local Church became established, the apostolic leaders moved on. But they chose and left behind local Church officers, whom they had ordained by the laying on of hands. These men were called by a number of different titles: *pastor* (which means "shepherd"), *teacher*, *presbyter* (priest or elder) or *bishop* (overseer). The words seem to have been used interchangeably because official titles had not yet been determined. Gradually the title of *bishop* was used only for the successors of the apostolic leaders. The title *presbyter* was used for the other local officers.

Note: For a clear statement and explanation of the question "Who can receive the sacrament?" see *Catechism*, 1577–1580.

◆ Discuss with the young people the statements they underlined. Have them highlight the main ideas highlighted on reduced pupil pages 96 through 101.

Be sure to stress that priests share in Christ's priesthood to the highest degree in the Eucharist. It is important to understand that the priest acts in the person of Christ himself.

Presentation (cont'd)

◆ To summarize the ritual of ordination of a bishop, you might like to ask these questions:

• What is the visible sign of the ordination of a bishop? (*the principal ordaining bishop laying his hands on the head of the bishop-elect*)

• What prayer is part of this sign? (*the prayer of consecration*)

• What oil is used in the ordination of a bishop? (*the same oil used in the sacraments of Baptism and Confirmation*) You may want to add that this oil is called *sacred chrism*.

• What does the bishop's ring symbolize? (*fidelity to the Church*)

◆ Ask a volunteer to summarize *Catholic ID*. Then discuss the **thought provoker** on page 98. Elicit suggestions from the group about ways you can support your bishop.

◆ Draw attention to *Scripture & My Life* on page 101. Ask a volunteer to read the Scripture passage suggested. Ask, "What does it mean to welcome our priests and bishops today?"

◆ If a videotape of a priest's ordination is available, show it to the young people now. After viewing the celebration, discuss the training and preparation a man makes before ordination day. If possible, invite a seminarian from the diocesan seminary to explain his courses of study and the steps he will take before being ordained.

The Ordination of a Bishop

A bishop is ordained by other bishops. The ordination takes place during the Eucharist, after the reading of the gospel. First a mandate, or letter, from the Holy Father is read, confirming the ordination of the new bishop. Then the people of the local church are asked to give their consent to the ordination. The congregation usually responds with enthusiastic applause. A homily is given by the principal ordaining bishop. He then asks the newly chosen bishop, or bishop-elect, a series of questions. By his answers the bishop-elect declares his readiness to serve his people.

The principal ordaining bishop prays that the Lord will anoint the bishop-elect, "with the fullness of priestly grace." Then, in complete silence, he lays his hands on the head of the bishop-elect. The other bishops then do the same. This ritual action, along with the prayer of consecration, is the visible sign of the ordination of a bishop.

While the Book of the Gospels is held above the new bishop's head, the principal ordaining bishop offers the prayer of consecration. The new bishop's head is anointed with oil, the same oil used in the sacraments of Baptism and Confirmation. The Book of the Gospels, which symbolizes the bishop's role as teacher and preacher of the word of God, is then given to the new bishop.

He is also given a ring as a symbol of fidelity to the Church. He receives the miter and the crosier, or pastoral staff.

The new bishop is then invited to take his seat in the chair of the bishop, the *cathedra*, and all the bishops exchange the sign of peace.

The miter is a traditional headcovering worn by the bishop during liturgical ceremonies. The word *miter* comes from a Latin word meaning "headband." As a symbol of his office, the miter has come to signify the role of the bishop as a "herald of truth," the principal teacher of the gospel in his diocese. During the liturgy the miter is removed whenever the bishop speaks to God in prayer.

98

At the end of the Eucharist, the new bishop blesses the people.

Who is the bishop of your diocese? What are some ways you can support your bishop?

The Priesthood of Christ

There are many bishops and many priests, but there is only one priesthood, the priesthood of Christ. Saint Paul explained that Jesus Christ is the one priest, the one mediator between God and the human race:

> For there is one God.
> There is also one mediator between God and the human race,
> Christ Jesus, himself human,
> who gave himself as ransom for all.
> 1 Timothy 2:5–6

The unique sacrifice of Jesus Christ on the cross is made present in the Eucharist. In the same way the one priesthood of Christ is made present in the priesthood of his ministers: our bishops, priests (presbyters), and deacons. This priesthood is the means that Christ chose to build up and lead the Church. Through the ordained ministry of bishops and priests, the presence of Christ as head of the Church is made visible. Through the sacrament of Holy Orders, bishops and priests are ordained to bring this unique presence of Christ to us.

Priests and bishops act not only in the name of Christ but also in the name of the whole Church, especially at the Eucharist, in which they present the entire body of Christ to God. It is because they represent Christ that they also represent the body of Christ, the Church. To share in the priesthood of Christ means to share in the work of Christ as mediator between God and the human race. It is the work of the priest, in all that he does, to serve the people of God.

In Holy Orders priests are united with the bishop in the priesthood of Christ. The priest is consecrated and ordained to preach the gospel, to celebrate the sacraments, and to guide the members of the body of Christ. He does this under the authority of his bishop.

At ordination, the new priest makes a promise of obedience to the bishop of the local church in which he will serve. At the end of the ordination rite, the bishop and the new priest exchange the sign of peace. Both actions are signs that the priest and his bishop are united in working for the kingdom of God. The bishop needs priests to help him and considers the priests of his diocese his "co-workers, his sons, his brothers and his friends" (*Catechism*, 1567).

 What do you think is the main work of a priest? Why is it essential to the Church?

The Ordination of a Priest

The ordination of a priest is very much like the ordination of a bishop. The essential rite of the sacrament—the laying on of hands and the prayer of consecration—is the same except that after the bishop lays hands on the candidate, the other priests present also lay their hands on him. This is a sign of their unity, of working together for the kingdom.

The rite of the ordination of a priest takes place during the Eucharist, after the reading of the gospel. The candidate is called forward and presented to the bishop. The bishop says:

We rely on the help of the Lord God and our Savior Jesus Christ, and we choose this man, our brother, for priesthood in the presbyteral order.

The consent of the people is then given, usually by joyful applause. The bishop then asks the candidate, in a series of questions, if he is willing to carry out the duties of a priest. The candidate answers, "I am, with the help of God."

The candidate promises obedience to the bishop of the local church. After the bishop leads a prayer for the candidate, the candidate prostrates himself during the Litany of the Saints. The bishop asks God the Father to pour out upon the candidate the blessing of the Holy Spirit and the grace and power of the priesthood.

Then, in silence, the bishop lays his hands on the candidate's head. Still in silence, all the priests who are present also lay their hands upon the candidate. The bishop, extending his hands over the candidate, offers the prayer of consecration. These two actions—the laying on of hands followed by the prayer of consecration—are the essential signs of ordination.

The new priest is invested with the stole and chasuble as symbols of the priesthood. Next the bishop anoints the palms of the new priest's hands with chrism, the same oil used in Baptism and Confirmation. After the gifts of bread and wine are presented, the bishop gives the paten and chalice to the new priest as symbols of the mystery of the Eucharist he will celebrate.

Then the bishop and the newly ordained exchange a sign of peace, and the celebration of the Eucharist continues.

Ordained for Service

The word *deacon* comes from a Greek word meaning "to serve." The first deacons served by providing food for the poor of the early Church. We read in the Acts of the Apostles that the Church in Jerusalem was growing so quickly that the daily distribution of food was not being taken care of properly. So the apostles met with the community and said, "'It is not right for us to neglect the word of God to serve at table. Brothers, select from among you seven reputable men, filled with the Spirit and wisdom, whom we shall appoint to this task. . . .' The proposal was acceptable to the whole community" (Acts 6:2–5).

Like the deacons of the early Church, deacons today carry God's message to us and share in the mission of Christ through the grace of Holy Orders. They are marked with an indelible spiritual character that conforms them to Christ, "who made himself the 'deacon' or servant of all" (*Catechism*, 1570). Deacons today may perform their service to the Church in many ways: in assisting the bishops and priests in the

99

◆ Discuss the ✦ **thought provoker** on page 99. Then distribute the handout *Following in Christ's Footsteps*. Allow about five minutes for the young people to write their questions. If possible, invite a priest to come and talk to the young people during this session or at a future one. The group may choose representative questions to ask during an interview at this time.

◆ Draw the group's attention to *Catholic Teachings*. Explain that, through the long history of the Church, the diaconate gradually lost its role as a distinct ministry. It became one of the ordained ministries on the way to ordination. All deacons became priests. The Second Vatican Council restored the diaconate as a permanent ministry for those who are called to it, not only for those planning to be priests.

◆ Ask the group if they know any deacons. List the names on the board. Ask, "What do deacons do?" After the group responds, ask if they can recall being present when a deacon was giving service in any of these ways. If a deacon serves in your parish, ask the young people if they can add specific examples of what a deacon does by using the parish deacon's ministry as an example.

FYI A man thinking about becoming a deacon feels a strong desire to live the gospel as deeply as possible in his own life, and wants to help others to do so. He is usually a dependable helper in his parish. Most dioceses have programs designed for those studying to become deacons. If a man wanting to become a deacon is married, he must have the understanding and support of his wife in his decision.

The term "lay deacon" is incorrect, because the deacon is truly ordained and is a member of the clergy of a particular diocese. He is not obliged to wear clerical clothing, and he is usually expected to receive his financial support from his secular occupation.

Presentation (cont'd)

◆ Ask, "How is the ordination of a deacon different from that of a bishop or priest?" (*Only the bishop lays hands on the candidate, to show the deacon's special attachment to the bishop of the diocese.*)

◆ Discuss *On Line with the Parish*. If a thank-you celebration is not possible, perhaps the group would like to send a card or letter of thanks to the pastor, priests, and deacons of the parish. You may want to send this card or letter to the men in connection with a special feast day meaningful to the parish or on the anniversaries of their ordinations.

Conclusion ___ min.

◆ Draw the group's attention to the chart. Have the young people form three groups: "Bishops," "Priests," "Deacons." Read sections of the chart at random. If a section refers to bishops, this group should stand. If to priests, the priest group will stand, and so on. Sometimes only one group will stand, sometimes all three.

Assessment: If you are administering *Chapter 12 Assessment*, page 101A, allow a brief period for the young people to complete the test.

---

liturgy, above all in the Eucharist; in the distribution of communion; in assisting at and blessing marriages; in the proclaiming of the gospel and in preaching; in presiding over funerals; and in works of service and charity. In all these tasks the deacon is guided first of all by the bishop of the local church and then by the pastor of the parish in which he serves.

The Ordination of a Deacon

The ordination of a deacon is similar to that of a bishop or priest except that at a deacon's ordination only the bishop lays hands on the candidate. This symbolizes the deacon's special attachment to the bishop in the tasks of his service.

The ordination of a deacon, like that of a bishop and a priest, takes place at the celebration of the Eucharist. After the reading of the gospel, the candidate is called forward, the bishop is assured of his worthiness, and the people assent to ordination by enthusiastic applause. In his homily the bishop explains the role of a deacon: "He will draw new strength from the gift of the Holy Spirit. He will help the bishop and his body of priests as a minister of the word, of the altar, and of charity. He will make himself a servant to all."

The bishop lays his hands, in silence, on the candidate's head. Then, with his hands extended over the candidate, the bishop prays the prayer of consecration.

The deacon is given a deacon's stole and the special deacon's vestment called the dalmatic. He wears the stole, not around his neck as a priest does, but diagonally across his chest. Now vested as a deacon, the newly ordained minister kneels before the bishop and receives from him the Book of the Gospels, a sign that he is to teach and practice God's word.

 In what ways is a deacon to be a servant and a herald?

Here is a brief summary of Holy Orders to help you recall the main ideas of this chapter.

Three Ranks	Who Ordains?	Essential Signs	Ministry
bishop (episcopate)	Only a bishop can ordain another bishop, a priest, or a deacon.	the laying on of hands and the prayer of consecration	successor to the apostles leader of his local church chief teacher, governor, and priest for his diocese in union with the pope and the other bishops, responsible for the teaching, governance, and sanctification of the entire Church
priest (presbyterate)	A priest is ordained by a bishop, usually the bishop of his diocese.	same as above	coworker with the bishop in preaching the gospel, celebrating the sacraments, and guiding the members of the body of Christ
deacon (diaconate)	A deacon is ordained by the bishop of his diocese.	same as above	assists the bishops and priests in works of service and charity and, in the liturgy, proclaiming the gospel and preaching

100

Answers for Chapter 12 Assessment

1. c	**2.** b	**3.** a	**4.** a	**5.** b
6. d	**7.** c	**8.** a	**9.** c	**10.** See page 97.

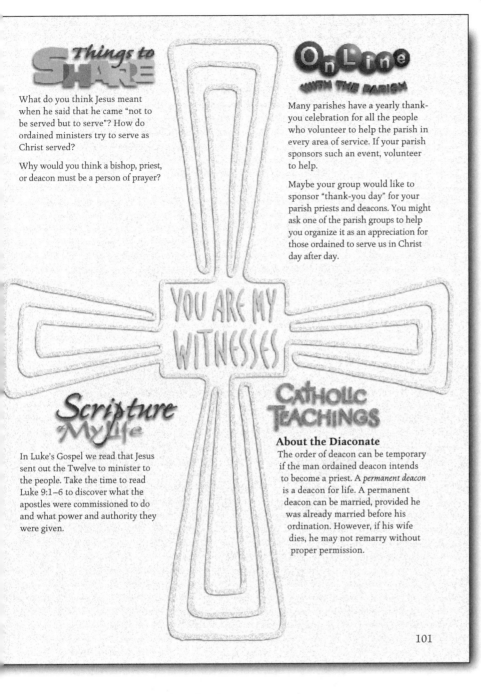

Things to SHARE

What do you think Jesus meant when he said that he came "not to be served but to serve"? How do ordained ministers try to serve as Christ served?

Why would you think a bishop, priest, or deacon must be a person of prayer?

OnLine WITH THE PARISH

Many parishes have a yearly thank-you celebration for all the people who volunteer to help the parish in every area of service. If your parish sponsors such an event, volunteer to help.

Maybe your group would like to sponsor "thank-you day" for your parish priests and deacons. You might ask one of the parish groups to help you organize it as an appreciation for those ordained to serve us in Christ day after day.

Scripture in My Life

In Luke's Gospel we read that Jesus sent out the Twelve to minister to the people. Take the time to read Luke 9:1–6 to discover what the apostles were commissioned to do and what power and authority they were given.

CATHOLIC TEACHINGS

About the Diaconate

The order of deacon can be temporary if the man ordained deacon intends to become a priest. A *permanent deacon* is a deacon for life. A permanent deacon can be married, provided he was already married before his ordination. However, if his wife dies, he may not remarry without proper permission.

YOU ARE MY WITNESSES

101

Conclusion (cont'd)

◆ Direct attention to *Things to Share* on page 101. Stress that people who do things for others need to be in touch with God for their own strength and also for sensitivity to others' needs. People of prayer know that they can call on God for help.

FORUM Assignment

✔ Read pages 102–109. Underline in pencil the statements that express six key ideas.

✔ Find three examples in music, poetry, greeting cards, or videos of expressions of the kind of love on which a lasting commitment in marriage can be founded. Be prepared to share your examples.

Closing Prayer: Lead the group in the following prayer for priests.

Lord Jesus Christ,
   we place in your hands the priests of the world,
Offer them to the Father in the joy of the Holy Spirit.
Help them to minister with joy and energy.

Evaluation: Do the young people understand the purpose of the priesthood and its three orders? Do they appreciate the symbolism of the rite of ordination? Do they understand that bishops, priests, and deacons are following in the footsteps of Christ through ministry, divine worship, and authority?

FOR CHAPTER 13

- copies of handout *Happily Ever After?*, page 102C
- *Chapter 13 Assessment*, page 109A
- *Highlights for Home*, page 109B
- hymns or songs on the theme of faithful love
- cassette and CD player and VCR for *Forum*

Assessment

1 The sacrament of Holy Orders
  a. is given to anyone who wishes.
  b. is given more than once.
  c. is given only once.
  d. none of the above

2 A bishop is ordained
  a. by the pope alone.
  b. by other bishops.
  c. by the people of the diocese.
  d. by the priests of the diocese.

3 _____ signifies the bishop's role as a "herald of truth."
  a. The miter
  b. The bishop's ring
  c. The bishop's staff
  d. Prostration

4 The bishop is given _____ as a symbol of fidelity to the Church.
  a. a ring
  b. a miter
  c. a staff
  d. the Book of the Gospels

5 The _____ symbolizes the bishop's role as teacher and preacher of the word of God.
  a. staff
  b. Book of the Gospels
  c. miter
  d. ring

6 The essential signs of ordination are the laying on of hands and
  a. the stole and chasuble.
  b. the exchange of the sign of peace.
  c. the Litany of the Saints.
  d. the prayer of consecration.

7 If the man being ordained intends to become a priest, the order of deacon is
  a. permanent.
  b. invalid.
  c. temporary.
  d. indelible.

8 In Holy Orders a man shares in the priesthood in three essential ways: ministry, _____ , and authority.
  a. divine worship
  b. teaching
  c. healing
  d. none of the above

9 Circle the letter beside the phrase that does *not* describe a deacon's task.
  a. blessing marriages
  b. distributing Holy Communion
  c. ordaining other deacons
  d. preaching

10 Explain briefly the responsibilities of a bishop. Write your response on the reverse side of this page.

Highlights for Home

Focus on Faith

Bishops, priests, and deacons are ordained to bring the good news of salvation to us. In this chapter, your son or daughter learned the vital importance to the Church of our ordained ministers. This chapter also introduced them to the beauty and symbolism of the rites of ordination.

It is hoped that in this chapter the young people also glimpsed the beauty of a life dedicated to God in the Church. For beautiful are the hands that baptize our children, offer the Eucharist, and anoint the sick among us. Beautiful the voice that preaches the gospel, assures us of God's forgiveness, and asks us to repeat wedding vows. Beautiful the life given to the service of God's people.

Conversation Starters

. . . . a few ideas to talk about together . . . .

◆ Do we take the ministry of the priests of our parish for granted? What can we do to show priests our appreciation and support?

◆ Do we consider it our responsibility to pray for priestly vocations? What words can we pray?

Feature Focus

Catholic ID explains that the miter, the traditional headcovering worn by the bishop during liturgical ceremonies, symbolizes the bishop's role as a "herald of truth." The bishop is the principal teacher of the gospel, the main messenger of the good news of Jesus Christ.

Reflection

Saint Francis de Sales (1567–1622) was ordained a priest during the time when many Catholics were joining the churches of the Protestant Reformation. Through his tireless efforts he re-established Catholicism in Switzerland. In 1602, he was appointed Bishop of Geneva. As the shepherd of his diocese, he counseled many people and helped them to see that through their own unique callings they could deepen their friendship with God.

Reflect on his words of advice:

Go courageously to do whatever you are called to do.
  Go simply.
If you have any fears, say to your soul:
  "The Lord will provide for us. . . ."
The apostles were mostly unlearned fishermen,
  but God gave them learning enough
  for the work they had to do.

Trust in him, depend on his providence, fear nothing.

THE SACRAMENT OF MATRIMONY

Adult Focus

The focus of this chapter is to encourage the young people to move beyond a romantic conception of marriage that focuses on a beautiful wedding and a hazy idea that "love will keep us together." It explores the sacrament of Matrimony as a lifelong commitment between a baptized man and a baptized woman whom God has brought together. Through the marriage covenant, they become one. By God's grace, they mirror for others the relationship between Christ and his beloved Church. By their free gift of self they are united in body, heart, and soul. Their indissoluble union and openness to having children is a sign of God's faithful love present in them and in the Church.

Our young people need to recognize that this exalted yet seemingly "ordinary" sacrament requires long-range preparation and self-discipline. The chapter provides them with a useful questionnaire to discern which interpersonal skills they need to develop in order to establish healthy relationships.

The young people are encouraged to pray for married and engaged couples, as well as for themselves, for they are members of the domestic Church (the family), and may one day be called to seek their own holiness in the sacrament of Matrimony.

Catechism Focus

The theme of Chapter 13 corresponds to paragraphs 1601–1605, 1638–1645, 1652, 2331 and 2335 of the *Catechism*.

Enrichment Activities

Marriage Medleys

To encourage the young people to discern popular songs that extol or describe true love, invite them to put together taped medleys. They might intersperse Christian rock, pop, and spiritual music dealing with faithful love, friendship, and marriage. If possible, make available to them the album *United As One*, Volumes 1 and 2 (OCP). The medleys may be used in class or at a youth retreat.

Anniversary Action Plans

Recognizing a married couple on their anniversary year after year is a sign of the Christian community's support for their gift of faithfulness. Suggest that the young people compile "Anniversary Action Plans" for all married couples in their extended families (as well as others of their choice). Have them list anniversary dates and one affirming action such as: making a greeting card, serving a meal, offering a service (free babysitting or praying a rosary for the couple's intentions).

Teaching Resources

Overview

To discover the meaning and importance of the sacrament of Matrimony.

Opening Prayer Ideas

Look at the photo on pages 102–103. Pray together 1 John 4:16.

or

Ask two volunteers to take turns reading 1 Corinthians 13:1–7. Pray for all married couples.

Materials

- Bibles, journals, and highlighters
- hymns or songs on the theme of faithful love (See page 107.)
- cassette and CD player and VCR for *Forum* activity

REPRODUCIBLE MASTERS
- copies of handout *Happily Ever After?*, page 102C
- *Chapter 13 Assessment*, page 109A
- *Highlights for Home*, page 109B

Liturgy and Worship Journal:
For Chapter 13, use pages 52–55.

Supplemental Resources

PAMPHLETS
Catholic Youth Update
- "Finding 'Forever' Friends"
- "Marriage Insurance: Never Too Soon to Invest"
- "Marriage: Supernatural and Sacramental"

St. Anthony Messenger Press
1615 Republic Street
Cincinnati, OH 45210

Happily Ever After?

Write a thoughtful response to each of these letters to "The Marriage Counselor."

Dear T.M.C.,

Joe and I are getting married soon. There's only one problem. He wants to be the boss. I think we should be equal partners. Do you think we can live happily ever after?

Hopeful in Houston

Dear Hope,

_____

_____

_____

_____

Sincerely, T.M.C.

Dear T.M.C.,

Should I get engaged to Teresa? I really love her. We are both Catholics, and we pray together sometimes. We enjoy hiking, dancing, and just being together. But my parents are divorced. I'm afraid Teresa and I will wind up the same way.

Doubtful in Dubuque

Dear Doubtful,

_____

_____

_____

_____

Cordially, T.M.C.

Dear T.M.C.,

Help! My wedding date is only two weeks away. I just found out my sweetheart doesn't want any children—ever! Should I let this discovery ruin everything? Or should I go ahead and hope for the best? Please respond by EXPRESS MAIL!!!

Frantic in Frankfurt

Dear Frantic,

_____

_____

_____

_____

Advisedly, T.M.C.

The Sacrament of Matrimony

God is love,
and whoever remains
in love remains in God.
1 John 4:16

103

Objective: To discover the meaning and importance of the sacrament of Matrimony.

Introduction ___ min.

Opening Prayer: Invite the young people to look at the photograph on pages 102 and 103 as you share the following account.

> In an essay on youth, Pope John Paul II points out that the origin of all vocations—including marriage—is the call to become "a free gift for others." He tells the story of a young Polish student who hungered after holiness. The student knew that he was not called to holy orders or religious life. So "he sought a companion for his life and sought her on his knees, in prayer." When he later recognized the woman who would be his wife, he saw her as having been sent to him by God.

Invite the young people to write a prayer to Jesus. Ask his help in finding and becoming a good and loving marriage partner or friend. Assure the group that sharing of this reflection will be on a voluntary basis.

Forum: If possible, have a cassette and CD player as well as a VCR available for the young people's use. Have the young people conduct the *Forum* as a TV talk show on the theme "Recognizing Real Love." Two co-hosts invite members of the audience to share their examples of expressions of true love in music, poetry, greeting cards, or videos. The co-hosts question participants about ways they can tell the difference between real love (on which a lasting marriage can be built) and false love (which dies when romance evaporates or infatuation runs its course). When all have participated, the co-hosts summarize key ideas expressed.

Presentation ____ min.

◆ Have someone read aloud the introductory quote and opening question at the top of page 104. Seek a few responses clarifying the difference in importance between the wedding event and the vocation of marriage.

◆ On the board draw two interlocking wedding rings. Ask the young people to define *the sacrament of Matrimony.* (*It is a sacred covenant uniting a baptized man and a baptized woman as partners for the whole of life. Matrimony mirrors the relationship between Christ and the Church.*)

Then invite volunteers to write in the space surrounding the rings words and phrases describing the Christian ideal of marriage. (*equal partners, true love, commitment to each other's good, finding God at the center of their mutual love, sharing love with children, a gift to the Church and the world*)

◆ Discuss with the young people the positive and negative ways the media presents love and sexuality. Stress the importance of remembering that these expressions do have a deeper meaning to those who share in respectful love. Share with them the FYI story that reminds us of the truth and strength of a loving relationship.

"A wedding lasts an hour; a marriage lasts a lifetime." What do you think this means?

The Sacrament of Matrimony

Weddings are beautiful ceremonies. Whether large or small, weddings are intended to be celebrations of love. But is there more to marriage than the feeling of romance we see so often in movies, on television, and in the books and magazines we read? Let's take a look at the wonder and mystery of marriage.

Obviously the civil authorities think there is more to marriage than movies or television portray. In the United States, for example, thousands of men and women each year obtain a civil license from the state in which they want to be married, and

104

104

each state has special requirements that must be fulfilled if a marriage is to be considered legal. These may include an age requirement or even the taking of a blood test as a check to keep society free from communicable diseases. Then every couple must go for a marriage license.

Why is the state so interested in marriage? Because marriage is so important for society. In fact society is built on marriage and the family. We as a society must know when two people are promising to share responsibility for rearing children, owning property, and paying taxes. Without marriage and family life, society would fall apart in ruins. The state wants to make sure that all is well for those who want to be married. Healthy marriages mean a healthy society everywhere in the world.

For Catholics, however, marriage goes far beyond what society demands. The Church teaches us that marriage between two baptized persons is more than a legal arrangement, more than a contract, and more than romance. Marriage is a sacrament in which a baptized man and a baptized woman commit themselves to each other as partners for life. This partnership is a sacred covenant that mirrors the relationship that Christ has with the Church.

In the *sacrament of Matrimony*, a man and woman commit themselves totally to each other in Christ. They vow to love and help each other for the rest of their lives and to share this love with their children.

In this Christian ideal of marriage, then, a man and a woman are equal partners, devoted to each other in true love, committed to each other's good, and ready to find God at the very center of their love for each other. Such a love cannot help but be open to new life—to the procreation and education of children.

This is a sacrament filled with great joy and love but it is also a serious and solemn obligation. Not everyone is ready to make such a commitment. It takes time, hard work, and deep dedication before two people are ready to walk down the aisle of a church and speak the vows of marriage to each other.

A Life-giving Sign of Grace

The sacrament of Matrimony is a life-giving sign of grace, not just at the wedding ceremony when the wedding vows are made, but for the lifetime during which the vows are lived out by a man and a woman.

Like each of the sacraments, the sacrament of Matrimony is a public act. The bride and groom speak their vows aloud before God and the community. The priest or deacon accepts these vows as the Church's official witness. There must also be two other witnesses. For a Catholic marriage to be considered valid, Catholics must marry in the presence of a priest or deacon and two witnesses. Unless otherwise dispensed, or excused, from this by the local bishop, any other marriage by Catholics would be considered invalid.

It is a surprise to many Catholics that the bride and groom themselves are the ministers of the sacrament. When the marriage vows are pronounced, the couple begins a whole new way of life. They are no longer two; they are one. The grace of this sacrament will enable them to put aside selfishness and to be open to each other in mutual support and generosity. The sacrament will strengthen them to approach an unknown future, with its joys and sorrows. It will help them to build their family life on the rock foundation of faith in Christ.

CATHOLIC ID

The banns of marriage are customary in the Church. The word *banns* means "proclamations" or "announcements." For three weeks before a wedding, the parish prints in the weekly bulletin or announces at Mass the names of the bride and groom and the date of the wedding. Because we are a community, we need to know when our sisters and brothers in faith are taking this decisive step in their lives. When you read or hear the banns of marriage, pray for those entering into this beautiful sacramental commitment.

105

◆ Discuss with the young people the statements they underlined in the chapter. Have them highlight the statements highlighted on the reduced pupil pages 104 through 109.

◆ Have a volunteer summarize *Catholic ID*. If possible, read any banns currently appearing in the parish bulletin, and write the names of the engaged couples on the board. Offer a brief prayer for these couples.

◆ Direct attention to *Catholic Teachings* on page 109. Emphasize that the Church values both the loving intimacy expressed in a married couple's sexual relationship and the children who are a sign of their covenanted love.

◆ Call on volunteers to clarify the respective roles of the priest and the bride and groom during the celebration of the sacrament. (*The priest is the Church's official witness. The latter are the ministers of the sacrament.*)

FYI To remove a tumor in the young woman's face, the surgeon had to cut a nerve. Now her mouth was crooked like a clown's with a goofy expression. She asked if it would always be that way, and the surgeon said, "Yes." Her young husband said, "I like it. It is kind of cute."

The surgeon watched as the husband bent over to kiss his wife. "I can see how he twists his own lips to accommodate to her, to show her that their kiss still works," the surgeon later wrote. He knew that he was in the presence of a true and faithful love.

Presentation (cont'd)

◆ Print *indissoluble bond* on the board. Ask the young people to define the term. (*a bond formed in Matrimony that can never be broken*) Challenge the young people to name at least three reasons why some people are incapable of honoring an indissoluble bond. (*They get married before they are ready; they are immature; they fail to work at marriage; they remain self-centered; they fail to pray and trust in God.*)

◆ Direct attention to the ☀ **thought provoker** on page 106. Discuss briefly.

◆ Present the following "What if?" situation. Have the young people role-play a family conference discussing the situation.

> What if your favorite cousin got engaged but was reluctant to get involved "in those weird Pre-Cana classes"? What if you, because of what you have learned about the Catholic way of preparing for the sacrament of Matrimony, could help your cousin by explaining the "whats" and "whys" of the preparation process?

◆ Distribute the handout *Happily Ever After?* Allow five to ten minutes for the young people to write their responses. Then have participants fold their handout sheets twice (as in a business letter) and drop them in a "mail bag" (a large purse or briefcase). Ask a designated delivery person to redistribute the letters. Have each person read aloud the responses from "The Marriage Counselor." When all have shared responses, the host summarizes the Catholic point of view on each of the three imaginary situations.

Getting Ready

When a couple decides to marry, it is because they have chosen to spend the rest of their lives together. They become engaged and announce their intention to marry. When one or both of them is Catholic, they meet with the parish priest, deacon, or other minister to begin a time of preparation. The sacrament of Matrimony requires special preparation because of the serious nature of the commitment. The couple must know of marriage's responsibilities, challenges, and graces. No one must enter into marriage lightly or without thought.

The priest or deacon will help the couple to determine whether or not they truly are free to marry to be certain that nothing or no one holds them back from making a free commitment in love. When we marry, we promise fidelity to one person with a permanent commitment. Marriage is not something that we try out for a while! We promise to be true to the other "in good times and in bad, in sickness and in health" until death.

Sadly, some people cannot make this type of commitment in Christ. Others try too early when

106

they are still immature. Others fail to work at marriage. Those who succeed at marriage are those who work at the kind of love Saint Paul describes, a love that "bears all things, believes all things, hopes all things, endures all things" (1 Corinthians 13:7).

☀ *Think about important events in your life that have taken preparation on your part. Why is preparation for marriage so important?*

Real Love

Catholics can never take the attitude that "we can always divorce if it doesn't go well." We believe that the sacrament of Matrimony forms an *indissoluble bond*—a bond that can never be broken. Real love based in Christ is not here one day and gone the next; real love is forever.

Celebrating Matrimony

Like every other sacrament Matrimony reveals something of the paschal mystery. When two Catholics celebrate the sacrament of Matrimony, they celebrate their willingness to imitate and encounter Christ in their lives of service, in the dyings and risings, sorrows and joys of family life.

The meaning of Catholic marriage is expressed in the rite of marriage. It is most fitting that the rite be

celebrated with a nuptial Mass. In this way the bride and groom unite themselves to the self-offering of Christ in the Eucharist. It is also fitting that they receive the Body and Blood of Christ in Holy Communion, which seals their union in Christ.

The sacrament of Matrimony has the same basic shape as all the other sacraments.

Gathering   The priest or deacon greets the bride and groom, welcoming them and their families and friends in the name of the Church.

Storytelling   The couple often selects the Scripture passages from the rite that correspond to the religious meaning they wish to express in their wedding.

Exchange of Vows   It is the bride and groom who, by their free consent and mutual vows, are the ministers of the sacrament. The pledging of vows must be *witnessed* by a priest, the Church's official witness, and two other people, usually the maid of honor and the best man. The free consent of the couple and the presence of a priest and two witnesses are the essential signs of the sacrament. The bride and groom stand before the congregation and vow "to give themselves, each to the other, mutually and definitively, in order to live a covenant of faithful and fruitful love" (*Catechism*, 1662).

The couple must reflect God's faithful love in three ways: in *unity* of body, heart, and soul; in *indissolubility*, that is, lifelong faithfulness; and in *openness to having children*. These three qualities are essential to Christian marriage.

Meal Sharing   As we have seen, when two practicing Catholics exchange their vows, they usually do so in the context of the Eucharist at a nuptial Mass. All that marriage says about union with Christ in sacrificial love is said even more eloquently in the Eucharist.

Commissioning   The blessing at the end of Mass is directed especially to the bride and groom. One blessing asks that the peace of Christ may always be in their home.

Recall a wedding liturgy in which you have participated. Can you describe the main elements based on the outline given here?

Are You Ready for Marriage?

The correct answer to the question above is, of course, no. Readiness for a lifelong commitment demands a certain maturity, an ability to care for and support a family, and an awareness of the challenges and responsibilities that joining one's life to another's demands. Still most of you are, whether you know it or not, preparing for marriage right now.

As we grow through life, we become aware of our own unique characteristics. Some of these we can do nothing about. The color of our hair and eyes is based on genetics, not personal preference. Other characteristics, however, are not fixed forever. We can make decisions about our personality traits. We can decide, for example, to be kind, to be more patient, to listen to others, to keep our promises. In other words, we can begin now to decide what kind of person we want to become, what kind of interpersonal skills we want to learn.

The vocation of marriage requires interpersonal skills. Marriage is a union of two compatible but often very different people. Two unique personalities must learn to make important decisions together, to discuss their differences of opinion, to allow themselves to reveal deep feelings to the other. This is not easy for anyone!

107

◆ Ask, "Why do you think it is important for the couple to participate in the planning of the liturgy for the wedding?"

Have a different volunteer read each of the passages listed in *Scripture & My Life* on page 109. Have the young people choose their favorite reading and write their reflections on this passage in their journal. You may also want to play one or all of the following songs (or any other on the theme of faithful love):

• "United As One" by Owen Alstott from the album of the same title, Vol. 1 (OCP)

• "Wherever You Go" by Gregory Norbet/Weston Priory from the album of the same title

• "First Corinthians 13" from the album *Like A Seal On Your Heart: Music for the Christian Wedding* (OCP).

If time allows, have the young people write in their journals their reflections on the lyrics of their favorite song.

◆ Direct attention to the **thought provoker** on page 107. Have a few volunteers offer their descriptions.

FYI   Together with their pastor, Alan and Lynn carefully planned their nuptial liturgy. They included a blessing of their parents. They reflected on several possible Scripture readings before choosing those which best expressed their vision of marriage. As their theme, they chose the lines: "Your people shall be my people, and your God my God" (Book of Ruth 1:16). Alan and Lynn also chose liturgical music that helped them focus on the meaning of Christian marriage.

Presentation (cont'd)

Have the young people form small groups to work with the questionnaire on page 108. Read the introduction and directions aloud. Suggest that the young people work individually in their journals for the first three to five minutes. Then encourage them to share ideas and solutions. After a brief group session, call on volunteers to identify those interpersonal skills that are most difficult for them. Identify ways of practicing the most needed skills. (*counting slowly to three; volunteering to help with younger children*)

◆ Call for brief responses to the **thought provoker** on page 108.

◆ Have a volunteer read *On Line with the Parish.* Be prepared with information about the kind of marriage preparation offered in your parish. Encourage the young people to share this information with those who may need it.

Conclusion ___ min.

◆ Discuss with the entire group the questions posed in *Things to Share.*

◆ Encourage the young people to share *Highlights for Home,* page 109B, with their families.

Assessment: If you are administering *Chapter 13 Assessment,* page 109A, allow a brief period for its completion.

The following questionnaire is a sample of the kinds of questions engaged couples are asked. Such a questionnaire can help the couple to become more aware of their own personalities and their ability to communicate with others. You have probably used these skills in friendships, in groups or teams you might belong to, or in group projects in school. Everyone needs these skills. Those who work on developing their interpersonal skills are headed toward satisfying friendships and, in time, a good marriage.

You may want to write your personal responses to these questions in your journal and then share your ideas and solutions in small groups. Check those skills you wish to improve.

MY INTERPERSONAL SKILLS

☐ Am I a good listener? How do I show this?

☐ How do I deal with criticism?

☐ What do I do when I am angry? How do I solve the problem?

☐ Do I spend money wisely?

☐ Do I give positive feedback? Do I affirm others and thank them when I am grateful for their help or support?

☐ Do I talk over problems with the person or persons directly involved?

☐ If I have a serious problem or need, do I talk it over with an adult I can trust?

☐ Do I look for ways to help others when I can?

☐ Do I show respect for others in my speech, saying "please," "thank you," and "pardon me"?

☐ Do I apologize when I've made a mistake or caused a problem?

☐ What is my reaction when my plans are upset for some reason?

☐ Have I learned to play with and watch over young children safely?

☐ Do I speak with adults respectfully and courteously?

☐ How do I treat the elderly persons I meet?

 How do you think developing interpersonal skills can prepare you for marriage?

108

Answers for Chapter 13 Assessment

1. a   **2.** c   **3.** b   **4.** a   **5.** b

6. d   **7.** c   **8.** d   **9.** a   **10.** See page 107.

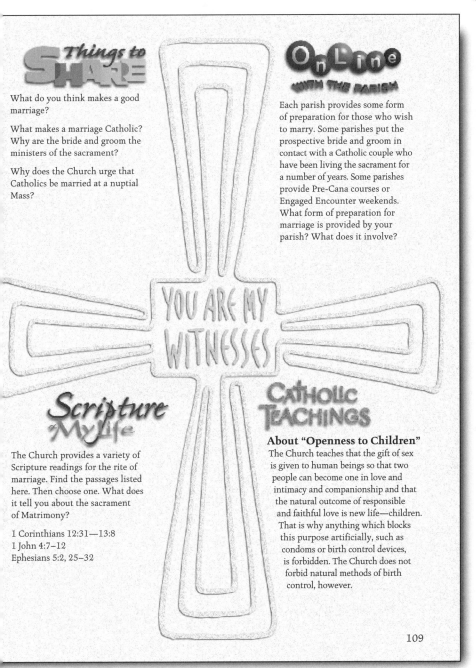

Things to SHARE

What do you think makes a good marriage?

What makes a marriage Catholic? Why are the bride and groom the ministers of the sacrament?

Why does the Church urge that Catholics be married at a nuptial Mass?

OnLine WITH THE PARISH

Each parish provides some form of preparation for those who wish to marry. Some parishes put the prospective bride and groom in contact with a Catholic couple who have been living the sacrament for a number of years. Some parishes provide Pre-Cana courses or Engaged Encounter weekends. What form of preparation for marriage is provided by your parish? What does it involve?

Scripture of My Life

The Church provides a variety of Scripture readings for the rite of marriage. Find the passages listed here. Then choose one. What does it tell you about the sacrament of Matrimony?

1 Corinthians 12:31—13:8
1 John 4:7–12
Ephesians 5:2, 25–32

Catholic Teachings

About "Openness to Children"
The Church teaches that the gift of sex is given to human beings so that two people can become one in love and intimacy and companionship and that the natural outcome of responsible and faithful love is new life—children. That is why anything which blocks this purpose artificially, such as condoms or birth control devices, is forbidden. The Church does not forbid natural methods of birth control, however.

109

Conclusion (cont'd)

FORUM Assignment

✔ Read pages 110–117. Underline in pencil the statements that express six key ideas.

✔ Discuss with the adults of your family the saints to whom they have particular devotion. Include in your discussion ways these saints reflected the light of God's love to others. Plan a simple way for your family to observe these saints' feast days.

Closing Prayer: Read aloud the following prayer. Pause at the places indicated. Invite the young people to repeat these words.

Jesus, teach us the meaning of true love. (*Pause.*) Give us the wisdom to know the difference between love and infatuation, (*Pause.*) between false friends and faithful companions. (*Pause.*) Give us a deep respect for marriage (*Pause.*) and a desire to help others who are struggling with their commitment to this lifelong vocation.

Evaluation: Do the young people understand the meaning and importance of the sacrament of Matrimony? Do they understand the need for maturity, faith, and preparation before accepting the responsibility of a lifelong commitment?

FOR CHAPTER 14

- skein of yarn
- rosary or rosaries
- copies of handout *Nine Days of Prayer*, page 110C
- *Chapter 14 Assessment*, page 117A
- *Highlights for Home*, page 117B

Assessment

 1 Marriage is important
- **a.** to the Church and society.
- **b.** as a political tool.
- **c.** to the couple alone.
- **d.** economically.

 2 The sacrament of Matrimony involves
- **a.** unbaptized persons.
- **b.** only a legal contract.
- **c.** a covenant between a baptized man and a baptized woman.
- **d.** none of the above

 3 Saint Paul compares marriage
- **a.** to a court case.
- **b.** to the love of Christ and the Church.
- **c.** to a business deal.
- **d.** to a Baptism.

 4 Catholic marriage vows require
- **a.** the witness of a priest or deacon.
- **b.** a doctor's certificate.
- **c.** that the children be present.
- **d.** all of the above

 5 The ministers of Matrimony
- **a.** are the priest and deacon.
- **b.** are the bride and groom.
- **c.** are the wedding party.
- **d.** are not necessary.

 6 Marriage preparation is
- **a.** required by most dioceses.
- **b.** only for certain couples.
- **c.** a recognition of Matrimony's challenges and responsibilities.
- **d.** both a and c

 7 An indissoluble bond
- **a.** is water solvent.
- **b.** is only a legal term.
- **c.** can never be broken.
- **d.** has nothing to do with marriage.

 8 Married couples reflect God's faithful love in
- **a.** their unity of body and soul.
- **b.** their lifelong faithfulness.
- **c.** their openness to children.
- **d.** all of the above

 9 Interpersonal skills are
- **a.** needed in marriage.
- **b.** not needed by youth.
- **c.** unimportant.
- **d.** none of the above

10 Describe the process of celebrating a nuptial Mass.

_____

_____

_____

_____

CHAPTER 13: The Sacrament of Matrimony

Highlights for Home

Focus on Faith

In a culture of quick change, temporary relationships, and the ready availability of divorce, society no longer provides the unqualified support that once strengthened spouses and families. Because we want our young people to be prepared for a good marriage, if that is their call from God, Chapter 13 helps them to take a clear-eyed look at what the sacrament of Matrimony is all about. In the eyes of the Church this beautiful sacrament unites a baptized man and a baptized woman in a lifelong covenant of love before God. As ministers of the sacrament to one another, they pronounce their vows before the community and are "united as one." By their gift of self to each other, their openness to having children, and their acceptance of the indissolubility of marriage, they are a sign of God's grace active in them. Christ is in them helping them to love each other "with a tender and powerful love" (*Catechism*, 1642).

Conversation Starters

. . . . a few ideas to talk about together . . . .

◆ What are ten characteristics of a good marriage?

◆ What interpersonal skills can I work on to prepare for a marriage in which these characteristics are present?

Feature Focus

The *Catholic ID* feature explains the custom of announcing a couple's intention to marry in the parish. Printed in the weekly bulletin, these "banns" (or proclamations) inform us about who is to be married and when the wedding will take place. As members of the faith community, we offer our prayers for those who are about to celebrate the lifelong sacrament of Matrimony.

Reflection

When a baptized couple marry in the Church, they promise each other, "I will love you and honor you all the days of my life." Perhaps you, too, will make that promise one day to the man or woman you believe God wants you to marry. To prepare for that day, ask yourself:

• How well am I doing at loving and honoring the members of my immediate family right now?

• Why is it often difficult to love and honor the people we live with, day in and day out?

• What improvements are needed in my actions or attitudes? When will I begin?

MARY AND THE SAINTS

Adult Focus

By her complete acceptance of God's will, her total cooperation in her son's work of redemption, and her adherence to every prompting of the Holy Spirit, "The Virgin Mary is the Church's model of faith and charity" (*CCC*, 967). The Church rightly honors Mary with special devotion, especially with four principal titles: Mother of God, Virgin, the Immaculate Conception and the Assumption. Because of her singular vocation, she is solemnly honored on January 1, December 8, and August 15. These liturgical feasts express her relationship to the Church and to all humanity: she is mother to us all "in the order of grace" (*CCC*, 968).

Mary continually intercedes for us before God. But hers is not the only voice raised on our behalf. The entire communion of saints intercedes for us. We do not worship or adore Mary or the saints. However, we do ask for their prayers, support and intercession with God as we attempt to walk the path of holiness. Our young people need to know that, as part of the communion of saints, they are surrounded and cherished by holy friends, and guarded and loved by the Mother of God. It is a realization that strengthens our faith and enlivens our hope on our journey to eternal life.

Catechism Focus

The theme of Chapter 14 corresponds to paragraphs 490–507, 964–971, 946–948, 2673–2679 of the *Catechism*.

Enrichment Activities

Making a Pilgrimage

Plan a group pilgrimage to a Marian shrine or a retreat center dedicated to Mary. Include plans for a picnic, Christian music concert or sing-along, and praying the rosary. The young people might invite a youth group from a different parish to join them for this day-long or weekend outing.

Viewing Videos

Invite a few volunteers to preview with you selected segments from the following videos. We suggest showing to the entire group a ten-minute segment from "The Road to Sainthood" in which the process of canonization is explained and illustrated. (See *Passion of the Saints*, Volume III. Fast-forward to the second half of this 100-minute video.) You may also wish to show "Saints for All Seasons" included in the third volume of *Saints' Gallery*.

Both series are available from:
Videos with Values
7315 Manchester Road
St. Louis, Missouri 63143

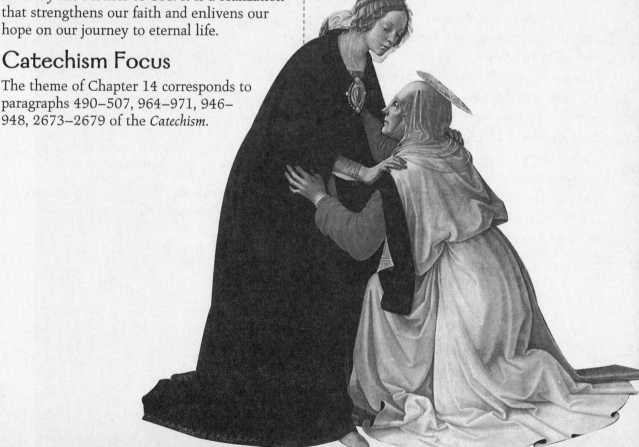

Teaching Resources

Overview

To discover our connection with the communion of saints; to explore the three types of liturgical celebrations of the lives of Mary and the saints.

Opening Prayer Ideas

Pray Hebrews 12:14. Reflect on one or more ways to strive for holiness.

or

Reflect on Luke 1:49. Name the great things God has done for you and your family.

Materials

- Bibles, journals, and high-lighters
- skein of yarn
- rosary or rosaries
- words to a traditional Marian hymn

REPRODUCIBLE MASTERS
- *Nine Days of Prayer*, page 110C
- *Chapter 14 Assessment*, page 117A
- *Highlights for Home*, page 117B

Liturgy and Worship Journal:
For Chapter 14, use pages 56–59.

Supplemental Resources

VIDEOS
The Madonna
Palisades Home Video
P.O. Box 2794
Virginia Beach, VA
23450–2794

Communion of Saints
Paulist Press
997 Macarthur Blvd.
Mahwah, NJ 07430

Nine Days of Prayer

A novena is a traditional prayer practice commemorating the nine days the followers of Jesus spent praying with Mary as they waited for the coming of the Holy Spirit on Pentecost Sunday. (The word *novena* comes from the word "nine" in Latin.)

Usually a novena is made for a particular intention. It can be made privately or with others.

It can be prayed for nine consecutive days or once a week for nine consecutive weeks (for example, nine consecutive Fridays).

Make a novena to Mary. Pray to her under nine of her special titles. A sample has been started for you. Begin to plan your prayers here and continue on the back of this sheet.

The First Day
Our Lady of Good Counsel, help us and guide us when we face difficult situations.

The Second Day
Title:

Prayer:

The Third Day
Title:

Prayer:

Mary and the Saints

Lord, this is the people that longs to see your face.
Solemnity of All Saints

111

Objective: To discover our connection with the communion of saints; to explore the three types of liturgical celebrations of the lives of Mary and the saints.

Introduction ___ min.

Opening Prayer: Invite the young people to look at the artwork on pages 110 and 111. Ask the young people to respond to the following acclamation with the prayer on page 110.

> With all God's holy people who have died and gone on before us, we belong to the body of Christ.

Continue the group's prayer with the following activity to demonstrate that the communion of saints is a network of support and companionship on our journey of faith.

1. Ask the group to stand in a circle.
2. Designate one person as the beginner. Ask this person to think of a saint, say the saint's name

aloud, and give a short biographical statement about the saint. An example statement is "Saint Joseph was the foster-father of Jesus." Ask the group to respond: "(Saint's name), support us on our journey of faith." Then this first person should hold tightly to the end of a skein of yarn, and, still holding the end, gently throw the skein across the circle to a person on the opposite side.

3. Each person who catches the skein should say a saint's name aloud and give a short statement about the saint. After the group responds, the catcher should hold a section of the string tightly and throw the skein to another person.
4. Repeat this process until everyone standing in the circle is part of the network. Then all take one step backward to tighten the net. The prayer can conclude with one person (the teacher or the appointed leader) saying, "Mary and all the saints, your shining lives are examples for us to follow. We ask you to continue to support us on our journey of faith." All respond: Amen.

Forum: Begin the *Forum* by explaining that, to prepare for the celebration of certain holidays, many home shows discuss special recipes and certain traditional customs well in advance of the actual day. Suggest the use of this format to enable the young people to share their ways of observing feast days of patron or favorite saints. Have co-hosts ask their guests to share ways these faith-filled ancestors reflected the light of God's love to others.

Presentation ___ min.

◆ Have a volunteer read the introductory paragraph on page 112. Discuss the question about asking in prayer for Mary and the saints' intercession.

◆ Ask the young people to skim pages 112 and 113. List on the board the images used to describe our union in holiness with the saints: communion of saints, body of Christ, and family. Ask all to highlight the key concepts highlighted on reduced pupil pages 112 through 116.

◆ Discuss the ☀ **thought provoker** on page 113. Draw a house framework on the board. Write on the frame strengths the young people suggest that they can use to build up the communion of saints. Then ask the young people to draw a framework in their journals. Have them write their own individual strengths as well as strengths they think they need to work on.

◆ Have someone summarize *Catholic Teachings* on page 117. Be certain the young people understand that God alone is adored or worshiped. Although these words are used loosely in our society ("I just adore your new car"; "I worship that rock idol"), we should practice using them only when we are referring to acts of honoring God.

All Christian prayer is directed to God the Father in the name of Jesus. Our Catholic tradition is filled with prayers calling upon the saints and uniquely upon Mary the mother of Jesus. Why do Catholics call upon Mary and the saints to intercede for us?

The Communion of Saints

Sometimes on headstones in a cemetery, there is a request: "Please pray for me," or "Pray for the repose of the soul of. . . ." We find such inscriptions in the early Christian cemeteries, too.

On the tombs of the martyrs, however, the inscriptions are different: They ask the martyrs to pray for us! These inscriptions are our earliest evidence of Christian prayer to the saints. From the beginning Christians have called upon Mary and the saints to intercede with God for them. Why?

In the preface for Masses on saints' days, we thank God because:

You renew the Church in every age
by raising up men and women outstanding in
    holiness,
living witnesses of your unchanging love.
They inspire us by their heroic lives,
and help us by their constant prayers
to be the living sign of your saving power.

We honor the saints because of their example and their intercession. They show us how to follow Christ, and they help us by their prayers.

The holiness of the saints is a reflection of God's holiness. In the sacraments the Father shares his holiness with us through the Son and the Holy

112

Spirit. Through the sacraments we enter into a "holy communion" and share, in union with the saints, God's life. Our union with God's holiness and with his holy ones (the saints) is called the *communion of saints*.

The doctrine of the communion of saints has very important consequences for our daily lives. Think of what it means — we are united with the saints in a common holiness!

Think, for a moment, of your physical body. When you exercise and strengthen your arms, your whole body benefits. When you do aerobics to strengthen your lungs and your heart, your whole body benefits. So it is with the body of Christ. "Since all the faithful form one body, the good of each is communicated to the others" (*Catechism*, 947).

Because we are members of the same body of Christ, all the good works, the merits, and the graces of the saints are communicated to us. The communion of saints assures us that *together* we form one family in Christ. What an encouragement this can be as we struggle and often fail in our efforts to follow Jesus. God's holiness is a *shared* gift.

What, then, does holiness mean for each one of us? We grow in holiness through a continual process of turning our lives toward God. We keep trying to empty ourselves of selfishness and sin in order to allow God's Spirit to fill us and to work in us. The saints have accomplished this to such a degree that when we look at their lives, we see and understand what Saint Paul meant when he wrote, "I live, no longer I, but Christ lives in me" (Galatians 2:20).

The communion of saints is both a tremendous responsibility and a source of great hope. Our responsibility is to follow Christ faithfully, as members of his body. Our hope is that we, together with all the saints, will share eternally in his final victory.

 How can you build up the communion of saints?

Celebrating the Saints

Devotion to Our Lady and the saints goes back to the earliest days of our Church. There is a rich liturgical tradition in the Church that celebrates Mary and the lives of the saints.

Liturgical celebrations are divided into three degrees. The most important days are called *solemnities*. For example, the days on which we celebrate the Trinity, Our Lord, or the Holy Spirit—Trinity Sunday, Christmas, Easter, Pentecost — are solemnities. In addition, we celebrate eight solemnities in honor of Mary or the saints each year. These include the solemnities of Mary, the Mother of God (January 1); Joseph, patron of the universal Church (March 19); John the Baptist (June 24); and the Apostles Peter and Paul (June 29).

Second in order of importance is that of *feast*. This rank includes, among others, the feasts of apostles and evangelists; the feast of the angels and archangels (September 29); and the feast of the first martyr, Stephen (December 26).

The final rank is *memorial*. On memorial days we celebrate the *memory* of a saint. Just as you might mark the birthdays of your friends on your calendar, the Church marks the birthdays of individual saints. However, there is one important difference. The Church does not celebrate the day the saints were born on earth but instead the day on which they were born into eternal life—that is, the day on which they died. It is their passage into new and eternal life that we celebrate, affirming that Christ's victory over death became fully real in their lives.

Reflections of the Holy

What does it mean when we call someone a *saint*? The word means "holy." In order to understand the holiness of the saints, we must start with the realization that only God is holy. If we call anyone other than God "holy," it is because the person reflects God's holiness. When we honor a saint's achievements, we are honoring what God did through the saint. Holiness is achieved, not by doing great things, but by allowing God's greatness to work in us.

113

◆ Share the following fictional case with the group. Call on volunteers to describe the process the parishioners should follow, step by step.

The people of St. Thomas Parish are determined to have one of their members recognized as a saint. She is Sister Maria Gonzalez, a missionary who spent forty years working among the poor in Latin America. Through her letters over the years and through testimony given by those she served, the pastor of St. Thomas has proof of Sister Maria's heroic self-sacrifice. She risked her life several times to save others, and died while caring for those afflicted by an epidemic. What advice can you give the pastor and people of St. Thomas? How should they proceed in this matter?

(Responses should include the following: *Call on an expert in Church matters to study Sister Maria's life; have the expert produce a report on the faith and good works of Sister Maria; submit this report to the bishop; cooperate with the continuing investigation into her holiness; encourage the bishop to submit the final results of Sister Maria's case to the Congregation for the Causes of Saints in Rome. Keep track of any miracles attributed to her intercession. Pray that she will one day be a canonized saint.*)

Presentation (cont'd)

◆ Invite the young people to look at the art on pages 114 and 115. Share with them the way each saint reflected the holiness of God.

• Blessed Katharine Drexel shared the gospel with Native Americans and African Americans.

• Saint Frances Xavier Cabrini founded many schools, hospitals, and orphanages for immigrants in the United States.

• Saint Charles Lwanga encouraged others to resist immorality and was martyred for his courageous faith.

• Blessed Juan Diego, through his sharing of his encounter with Mary, gave hope to the oppressed Indians of Mexico.

• Saint Andrew Kim helped missionaries to enter Korea and gave his life for the spread of the good news of Christ.

• Blessed Kateri Tekakwitha chose a life of chastity, prayer, and service.

◆ Invite responses to the Marian art on page 116. Why is it important for members of a universal Church to picture Mary in many different racial and ethnic representations? If you were an artist, how would you most like to depict Mary?

◆ Print the term *immaculate conception* on the board. Call for explanations of its meaning. Be certain the young people understand that the term applies to Mary's freedom from sin from the moment of her conception. The Church believes that this singular grace and privilege was bestowed by God on Mary because of her singular vocation to be the Mother of the Savior.

The Church is aware that millions of Christians have lived holy lives and that they now share in the happiness of God's life in heaven. They are all saints in the general sense of the word. However, in order to recognize the holiness of particular saints in a formal way, the Church has instituted the process called *canonization*. In order for a holy person to be canonized, a careful investigation is made of the person's life. The final results are sent to the Congregation for the Causes of Saints in Rome. The holy person may then be given the title of "Blessed."

Usually, three miracles attributed to the holy person's intercession are required before formal declaration of sainthood. Then the pope, in a beautiful and solemn ceremony, canonizes the saint, declaring that this holy person is truly a saint and extending veneration of this newly canonized saint to the whole Church.

The diversity in the lives of the saints teaches us that all Christians are called to holiness by imitating Christ in their particular circumstances. The life stories of the saints can often help us face the challenges in our own lives. And these great heroes and heroines can become our role models in living the Christian life.

Mary, Mother of Jesus

Mary has been honored in many ways through the centuries. However, everything that can be said about Mary, all the honor given to her, is due to two important facts: She is the mother of Jesus, and she is his first disciple. By understanding these two relationships, we can understand the role Mary plays in our salvation.

First of all, we honor Mary because of her relationship to Jesus: She is his mother. Mary does not draw attention to herself; she always points to Jesus. Each of the honors given to

Blessed Katharine Drexel

114

Mary is best understood in relation to Christ. We can see this in the four principal privileges for which the Church has traditionally honored Mary: Mother of God, the Blessed Virgin, the Immaculate Conception, and the Assumption.

What we believe about Mary is based on our understanding of Jesus. For example, when the second Council of Ephesus (A.D. 431) proclaimed Mary the Mother of God, it was declaring who *Jesus* was. The child that Mary bore in her womb was divine and therefore Mary, the mother of that child, is indeed the Mother of God. We celebrate the Solemnity of Mary, Mother of God on January 1.

We call Mary the Blessed Virgin because the Church has always believed and taught that Jesus was conceived by the power of the Holy Spirit.

Because God chose Mary to be the Mother of the Savior, it is fitting that she was the first to be saved. We believe that she was redeemed and free from all sin from the very beginning of her life—that is, from the moment of her conception. We call this privilege the immaculate conception. We celebrate the Solemnity of the Immaculate Conception on December 8.

We believe that when Mary's life on earth was over, God took her into heaven body and soul.

Saint Frances Xavier Cabrini

Saint Charles Lwanga

This participation in the resurrection and ascension of her son is called the assumption of the Blessed Virgin. We celebrate the Solemnity of the Assumption on August 15.

Mary, First Disciple of Jesus

The second reason we honor Mary is because of her relation to the Church: Mary is the first member of the Church, the model disciple. What does it mean to be a disciple? A disciple follows Jesus in doing the will of his Father.

No one has lived this more perfectly than Mary. Mary shows us what it means to be a disciple of Jesus, what it means to be a member of the Church.

We, too, are disciples. Mary, as Mother of God, bore Jesus in her womb and gave him birth. Today we, the Church, bear Christ in our bodies by Baptism and Eucharist. We are to bring forth Christ to our world by word and example. This is how we live as Jesus' disciples.

What does Mary's life say to you about discipleship?

The Hail Mary

The most common prayer to Mary, the one all Catholics know by heart, is the Hail Mary.

The prayer consists of two greetings and a petition. The two greetings are taken from the first chapter of Luke's Gospel. The first is the greeting of the angel Gabriel (Luke 1:28); the second, that of Mary's cousin Elizabeth (Luke 1:42).

The greeting of the angel Gabriel reminds us of the Book of Zephaniah: "Shout for joy, O daughter Zion! . . . The LORD your God is in your midst" (Zephaniah 3:14, 17). In the Hail Mary we pray, "Hail Mary, full of grace, the Lord is with you." The word we translate as "Hail" is the same word Zephaniah used: "Rejoice" or "Shout for joy." In Gabriel's greeting to Mary, it is as if he were saying to her, "Shout for joy, O highly favored one! The Lord is in your midst."

CATHOLIC ID

Do you have a patron saint? The Church encourages Catholics to be given the name of a saint when they are baptized as infants. Parents are not required to name their child after a saint, but it is an excellent tradition. A patron saint serves as an example of Christian life, and the child who is given a saint's name is assured of the saint's intercession.

Catholics may also choose another saint's name when they are confirmed. They do this in order to have another personal example of the Christian life to imitate. Today, however, some Catholics keep their baptismal names when they are confirmed in order to emphasize the connection between Baptism and Confirmation.

Blessed Juan Diego

Saint Andrew Kim

Blessed Kateri Tekakwitha

115

◆ Call on volunteers to respond to the **thought provoker** on page 115. *(Mary's life tells us that disciples place God's will above their own. They pray often, listen carefully to the word of God, and do whatever Jesus tells them.)*

◆ Form small groups of "Mary Communicators." Have writing and drawing materials available. Give the following assignment:

> Your task is to communicate the Hail Mary, either in part or in its entirety, to an audience of young people who are unfamiliar with the prayer. How will you teach the prayer in a way that will appeal to your peers? Here are a few ideas: write a respectful rap version; find a familiar melody to use for the prayer; present it in some artistic fashion with attractive lettering and symbols. Or, the young people may come up with completely original ways of communicating the prayer.

FYI Christian monks in the second century used beads or pebbles found in the Egyptian desert to count their prayers. The rosary as we know it originated in the twelfth century when devotion to Jesus and Mary was very popular. The word "bead" comes from the Middle English *beda*, meaning "prayer." The word *rosary* comes from the Latin *rosarium*, meaning "rose garden."

Presentation (cont'd)

◆ Ask a volunteer to summarize *Scripture & My Life* on page 117. Encourage the young people to try to learn the names of the fifteen mysteries by heart. Also encourage them to consider what other events in the lives of Jesus and Mary they might want to commemorate while praying the rosary.

◆ Discuss with the group the questions in *Things to Share*.

Conclusion ___ min.

◆ Have a volunteer summarize *On Line with the Parish*. If possible, have a parish calendar on hand for the group to use. Seek responses to the parish questions.

Assessment: You may want to administer a cumulative review test by having the young people work with partners to complete the *Final Assessment*, pages 126 and 127.

If you are administering *Chapter 14 Assessment*, page 117A, allow five to ten minutes for its completion.

Some of the many cultural representations of the Blessed Virgin Mary in art

When we say "Hail Mary," then, it is helpful to remember that this greeting is a joyful reminder of God's goodness and favor: Shout for joy!

The second greeting of the Hail Mary is that of Elizabeth: "Most blessed are you among women, and blessed is the fruit of your womb" (Luke 1:42). Mary is always seen in relation to her son. As Jesus is the source of every blessing, Mary, who bore Jesus in her womb and brought him forth to the world, is indeed worthy to be called blessed.

The second half of the Hail Mary is a traditional prayer of petition whose origins are lost in history. In it we ask that Mary will intercede for us "now and at the hour of our death."

The Rosary
There came a time when many Christians no longer knew the psalms by heart, so they began to meditate on the life of Jesus while reciting the Hail Mary or the Lord's Prayer. Eventually this practice was called praying the rosary. By the fifteenth century it had become a popular devotion.

The rosary can be prayed alone or with others. Usually we start with the Apostles' Creed, one Our Father, three Hail Marys, and one Glory to the Father. Following this introduction, we begin our meditation on the mysteries. Meditation—thinking and praying about the wonderful events of our salvation—is at the very heart of the rosary.

Each decade of the rosary is made up of one Our Father, ten Hail Marys, and one Glory to the Father. At the beginning of each decade, we select the mystery on which we are going to meditate. Then we think of this event in the life of Jesus or in the life of his mother while praying the ten Hail Marys. We usually end the Rosary with a centuries-old prayer to Mary, the Hail, Holy Queen.

Recall the words of Gabriel and Elizabeth to Mary: joy and blessing. Then quietly pray the Hail Mary together.

116

Answers for Chapter 14 Assessment
1. b **2.** d **3.** d **4.** b **5.** b
6. b **7.** d **8.** a **9.** d **10.** See page 116.

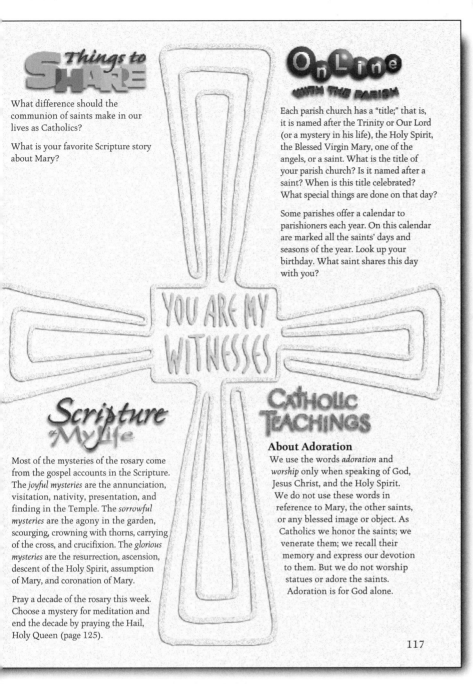

Things to SHARE

What difference should the communion of saints make in our lives as Catholics?

What is your favorite Scripture story about Mary?

OnLine WITH THE PARISH

Each parish church has a "title;" that is, it is named after the Trinity or Our Lord (or a mystery in his life), the Holy Spirit, the Blessed Virgin Mary, one of the angels, or a saint. What is the title of your parish church? Is it named after a saint? When is this title celebrated? What special things are done on that day?

Some parishes offer a calendar to parishioners each year. On this calendar are marked all the saints' days and seasons of the year. Look up your birthday. What saint shares this day with you?

Scripture of My Life

Most of the mysteries of the rosary come from the gospel accounts in the Scripture. The *joyful mysteries* are the annunciation, visitation, nativity, presentation, and finding in the Temple. The *sorrowful mysteries* are the agony in the garden, scourging, crowning with thorns, carrying of the cross, and crucifixion. The *glorious mysteries* are the resurrection, ascension, descent of the Holy Spirit, assumption of Mary, and coronation of Mary.

Pray a decade of the rosary this week. Choose a mystery for meditation and end the decade by praying the Hail, Holy Queen (page 125).

Catholic Teachings

About Adoration

We use the words *adoration* and *worship* only when speaking of God, Jesus Christ, and the Holy Spirit. We do not use these words in reference to Mary, the other saints, or any blessed image or object. As Catholics we honor the saints; we venerate them; we recall their memory and express our devotion to them. But we do not worship statues or adore the saints. Adoration is for God alone.

117

Conclusion (cont'd)

Closing Prayer: Direct attention to the ✦ thought provoker on page 116. Pray the Hail Mary together. Then distribute the handout *Nine Days of Prayer.* Read together the explanation and origins of the novena. Ask the young people to name titles of Mary with which they are familiar. List these titles on the board. Allow a few minutes of quiet time for all to choose three titles and write a prayer for each. Explain that the young people may want to complete the novena prayers for the remaining days in their free time. Encourage the group to pray to Mary often. Invite any person who wishes to share one of his or her novena prayers.

Close by saying a decade of the rosary and singing a traditional Marian hymn such as "Immaculate Mary." The lyrics may be found in most parish hymnals.

Evaluation: Do the young people understand why and how we celebrate Mary and the saints? Are they familiar with the Blessed Mother's four privileges? Do the young people understand the meaning of the words of the Hail Mary and the reasons Catholics are encouraged to pray the rosary?

Assessment

 1 The communion of saints
a. is the Eucharist.
b. is our union with God's holiness and with his holy ones.
c. includes only holy people.
d. means eternal life.

 2 Images of our unity include
a. the household of God.
b. the body of Christ.
c. the Christian family.
d. all of the above

 3 The saints
a. intercede for us.
b. have nothing to do with us.
c. share their graces with us.
d. a and c

 4 Solemnities are
a. serious discussions.
b. the most important days on the Church calendar.
c. just like feasts and memorials.
d. Vatican Councils.

 5 Canonization is a process of
a. building cannons.
b. recognizing saints.
c. making Church laws.
d. recognizing the holiness of particular people.

 6 Saints who served in America
a. have not been canonized.
b. include Elizabeth Seton and Isaac Jogues.
c. include Andrew Kim and Charles Lwanga.
d. none of the above

 7 Mary's principal privileges are:
a. Mother of God and Virgin.
b. the immaculate conception.
c. the assumption.
d. all of the above

 8 The immaculate conception means that
a. Mary was free from sin from the time of her conception.
b. Jesus was free from sin.
c. the saints have no sin.
d. Mary is a virgin.

 9 The Hail Mary
a. was given to us by Jesus.
b. includes the Magnificat of Mary.
c. is called a solemnity.
d. is the most common Catholic prayer to Our Lady.

10 Explain how we pray the rosary.

_____
_____
_____
_____
_____

Highlights for Home

Focus on Faith

Many tourists visit Mary, Queen of the Universe Shrine in Orlando, Florida. Here Mass is celebrated daily. Tourists are impressed by the beautiful rosary windows depicting saints of the North American Church.

Whether we can get to Orlando or not, the Church gives us the opportunity each year to honor Mary, mother of Jesus and his first disciple. We celebrate her as Mother of God on January 1, as the Immaculate Conception on December 8, and in her Assumption on August 15. As families, we honor Mary by making her part of our home life (praying a Hail Mary or the rosary together, displaying an icon or statue, dedicating a garden to her, or perhaps pursuing a justice project for the "lowly").

Together with Mary, the entire communion of saints stands ready to befriend and intercede for us. Our prayers to them are ultimately prayers to God from whom all graces and blessings flow. To encourage your sons and daughters to get in touch with Mary and the saints is to share the treasures of your faith with them.

Conversation Starters

. . . . a few ideas to talk about together . . . .

◆ How does Mary's example challenge us to be more courageous disciples?

◆ How has Mary been a source of comfort or help to you?

◆ In what ways do you find the saints companions and examples of hope?

Feature Focus

The *Catholic ID* feature reminds us that Catholics are encouraged to have patron saints as their special intercessors in heaven. The patron saint can also serve as a role model for the young person who has been given the saint's name at Baptism or Confirmation.

Reflection

In Mary's song of praise, the Magnificat, she proclaims thanksgiving for the privilege of her vocation as Mother of God and the first disciple of Jesus. Let us pray Mary's song with her to proclaim our thanks to God for all the great things that God has done for us. Reflect quietly on the following verses (Luke 1:46, 49–50).

*My soul proclaims the greatness of the Lord;
    my spirit rejoices in God my savior. . . .*

*The Mighty One has done great things for
    me
    and holy is his name.
His mercy is from age to age
    to those who fear him.*

PATHS OF PRAYER

Adult Focus

Just as the young people practice math, vocabulary, or sports skills, they can also develop the habit of praying daily—even when they are weary or "not in the mood." The Catholic tradition of prayer is rich and varied, rooted in daily praise, petition, intercession, and thanksgiving.

You may want to use the three prayer sessions in this section during a retreat day, an evening during Lent or Advent, or before the young people celebrate Confirmation. You may also use one of the sessions as an alternate *Opening Prayer* or *Closing Prayer* for any of the fourteen sessions of the course.

Review *Prayer and the Young Person* in this guide on page G14. It is important that you examine the three sessions in order to plan their use and to gather materials needed for their presentation. You may want to conduct these prayer sessions in a place that is different from where you usually meet as a group.

Catechism Focus

The theme of this session corresponds to paragraphs 2759–2776, 2700–2724, 1174–1178, 2697–2699, and 435 of the *Catechism*.

Enrichment Activities

🖥 Computer Connection

Have the young people design a screen saver that is a visual aid to them for one of the paths of prayer mentioned in the chapter. Have the young people exchange E-mail prayers with those with whom they communicate by computer.

Planning a Prayer Service

Involve the young people in choosing a theme of concern in their daily lives. Examples include: relationships with parents, loneliness, addictions, love and sexuality. Have them plan a prayer service integrating scriptural readings with popular music or video segments that speak to the theme. They might also compose a litany to Jesus, Companion of Youth.

Doing Dance Meditations

This activity may be done with the guidance of a liturgical dancer from your diocese, or with the video "Movement Meditations: To the Songs of Taize" featuring Carla De Sola, with Thomas Kane (Paulist Press). The video offers fourteen meditations involving simple movement patterns which the young people can follow. A booklet of instructions is included.

Teaching Resources

Overview

To invite the young people to experience various forms of prayer in order to find the paths that will lead them closer to God.

Materials—Session 1

- Bibles and journals
- colored pencils or markers
- video *Notre Dame Cathedral*

Wellspring Media
65 Bleecker Street
New York, NY 10012

Materials—Session 2

- posterboard, markers, rulers
- missalette or liturgical calendar
- index cards or slips of paper
- box or basket
- video *St. Mark's Gospel*

Palisades Home Video
P.O. Box 2794
Virginia Beach, VA 23450

Materials—Session 3

 Liturgy and Worship Journal:
See pages 60–63.

- album *Instruments of Peace* by David Haas or other reflective music
- CD or cassette player
- video *To Everything There Is a Season*

Ignatius Press
P.O. Box 1339
Ft. Collins, CO 80522

Objective: To discover stained-glass windows as aids on the path of prayer.

Introduction ___ min.

Opening Prayer: Ask the young people to share prayerful experiences of joy. (These may include a great variety of memories from an athletic or artistic performance to the deep enjoyment of a sunset or a mountain to a wonderful experience of liturgy.) Encourage the group to be open to all the everyday and extraordinary joys that Jesus wants them to experience. Pray Psalm 16:11 aloud together.

Presentation ___ min.

Discussion: Point out that the cyclist in the photograph on page 118 may be praying while pedaling. Have the young people brainstorm other activities that may be considered spiritual "exercise." Have volunteer recorders write the responses on the board. You may want to add the following suggestions: talking to God while dribbling a basketball or shooting hoops; thanking God for his great gifts while walking; praying or singing while doing pottery work.

◆ Invite responses to the window on page 119. Discuss why the young people think stained-glass windows can help someone to pray. Encourage them to look more closely at the stained glass in their parish church (or other churches) to select those symbols or scenes that speak most effectively to them.

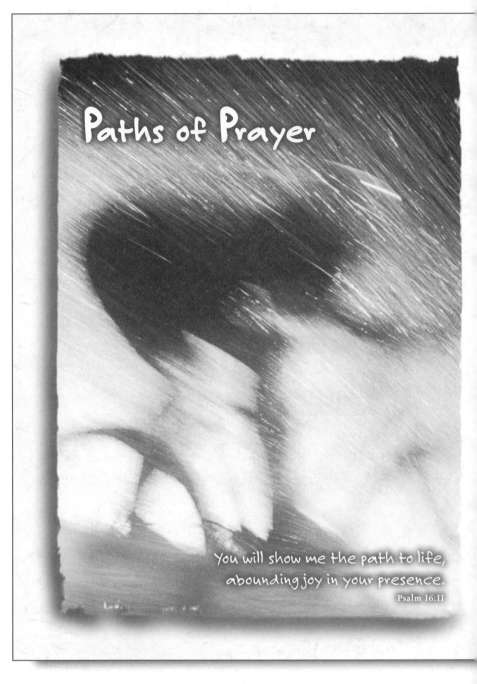

Paths of Prayer

You will show me the path to life, abounding joy in your presence.
Psalm 16:11

◆ Before beginning the window activity on page 119, you may wish to show the rose window and other stained glass shown on the video *Notre Dame Cathedral.* It is available from:

Wellspring Media
65 Bleecker Street
New York, NY 10012

*Prayer is a path that leads
to God; prayer is a window that reflects
God's light; prayer is a heart open to God's love.
What is prayer for you?*

Windows of Prayer

In *prayer* we raise our hearts and minds to God. We ask God for the good things we need, we thank him for his gifts, we express our sorrow for sin, we pray for others, and we praise him for his goodness. With the help of the Holy Spirit and the tradition of the Church, we can pray in many ways. Here is one you might like to try.

Look at the empty stained-glass window here. How would you complete it? Here is a suggestion: Make this window into an expression of your relationship with God. Like a stained-glass window, this relationship has many dimensions. Think about the sacraments you have celebrated; you may want to symbolize each one in a section of your window. Think about your times of prayer, both during the liturgy and alone. These could be symbolized in sections of your window. How do family and friends help you find God? Symbolize this in your window. Perhaps the Scriptures will find a place in your window as well.

What would you put in the center of your window? Perhaps you might insert a symbol of Jesus: the cross as symbol of the paschal mystery or bread and wine, the symbols of the Eucharist. What symbolizes the center of your relationship with God?

119

• palm branch (victory, triumph over death)
• thorns (suffering, sin)
• tree (abundant life)

Ask the young people to choose titles for their completed rose windows. Allow about fifteen minutes for this activity. Then have volunteers act as tour guides and explain the significance of their rose windows.

Conclusion ___ min.

Invite the young people to write their own definitions of prayer. Then ask them to write one brief prayer for each section of their rose windows, beginning with the center. Assure them that each prayer may be brief, such as, "God, help me to trust you like the sparrow does."

Closing Prayer: Gather in a prayer circle. Call on volunteers to share one or more of their window prayers. After each prayer, the group responds, "Lord, you are the light of the world!"

Prayer Activity: Distribute additional markers, colored pencils, paint and brush kits, if available. Invite the young people, working alone or with a partner, to complete the window activity described on page 119. If you choose, put a list of Christian symbols on the board to help them get started.

• butterfly
• fish (Christ, baptism)
• lamb (Jesus, Good Shepherd)
• sparrow (least ones, dependence on God)
• wheat and grapes (Eucharist)
• olive branch (peace)

FOR SESSION 2

• posterboard, markers, rulers
• missalette or liturgical calendar
• index cards or slips of paper
• box or basket

Objective: To explore ways of praying with Scripture.

Introduction ___ min.

Opening Prayer: Have a volunteer read Matthew 7:7–11. Invite the young people to reflect on Jesus' words.

 Write your reflections in your journal.

Presentation ___ min.

Prayer Activities: Have the young people form small prayer groups. Provide the groups with posterboard, markers, and rulers. Suggest that the group work on any or all of the following activities.

• *Praying the Our Father*
Look up both versions of the Our Father in the Gospels of Matthew and Luke. Make a poster of Luke's version of the Lord's Prayer. Be prepared to share how the two gospel stories and the prayer differ.

• *Praying Scripture Pictures*
Do the prayer exercise on page 120. Write your responses in your journal. Make a poster encouraging others to pray with imagined Scripture pictures or scenes.

• *Praying God's Word for the Day*
Follow the directions in the text on page 121. Choose some verses from the Old Testament and others from the New Testament. Make a poster illustrating the verse your group likes best.

• *Praying Today's Scripture*
(Be sure each group has a list of the liturgical readings for today. These may be found in the missalette or on a liturgical calendar.) Follow the directions on page 121. Make a poster illustrating the verse or ideas your group finds most meaningful.

• *Praying with Scripture and Music*
(If possible, have the groups meet in a separate space where they can sing out loud. Provide them with a parish hymnal for ideas.) Follow the directions on page 121. Make a poster of your chosen verse or verses. Be prepared to sing your prayer.

Praying with Scripture

The Sacred Scriptures can enrich our prayer immensely. They are the "faith record" of God's mysterious plan—what God has done in history and the revelation of God's plan for the world. A good way to pray is to take the Bible, read a passage, and then talk it over with God.

Praying with just one or two Scripture verses is a traditional and practical way to make prayer a part of our everyday lives. We can easily pray a short, easy-to-remember Scripture verse at work or play or during those "between times" we find ourselves in so often: between home and school, between lunch and recess, between the ending of one class and the beginning of another.

Here are several ways to pray with Scripture. Which appeal to you?

The Our Father

The whole gospel of Jesus Christ is summed up in the Our Father. It is the purest and most essential prayer of the Church. When we pray the Our Father, we pray with the attitude of Jesus and the Spirit of Jesus. We pray for what Jesus wants—that God's will be done on earth. As we pray the Our Father, we become one with Jesus and one with the Father in love and trust. The Our Father can be found in Matthew 6:9–13 and in Luke 11:2–4.

Scripture Pictures

When people asked Saint Ignatius Loyola for help in prayer, he advised them to picture a scene from Scripture and to put themselves into the scene. Try it with Matthew 8:23–27. Imagine the people, the sounds, the smells; and especially, see Jesus as he speaks and acts. What is he saying to you? When you finish, write your thoughts in your journal.

120

120

God's Word for the Day

Compile a list of at least seven favorite Scripture passages. Choose one each day as your special verse. Every time your mind is free or you are between activities, recall your verse and say it to yourself a few times. Here are two for your list:

• "Your word is a lamp for my feet,
    a light for my path" (Psalm 119:105).

• "I am the good shepherd, and I know mine and mine know me" (John 10:14).

Today's Scripture

Using the Church's calendar of Scripture readings, find the readings for today. Read them and the psalm carefully. If you find a verse or idea meaningful, stop and let it sink in. Stay with it as long as you like. Then go on. Choose one of the verses, and recall it often during the day.

Scripture and Music

Music is a traditional and beautiful way to focus on the words and meaning of Scripture. Try setting a favorite verse to a simple melody, perhaps in a chantlike style. Create a harmony as well! You may want to use a Scripture story or set of verses as the basis for an entire song. Saint John Chrysostom wrote many Scripture hymns for the Church. Ask his help!

Scripture Exchange

Spend some time looking through the New Testament. Write down, on an index card or a slip of paper, one or two verses you like. Collect them from the group in a box or basket. Then invite each group member to draw one. You may want to decorate or illustrate your verse on paper and display it.

The Prayer of the Name

"You shall name him Jesus" (Luke 1:31). The name of Jesus is a simple but powerful prayer, and using the holy name of Jesus in prayer is an ancient tradition in the Church. Begin by closing your eyes and becoming still. Breathe slowly and deeply. Then, as you breathe in, quietly say "Jesus." As you breathe out, you may want to say "Savior" or "peace" or another word that reminds you of Jesus. Continue this rhythm for as long as you wish.

Scriptural Meditation

The path of meditation is another path to union with God. *Meditation* is simply "thinking about God," and it can easily flow into *contemplation* ("being with" God). Most often we meditate on the Scriptures, but other spiritual books can be starting points as well, especially those that explain the Scriptures and inspire us to live the Christian life. A scriptural meditation has been prepared for you on the next page.

Conclusion ___ min.

◆ If time allows, share with the young people the Church's tradition of *lectio divina* or reading of the holy Scriptures. Anyone who can read and sit still for ten to twenty minutes can pray through holy reading. The process is:

• Choose a scriptural passage.

• Read it through once. Then reread it more slowly or aloud.

• Ask the Holy Spirit to help you mull over and ponder the word of God you have just read.

• Write in your journal the message you have received in your own words.

Closing Prayer: Have prayer group members display their posters and share their reflections on the seven ways of praying with Scripture.

• *Praying a Scripture Exchange*
  (Provide each group with index cards or slips of paper, and a box or basket.) Follow the directions on page 121. Make as many verse cards as there are young people in the class. Make a poster of the verse your group likes best.

• *Praying the Name of Jesus*
  (If possible, provide this group with a separate space where they will not be distracted.) Practice the prayer as outlined on page 121. Make a poster encouraging others to pray the name of Jesus.

FOR SESSION 3

• album *Instruments of Peace* by David Haas (GIA) or other music of choice

• CD or cassette player

• display of sacramental objects

Objective: To experience meditation and contemplation.

Introduction ___ min.

Opening Prayer: Do a breath meditation, praying the name of Jesus on each deep inhalation and exhalation.

Presentation ___ min.

Discussion: To prepare for this session, draw attention to the last paragraph on page 121, "Scriptural Meditation." Ask for examples of familiar or favorite passages from Scripture. Explain that today we will be meditating on a Scripture passage from the Gospel of Mark.

◆ Have the terms *vocal prayer, contemplation,* and *meditation* printed on three large candles sketched on the board. Call on young people whose names begin with *v, p, c,* or *m* to come forward and "light the candles" by defining each term and drawing a flame above each in yellow or orange chalk. Take a survey to find out how many young people feel most "at home with" each of these three ways of praying. Guide a brief dialogue on how our prayer choices may reflect our personalities and life experiences.

Prayer: Before sharing the Scripture meditation on page 122, invite the young people to occupy their own sacred spaces by separating from one another, sitting on cushions on the floor, or using any available prayer corners. (If possible, move outside or into a chapel.) Let the group know that they are about to experiment with a Scripture meditation. Their only task is to do their best to enter into the experience and focus their imaginations on the scene created by the narrator's voice.

To introduce the meditation, play a song such as "We Walk By Faith" or "Healer of Our Every Ill" from the album *Instruments of Peace* by Marty Haugen (GIA).

Then narrate the meditation on page 122. Pause after each question to allow for silent reflection. After the direction to "Take time to 'just be with Jesus,'" allow for a few minutes' silence. Then complete the meditation.

A Scripture Meditation

For now, let's choose a Scripture passage, Mark 10:46–52, for our meditation. Before meditating, it is a good idea to help yourself become calm, peaceful, and undistracted. Sometimes listening to soft background music can help. First sit in a straight but comfortable position and close your eyes. Now let's try it.

Imagine yourself sitting by the side of a dusty road. You look down the road. You are waiting for Jesus to come by. Already you see him in the distance, surrounded by a large crowd.

Suddenly, across the road, you notice someone—Bartimaeus, a blind man. He, too, is waiting for Jesus. You hear him call out, "Jesus, Son of David, have pity on me." Jesus and the crowd are coming closer. What do you hear? There is the calling of Bartimaeus, the buzz of the crowd, and someone scolding Bartimaeus: "Quiet, blind man!" What do you see? There is Jesus, coming down the road. There is Bartimaeus, alone and poor, the hot sun beating down on him.

Suddenly all is silent. Jesus is here—just a few feet away. "Call him," Jesus says. Someone runs to where Bartimaeus sits in the sun. "Take courage; get up, he is calling you."

Everything is happening right in front of you. You see Bartimaeus as he joyfully throws aside his cloak, springs to his feet, and comes to Jesus. You hear Jesus ask, "What do you want me to do for you?" Bartimaeus replies in a pleading voice, "Master, I want to see." Jesus tells him, "Go your way; your faith has saved you." Immediately Bartimaeus receives his sight and begins to follow Jesus.

But wait! Jesus is stopping again. He has seen you sitting there in your special place. Jesus calls to you, "Come here, my friend." You quickly stand up and go to meet him. Jesus looks at you with great love. "So—why were you waiting for me? What do you want me to do for you?"

Think a moment. What is your answer? What does Jesus say to you?

Take time to "just be with" Jesus a little while.

Now begin to say good-bye. Watch Jesus a moment as he turns to continue his journey of healing. Now begin your own journey back. Say good-bye to your special place. Then open your eyes slowly. Let us pray the Our Father together.

A Life of Prayer

In our Catholic life of prayer, we often pray with words, aloud, and usually with others. This prayer with words is called *vocal prayer* because we pray

LOOKING BACK

Think for a moment about your experience. If there is anything about your meditation that you would like to remember, write it in your journal now.

In prayer God always gives us exactly what we need. All prayer is a gift of God's life and grace. We need only take time to receive it.

122

not only with our minds and hearts but with our voices as well. The prayers we say during the liturgy are vocal prayers, as are traditional prayers such as the Our Father and the Hail Mary.

There are many paths to God in prayer. Vocal prayer is one of them. Once two sisters asked Saint Teresa of Avila how to find union with God. "Say the Our Father," responded Teresa. Sometimes when we say a familiar prayer carefully and thoughtfully, we gain insight into the meaning of the words. Then the words slowly fade away, and we find ourselves "just being" at peace in God. This is the prayer of contemplation.

Contemplation is the prayer of union with God. We might also call it the prayer of "just being with" God. If you look up the word *contemplation* in the dictionary, you will find: "the act of looking at attentively and thoughtfully." The prayer of contemplation is simply looking at God. As one saint described this kind of prayer, "I look at God and he looks at me."

We can also pray with sacramentals. Sacramentals are part of our daily lives. They are blessings, actions,

and objects that the Church uses to prepare us for the graces of the sacraments. By objects, we mean things such as statues, medals, rosaries, candles, and crucifixes. By actions, we mean actions such as the sign of the cross, the laying on of hands, the sprinkling of blessed water. Blessings include the blessing of people, places, food, and objects. We bless ashes on Ash Wednesday and palms on Palm Sunday. Can you think of other times when we use blessings?

Unlike sacraments, which were instituted by Christ, sacramentals were instituted by the Church. The Church teaches us that sacramentals are never to be used in a magical or superstitious way or looked upon as good luck charms.

What sacramentals are part of your everyday life? You may want to write your own prayer, asking God's blessing on yourself, your family, your home, and your everyday activities.

◆ From a display on the prayer table, pass around assorted sacramentals (words of blessings, rosaries, statues, medals, icons, candles, crucifixes). If possible, provide one for each young person. Invite responses to:

• How might these sacramentals help people to pray?

• Which of these examples are most appealing to you? Why?

Encourage the use of sacramental objects, actions, and blessings at home. Note that some families have small holy water fonts in their homes so that family members and guests can bless themselves before going to bed at night or whenever they choose. (Do not collect the sacramentals until after the *Closing Prayer*.)

Closing Prayer: Invite the young people to do the closing reflection on page 123. If they choose, they might sketch the sacramental object they have received. Then their original blessing (for family, friends, home, activities or self) may be written inside the sketch or around the border. Share these as time allows.

Conclusion ___ min.

Invite the young people to write a response to their meditation experience in their journals. Encourage them to write their responses to Jesus' question, "What do you want me to do for you?" They might also record what they believe Jesus' answer was or will be.

Chapters 1-7

Circle the letter beside the **best** answer.

 1 Catholic symbols and rituals are to be used

a. carelessly.

b. superstitiously.

c. reverently in worship.

d. sparingly.

 2 The paschal mystery of Jesus is

a. the story of Jesus' miracles.

b. the passion, death, resurrection, and ascension of Jesus.

c. the story of Jesus' birth.

d. the story of the Last Supper.

 3 *Liturgy* is

a. the public prayer of the Church.

b. the participation of the people in the work of God.

c. the celebration of the paschal mystery.

d. all the above

 4 The sacraments of initiation are

a. Baptism and Confirmation.

b. Baptism, Confirmation, and Holy Orders.

c. Baptism and Eucharist.

d. Baptism, Confirmation, and Eucharist.

 5 _____ is the liturgical act of remembering.

a. Anamnesis

b. Basilica

c. Lectern

d. Ambo

Define the following terms.

 6 symbol _____

_____

_____

_____

_____

7 ritual _____

_____

_____

_____

_____

 8 sacrifice _____

_____

_____

_____

_____

9 mystery _____

_____

_____

_____

_____

10 conversion _____

_____

_____

_____

_____

 11 sacrament _____

_____

_____

_____

_____

12 the sacrament of the Eucharist

_____
_____
_____
_____

Name the part or fixture of the church described.

13 The table of the Lord and the place where the sacrifice of the Mass is offered

_____

14 The space for celebrating Reconciliation

_____

15 The place in which the Eucharist is kept

_____

16 The reader's stand

_____

How would you reply if people asked you the following questions?

17 How can I become a member of the Catholic Church?

_____
_____
_____
_____
_____
_____

18 Why do Catholics reserve the Eucharist in the tabernacle?

_____
_____
_____
_____
_____
_____
_____

19 What are the effects of original sin?

_____
_____
_____
_____
_____
_____

20 How does receiving the Body of Christ at the Eucharist connect us to the body of Christ, the Church?

_____
_____
_____
_____
_____
_____
_____

For extra credit

How does celebrating the paschal mystery of Jesus help you follow Jesus Christ in your everyday life?

ASSESSMENT

Name _____

Chapters 8-14

Circle the letter beside the **best** answer.

 1 Another name for the Lord's Day is
  a. Sabbath.
  b. Sunday.
  c. Saturday.
  d. Christmas.

 2 The most important way Catholics praise God and honor the risen Christ is by
  a. spending time in quiet prayer.
  b. visiting the sick.
  c. participating in the Eucharist.
  d. spending quality time with family.

 3 *Mystagogy* is
  a. the time spent in preparation for Easter.
  b. the celebration of Pentecost.
  c. a time for learning about and meditating on the mysteries of faith.
  d. the three-day observance of Easter.

 4 The sacrament of Reconciliation
  a. celebrates our continuing conversion.
  b. is a celebration of love and forgiveness.
  c. strengthens us to grow in God's grace.
  d. all of the above

 5 The laying on of hands is a sign of the sacrament of
  a. Matrimony.
  b. Eucharist.
  c. Holy Orders.
  d. Baptism.

Define the following terms.

6 Triduum _____
_____
_____
_____

7 neophyte _____
_____
_____
_____

8 absolution _____
_____
_____
_____

9 viaticum _____
_____
_____
_____

10 deacon _____
_____
_____
_____

11 indissoluble bond _____
_____
_____
_____

F I N A L

Name the sacrament that is described.

12 The priest anoints each sick person with oil and makes the sign of the cross on the person's forehead and on the palm of each hand.

_____
_____

13 The free consent of the couple and the presence of a priest and two witnesses are the essential sign of this sacrament.

_____
_____

14 The candidate promises obedience to the bishop of the local church under whom he will serve.

_____
_____

15 Our relationship to God and to the community of the Church is restored.

_____
_____

How would you explain the following statements?

16 The communion of saints is both a tremendous responsibility and a source of hope.

_____
_____
_____
_____

17 As Catholics we honor the saints and express our devotion to them, but adoration is for God alone.

_____
_____
_____
_____

18 The liturgy enables us to pass from our past-present-future time into God's time of salvation.

_____
_____
_____
_____

19 Baptism is both a dying and a rising.

_____
_____
_____
_____

20 The gift of the Holy Spirit is a gift of mission.

_____
_____
_____
_____

For extra credit

What is your favorite liturgical season? Explain why.

ASSESSMENT

Answer Sheet for Semester Tests

Midsemester Test

1. c   **2.** b   **3.** d   **4.** d   **5.** a

6. something that stands for or suggests something else

7. a symbolic action expressing our deepest beliefs

8. a ritual action that brings about and celebrates our joyful union with God

9. a truth that continually calls us to deeper understanding

10. the process of coming to believe that Jesus Christ is the Savior of the world. Literally it means, "turning around, going in the other direction."

11. a visible and effective sign, given to us by Christ, through which we share in God's grace

12. The sacrament of the Eucharist is the sacrament of the Body and Blood of Christ.

13. altar

14. the reconciliation chapel

15. tabernacle

16. lectern or ambo

17. by joining the RCIA in your parish, becoming a catechumen, and receiving the sacraments of initiation (See pages 49–50.)

18. The consecrated Hosts can be taken to the sick and the dying; Catholics also have a long tradition of praying before the Blessed Sacrament reserved in the tabernacle.

19. The effects of original sin are weakness of will, tendency to sin, suffering, and death.

20. When we receive the Body of Christ at the Eucharist, we also receive Christ living in each member of the body of Christ, the Church. We must treat each member of Christ's body as we would treat Christ himself.

For extra credit: Accept reasonable responses.

Final Test

1. b   **2.** c   **3.** c   **4.** d   **5.** c

6. means "three days"—begins with the Lord's Supper on Holy Thursday and ends with evening prayer on Easter Sunday

7. newly initiated Christian

8. pardon, or being set free, from sin

9. means "on the way with you"—the Eucharist given to the dying

10. means "servant"—one of the ranks of Holy Orders

11. a bond that can never be broken

12. sacrament of the Anointing of the Sick

13. sacrament of Matrimony

14. sacrament of Holy Orders

15. sacrament of Reconciliation

16. It is a responsibility because everything we do, both good and bad, affects the rest of the body of Christ; it is a source of hope because we benefit by the holiness of the saints and the goodness of all the members of the body of Christ.

17. We adore and worship God alone because he is the creator of all. We honor the saints because they are friends of God, followers of Jesus, and can help us by their example and their prayers.

18. God's time of salvation is always now. In the liturgy, what happened in the past is made present now, and is a foretaste of the future (heaven). The liturgy does not divide up time, but makes God's salvation through Jesus Christ present now.

19. Baptism is a dying because it is a change from an old life to a new way of life, a Christian way of life. It is a rising because in Baptism we are given a new life in the risen Christ.

20. The gift of the Holy Spirit sends us out to others, just as the Holy Spirit sent the apostles out to tell others about Jesus on the first Pentecost. The Holy Spirit enables us to share in the mission of Jesus Christ, to help the kingdom to come in the world.

For extra credit: Accept reasonable responses.